TABLE OF CONTENTS

INTRODUCTION

An enormous amount of harm is done in God's name. All around the world, God and his contradictory wishes are blamed for every kind of religious strife, whether in Iran or Israel; in the Netherlands or Northern Ireland. The Christian God in particular is notorious for having promoted division, ignorance and suffering for the best part of two thousand years. Devout Christians, professing dependence on their God's guidance, have done, and continue to do, some outrageous things – from the butchery of the Crusades and the Inquisition to the calculated genocide of the Holocaust and Rwanda in more recent times – all as part of their professed quest to obey and spread God's revealed Word. I intend to show that God is innocent!

Today, there are said to be three-and-a-half billion monotheists in the world. These people are to varying degrees guided and controlled by elite individuals within each denomination who have assumed positions of power by virtue of their claims to be representatives on Earth of this One True supernatural God. They claim to be privy to His wishes, and enjoy the earthly privileges that this heavenly power brings. These are the men that I call 'clerics'. They are those executive religious leaders and spokesmen who determine doctrine, and who employ the worker priests, who I see largely as victims. Many clerics use Machiavellian devices to promote their competing brands of snake oil and maximise their own political influence, while vilifying those honest atheists and ethical freethinkers who dare to call their bluff. The circumstantial evidence suggests that at least some of them are '… an establishment of con artists who have dedicated their lives to propping up a sense of self-importance by claiming to talk to an invisible big kahuna' (biologist PZ Myers in the *New Statesman*, 25 July 2011).

Christian clerics preach a message that is authoritarian, sexist, homophobic, reactionary, intolerant, anti-socialist, anti-intellectual and anti-democratic. Theirs is a 'Christianity' that

1

owes more to fascism than to the Sermon on the Mount. Quite a few of them have so twisted Jesus' supposed teachings that they now preach war and greed; they worship wealth, and instead of giving to Caesar what is Caesar's, they seek political power and privilege for themselves. My thesis is that those pretenders, the powerful popes, prelates, preachers and presidents who presume to speak on God's behalf are either victims of their own indoctrination, or else they are artful opportunists, wolves in sheep's clothing. Either way, they threaten the wellbeing and even the survival of the human race, and they certainly don't deserve the obsequious respect that is usually accorded to them. These are the men for whom 'God loves a giver' means 'I love a giver'; 'God told me to invade Iraq' means 'I decided to invade Iraq'; and 'God will punish you if you tell anyone, little boy' means … well, you know what it means.

Increasing numbers of people resent being coerced and frustrated by the political and financial demands of God's spokesmen: by the shenanigans of the Vatican, the ambitions of the Islamists (i.e the OIC – Organisation of Islamic Co-operation) and the American Religious Right in world affairs; and by the security constraints caused by the daily fear of some Muslim victim of religious indoctrination seeking eternal glory and seventy-two virgins. These people are beginning to wonder about the God that Christians and Muslims profess to worship and obey.

Nietzsche offered a good alibi: 'God's only excuse is that he doesn't exist.' He certainly pretends not to exist, and even devout believers have to accept that the God that men once depended on to heal the sick and ensure a bountiful harvest was clearly illusory – we can see now that disinfectant and fertiliser would have been respectively more effective than prayer and sacrifice. It rather looks as if those ancient clerics were misleading the people about God's involvement with the world, whether intentionally or innocently. And they still are, for despite the fact that science has shown us some of the exquisite simplicity of the workings of the natural world, such as the concept of evolution by natural selection or the all-embracing elementary relationship between energy and matter, $e = mc^2$, those who inhabit the supernatural worlds of Christianity and Islam nevertheless claim three-and-a-half billion followers worldwide. These followers presumably acquiesce to the suffering and trouble promoted by their clerics, whether intentionally or innocently, in the name of their particular god (which may or may not exist – and, by definition, only one monotheistic God can be valid).

I call myself an agnostic and I reject the anthropomorphic God, the God with human-like emotions and characteristics that Christians worship, whilst conceding that something that might be referred to as 'God' may exist or once have existed. After all, pantheists identify God with the universe, and the universe surely exists. What also exists, if only in men's minds, is ScapeGod – the God who is blamed for all the religious strife.

Some senior clerics may indeed believe all that they preach. They may believe that God guides them and makes them infallible, and that all the suffering that is done in God's name is the price that must be paid if humankind is to be saved. But, as we will see, there have been some cynical opportunists among them – men who sought power and privilege for themselves by colluding with despots and suppressing the masses of ordinary people. They have put a devout and virtuous face on their actions, and claimed to be acting in God's name, secure in the knowledge that God wouldn't contradict them. I confess that I have no answers to the big questions about the purpose and destination of humankind, but I find that the childish 'explanations' provided by spokesmen for the main religions are neither probable nor even imaginative.

But whether or not God exists is not central to my thesis. My main argument is that the major religions don't know any more about God than I do, and yet their clerics have arrogantly taken over people's lives, invented 'sins' for which they threaten them with dire punishment for all eternity, demanded political and financial privileges and more, all on the highly dubious basis that they have a self-proclaimed 'special relationship' with God. It is not so much the organised religions *per se,* as their senior

3

clerics, the men who define and operate the various monotheistic religions in supposed accordance with their God's wishes, which, they assure us, they alone are privy to.

This book is largely about these clerics – the leaders who specify the beliefs of their followers, and who instruct them in what they should think and how they should behave in order to satisfy God's wishes. These religious leaders enjoy respect, privilege, power and wealth by virtue of their self-proclaimed positions as God's confidantes. They are the Ayatollahs, imams and mullahs who interpret and enforce Islamic law and tradition; they are the founders and leaders of the various Protestant denominations and sects; they are the pastorpreneurs and televangelists; they are the popes and the senior hierarchy of Roman Catholicism, and they are the political leaders like George Bush and Tony Blair, in that they all claim to be guided by God. Using God's name, men such as these have variously caused incredible harm: ignorance, suffering, division, wars, massacres, genocides and hatreds – hatred of freedom, of women, of Jews, of homosexuals, of atheists, of other-believers …. Let me hasten to add that for the purpose of the present thesis, the term 'cleric' does not include ordinary religious workers – priests, nuns, vicars, charity workers and the religious congregations – who I see as the primary victims of clerical indoctrination.

These comments apply to all three main monotheistic religions, though I focus on mainstream traditional Christianity because it is the largest and most notorious. If I appear to write excessively about Roman Catholicism, it is because nearly all Western Christianity was Roman Catholicism until Luther ignited the Reformation in 1517, and Protestantism was born. To the present day, however, the Roman Catholic Church still claims to be the only truly Christian church, insisting that all Protestant and Orthodox denominations are 'not proper churches', even though the Scriptures upon which the Protestant churches are variously founded were written and edited by ancient clerics with a Catholic agenda.

4

Part I of this book contains a very brief and inevitably biased review of the origins of Christianity. Here we see that Christian beliefs were initially formulated by St Paul, and subsequently distorted by the early clerics after Jesus' predicted Apocalypse had failed to materialise – distorted to the extent that Christ would not now recognise any of the thousand-odd religious denominations that bear his name, and would bitterly oppose many of them, including, one suspects, Roman Catholicism.

Part II reviews some of the enormous harm, suffering and waste that have been inflicted on the world as a result of those distorted teachings, and the efforts of clerics to enforce them in God's name, though without his authority. As we shall see, clerics are discovered to be at the root of most of the hatred, division, ignorance and trouble commonly attributed either to God or, more vaguely, to 'religion'.

Part III reviews the main foundational beliefs of Christianity and finds every one of them to be false. This obliges us to consider why two billion normal, thoughtful people profess total acceptance of Christian beliefs and teachings, and why they defend these beliefs so tenaciously whenever they are challenged. However, we soon discover that most traditional Christian beliefs are not as deeply held (or even understood) as they appear to be, and we note a worldwide trend towards dumbing them down even further.

In Part IV we follow the money. We will find that being a cleric can be lucrative, and that in fact money, privilege and political power clearly preoccupy many clerics. We consider the rocky relationship between self-serving clerics and self-serving legislators, one result of which is that non-religious citizens inevitably find themselves generously subsidising clerics, receiving only abuse in return.

Finally, Part V briefly reviews some urgently needed changes in our attitudes to religion in general, and to its senior clerics in particular, if humankind is to survive and flourish.

PART I

SETTING THE SCENE

CHAPTER 1

ONE OF MANY BIASED SHORT HISTORIES OF CHRISTIANITY

There was a time when religion ruled the world. It is known as the Dark Ages.

> Ruth Hurmence Green in *The Born Again Skeptics' Guide to the Bible* (1979)

The ancient Greek philosophers knew a thing or two. From 600 to 100BCE, they developed some very progressive ideas about such varied subjects as ethics, gymnastics, logic, music, economics, physics, sociology and human happiness. Significantly, perhaps, they weren't particularly interested in theology. Early Rome was much influenced by Greek philosophy and the Romans helped to disseminate it (in Latin, but otherwise without much change) throughout the empire, along with some of their own developments such as paved roads and aqueducts. They were quite advanced.

The Persians, meanwhile (since 400BCE), had been worshipping a pagan sun god called Mithras. According to various sources,[1] Mithras was born of a virgin on 25 December with shepherds in attendance. During his lifetime he was a celibate itinerant teacher who, with twelve disciples, performed miracles and promised that their benevolent god would grant eternal salvation to the souls of believers in a world to come. On the day of judgement, the dead would be resurrected after a final conflict when light would triumph over darkness.

---

[1] Including H Pomeroy Brewster, *Saints and Festivals of the Christian Church* (1904); Franz Cumont, *The Mysteries of Mitha* (1903) and *Oriental Religions in Roman Paganism* (1911); Amaury de Reincourt, *Sex and Power in History* (1974); SH Hooke, *The Siege Perilous: Essays in Biblical Anthropology & Kindred Subjects* (1970); Homer Smith, *Man and His Gods* (1952); Martin A Larson, *The Story of Christian Origins* (1977); and John Holland Smith, *The Death of Classical Paganism* (1976).

Mithraists had purification rituals involving baptism to remove sins, when a sign of a cross was made on the infant's forehead; they also had a eucharist involving bread and wine which signified body and blood; and followers saw Mithras as one of a Holy Trinity. Women were, of course, barred from the Mithraic priesthood. They believed in a celestial Heaven and an infernal Hell below. After a last supper, Mithras was crucified, but then rose from his tomb on the third day and returned to Heaven (venerated figures had been rising from the dead for thousands of years before Mithras. Gods were expected to do it – you weren't a proper god if you didn't rise from the dead). Mithraism was introduced into the Roman Empire in 68BCE, where it became popular with the soldiers and gentry, so it was already well established long before Jesus started preaching.

Jesus was a Palestinian Jew born in Galilee during the reign of the Roman Emperor Augustus (27BCE to 14CE). We know little of him until he reached the age of around thirty, when we find a poor itinerant preacher, a charismatic but vitriolic orator who openly despised the arrogant Jewish priesthood. The authorities therefore saw him as a troublemaker, especially when he arrived in Jerusalem and started a riot in the temple. Jesus was an apocalyptist – he believed that the world would end very soon, possibly with his own death, and so he could never have had any intention of establishing any sort of lasting religion. Despite this, he supposedly passed the leadership of his sect to his disciple Peter, Petra the rock, now revered by Catholics as the first pope.

Neither Peter nor any of the other disciples was present at the Crucifixion and, despite fanciful stories of Jesus supposedly appearing to them after the Resurrection and encouraging them to spread his message, Mark's gospel makes no such claim (verses 16:9–20 were added later). The tiny, exclusively Jewish sect that ultimately evolved into Christianity would surely have faded away but for the efforts of Paul of Tarsus, the zealous missionary whose letters to the fledgling Christian communities were the first Christian documents. Though he never met Jesus, Paul wrote thirteen of the 27 books in the New Testament, and so it was Paul rather than Jesus who may be said to have 'invented' Christianity.

Jesus had never been interested in saving uncircumcised gentiles. His message had been intended exclusively for Jews, but Paul preached all around the eastern Mediterranean to anyone who would listen. And so it was Paul, not Peter, who promoted the messianic cult that became Christianity, and turned it into a recognised political force. The rest of the New Testament was written long after Jesus' death by other people who never knew him. Presumably this was done to fill a political need that became apparent after Jesus' predicted Apocalypse had failed to materialise and Paul's Christianity was nevertheless clearly becoming a popular movement.

It seems that Paul was a bitter little man, obsessed to the point of psychosis with his weak physique – he was skinny, bald and probably sexually impotent (2 Corinthians 12:7–10). He believed, however, that he had a mandate to preach God's Word (incidentally, modern psychiatrists have identified 'psychic inflation' as a condition, usually rooted in feelings of deep inferiority, whereby an individual imagines that he has godlike attributes). It was presumably Paul's masochistic resentment of his physique that drove him to attack the love, pleasure, freedom and autonomy enjoyed by most of humanity. It was Paul, not Jesus, who loathed sexuality and bodily pleasure; who hated women and who praised chastity, abstinence and celibacy (1 Corinthians 7:8). Paul similarly made a virtue of his lack of philosophical education – he praised ignorance and publicly ridiculed the Stoic and Epicurean philosophers, calling on believers to refute 'the addled and foolish questionings' and 'hollow frauds' of philosophy (2 Corinthians 10:5; 1 Timothy 1:3–7). These sentiments appealed particularly to the uneducated.

So it was that the Greek veneration of democracy, happiness, wisdom and philosophy came to be despised by the early Christians. Paul the weakling who hated his impotent body got his revenge on the world by teaching all Christians to hate their bodies, to hate women and to hate pleasure, learning and happiness. He also taught that lowly social station, dire poverty and unfair treatment must be accepted gladly and without complaint, as God's arbitrary judgements on each individual.

Whatever he really thought of the Roman occupying forces, Paul urged his Christians to submit to them. He taught that all power comes from God and he encouraged his followers to obey the Emperor because, he said, disobedience to those in power was effectively disobedience to God. Small wonder then that, despite Mithraism's head start over Christianity, Emperor Constantine did a deal with the early Christian clerics: 'You keep on preaching that I am God's deputy on Earth and get them to pay their taxes, and in return, I will make Christianity the official religion within the Roman empire.' He did just that in 325CE at the Congress of Nicaea. This had been called to determine once and for all time exactly what it was that Christians should and should not believe. It resulted in the Nicene Creed, with Mithras being deposed and Jesus officially declared the Son of God. Henceforth, the traditional celebration of Mithras' birthday on 25 December was to become Christmas Day. The Manicheans (adherents of a dualistic religion which originated around 250 CE, and thrived over half the world between 3rd and 7th centuries) were now taught that 'Christ is the glorious intelligence which the Persians called Mithras' (*Ecclesiastical History*, Eusebius of Caesarea, 3rd Century, Part 2, Chap 5), after Christian clerics had adopted Mithraic traditions and re-ascribed them to Jesus.

Nicaea marked the beginning of Christianity as a powerful institutional religion. It simultaneously marked the demise of the historical Jesus and his ideals as reported in the gospels, since most of his teachings had now become 'inconvenient'. Now that they enjoyed political power, the early clerics could smell personal aggrandisement, and they used a twisted form of philosophy to justify their repressive dogma. As quickly as they could, they claimed for example that God had given them the 'certain gift of truth'. They demanded that it was therefore incumbent on the whole of humanity to accept their authority because, as Ignatius of Antioch explained, 'Your bishop presides over you in the place of God.' Thus they took ownership of 'the Truth' and all those who purported to disseminate it. They went on to announce that God was male, and that male dominance was therefore the natural order of things. Women were declared subservient and barred from the priesthood, 'because our Lord was a man' (as confirmed by Pope Paul VI as recently as 1977). In 380CE, a law was passed condemning all non-Christians to 'infamy' and introducing the death penalty for those who threatened the persons or the goods of Catholic ministers.

The clerics quoted Matthew (17:25–26):

'From whom do the kings of the earth collect duty and taxes –
from their own sons or from others?'
'From others,' Peter replied.
'Then the sons are exempt,' Jesus said.

This showed that, as God's favourites, they should be exempt from His generally applicable laws and entitled to special privileges. Constantine had already been persuaded to excuse them from paying taxes or serving in the army, with hundreds of them having further gained exemption from ever having to face trial in a secular court. The clerics made themselves comfortable. Their contacts with Hinduism would have introduced them to the caste system wherein, impressively, the priests are deemed to belong to the privileged Brahmin class, immune from birth from ever having to do any hard or degrading work. And so Christianity now evolved into the very kind of totalitarian religion whose arrogant and privileged high priests Jesus had so despised.

The pope effectively assumed the emperor's role after the sack of Rome by Visigoths in 410. As clerics took over, the world slipped into the Dark Ages: roads and aqueducts started falling apart; learning and knowledge (especially in the fields of medicine, science, education, history and commerce) was despised and forgotten; the schools of Athens were closed, books were burned and history was rewritten. Academies were closed and, in 435, the clerics announced that heresy was now a capital offence. They introduced rules concerning sex, pleasure, free will and the afterlife; they invented the Devil to explain away the existence of evil; and they devised philosophical-sounding arguments to justify their use of force to compel submission (*Cognite Intrare*) to themselves.

They even produced a document purporting to be a decree from the Emperor Constantine bestowing Old Rome and its western territories on the pope, and this so called Donation of Constantine was used as the basis of the pope's temporal power right through the Dark Ages, until it was exposed as a forgery in 1439CE. As clerics took control, hygiene and health declined and, in 540, a bubonic plague broke out which ultimately killed tens of millions. Naturally, the clerics capitalised on this, calling it God's punishment for not heeding their warnings. Thus fear of their vindictive God was placed firmly into the minds of the superstitious masses.

By the ninth century, all of Europe had been Christianised and the clerics had become extremely rich and powerful. As the Dark Ages proceeded, more than a quarter of all Western Europe was 'held' by the Church; its bishops also owned land in feudal tenure as well as property and land they confiscated and took by force.

In the early fourth century, Emperor Diocletian had divided the Roman (Christian) Empire into a Greek-speaking eastern bloc and a Latin-speaking western bloc. Each had continued to evolve separately, so that the differences in tradition, liturgy and theology eventually became unbridgeable. The Eastern and Western churches formally separated in the Great Schism of 1054, with the Eastern (Orthodox) Church no longer subservient to the pope.

In the West, Christians had continued following the Bishop of Rome, but by now Rome had become so outrageously corrupt, so obsessed with power and possessions, and so obviously at odds with Jesus' ideals, that in 1326 the Pope issued a bull *Cum Inter Nonnullus,* making it a heresy even to suggest that Jesus was not himself a rich man of property. Sources of clerical wealth included tithes, benefices, wills, donations, sales of indulgences and simony and, for the Crusaders and Inquisitors, bribes and confiscations of alleged heretics' property (even though the Inquisitors were mostly Franciscans and Dominicans, who were sworn to poverty).

Having bled the countryside dry, Pope Clement V turned his attention inwards, to the wealthy Order of the Templars. In 1307 he spuriously accused them of heresy and arranged for the senior Templars to be arrested. The Order was suppressed in 1313, in order that all its property could be confiscated and shared between King Philip IV (of France) and the Pope. Many believers were disgusted, and some reacted.

Meanwhile many clerics showed absolute disdain for Jesus' message of peace. For example, in 1095 Pope Urban II initiated the first of the Crusades against the Muslims. This ultimately resulted in the butchery of twenty million innocents 'in God's name'. In 1229, the pope formalised the Inquisition, while in Northern Europe clerics were promoting witch hunts; and in the 1530s, in North and South America indigenous populations were methodically slaughtered 'for the glory of God', and millions of slaves were brought from Africa to replace them. So much for peace and goodwill to all men.

From the 1400s to the 1600s, Europe started to emerge from the Dark Ages. There was a period of rebirth, the Renaissance, when, despite Rome's best efforts, culture and technology started to creep forward. This was mainly thanks to the example set by educated Moors in Spain and the invention of the printing press, gunpowder and the navigational compass. These developments eventually led in 1517 to a second and more devastating schism, the Reformation. Martin Luther and the Protestants now stressed the importance of biblical teaching (which, thanks to the printing press, could now be widely disseminated), splitting away from the Roman church and its dependence on the pope's authority.

Protestantism turned out to be highly fissile, and almost immediately split into three branches: The Lutherans, John Calvin's Reformed Church and the born-again Anabaptists, who in due course subdivided further into Presbyterians, Anglicans, Free Churches and so on. They were all united in rejecting Catholic dogma in favour of the Bible, with some, such as the Methodists, further rejecting the whole notion of ordained priests and bishops in favour of lay teachers and even (Shock! Horror!) women preachers. As the Protestants fragmented, the clerics of each denomination laid claim and counter-claim to the unique truth about God and his wishes.

The Vatican reacted to its loss of power at the Council of Trent (1545–63), where it initiated the Counter Reformation – involving 130 more years of hatred and bloody warfare between Protestants and Catholics and the killing of millions more throughout Europe. Despite the fighting, the break from Rome's arthritic hand had freed up progress in scholarship in social, political and economic affairs. The seventeenth and eighteenth centuries saw the dawn of the Enlightenment. The prosperity that attended it brought literacy and independence to ordinary Europeans who had begun to question the whole Christian message, especially as the traditional churches had only hellfire, sacrifice and misery to offer.

The French Revolution of 1789 was a popular challenge to Rome, which still openly condemned the ideals of *liberté, egalité* and *fraternité*, persisting with its teaching that basic human rights were the God-given privilege of a wealthy few. The nineteenth century witnessed the Industrial Revolution, when religious control was finally separated from science. Charles Darwin was also born and Nietzsche announced the death of God.

Christianity continued to decline in Western Europe until it hit bottom in 1972: David L Edwards, the Speaker's Chaplain in the British House of Commons, described the Anglican Church as 'a museum', adding that people no longer believed in a supernatural soul, or that crops could be made to grow by casting spells over them: '[I]f we make any claim to be educated, we have to live in a universe which looks very different' from that of traditional Christianity (David L Edwards in *What is Real in Christianity*, Fontana, London, 1972). A lot of Western Europeans shared these views.

Yet Christianity didn't die, even in Western Europe. The psychological need to belong turned out to be stronger than the need to believe, and cultural roots can be surprisingly difficult to cut. Despite their loss of belief, many people have stayed on as superficially loyal members of their Protestant communities. Others have continued to pay lip service to Rome, going through the liturgies and reciting the creeds of their respective churches, openly professing their allegiance to Christianity. More recently, in underdeveloped countries, there has been a huge upsurge of interest in newer forms of Protestantism – such as born-again Pentecostalism, promoted by more obviously business-minded clerics.

There are now thousands (over twenty thousand, according to AC Grayling in *To Set Prometheus Free*, Oberon, 2009) of mutually contradictory denominations within Christianity. At one extreme are the authoritarian, conservative churches, such as the Roman Catholics and the Lutherans, whose teachings are based on tradition and the authority of clerics. With these we can bundle the Puritans, the fundamentalists and evangelists who recognise only the authority of the Bible. At the other extreme are the subjective empowerment churches, based on personal emotional relationships with God, such as the Charismatics and the Pentecostals. And between these extremes are the liberals who variously depend on authority, the gospels and inner mystical sources for their beliefs, but who are generally less dogmatic and more tolerant. Beyond these extremes are nihilism and post-modernist new-ageism, loosely based on Christianity though strongly influenced by mystical Eastern cultures such as spiritual yoga, tai chi and reiki in one direction, and pantheism and deism in the other. Jesus would recognise none of them.

We have seen that the history of Christianity is largely the chequered history of its senior clerics and their bloody quest for wealth and power over the masses, even though they presented themselves sanctimoniously as holy men, piously sacrificing themselves to God's will. Today, when Christians talk of 'God', or 'the Church', or 'the Holy Scriptures', they tend to think of these things as being not of this world but in some way spiritual, transcending human experience, absolute and impenetrable. But as we have just seen, they are in fact only whatever a few senior clerics have chosen to tell us they are: God and his supposed wishes are known to us only through the words of self- or mutually-appointed clerics. The Church's structure and teachings were determined by its clerics; the scriptures were written by ancient clerics and edited by subsequent clerics to suit their own political purposes. It is clear that the Christian God, the Christian churches and the scriptures are together no more than a man-made façade that conceals clerics at work, and the whole concept of Christianity as a 'revealed religion' is based on a handful of clerics 'revealing' scriptures that earlier clerics had written. It remains to be seen whether or not those clerics were high-minded and holy, or self-serving and cynical – we will keep an eye on them in Part II.

PART II

THE HARM DONE IN GOD'S NAME

In 1999, Pope John Paul II formally apologised on behalf of his predecessors for their unspeakable crimes against humanity (though he called them mere 'errors'). He was probably referring to the sadistic torture and wholesale slaughter of millions of innocents as devout Christians gratuitously attacked and murdered Muslims, Jews, Orthodox Christians and so-called heretics in the Crusades, the Inquisition, and the several religious wars; or maybe it was his Church's contribution to the Spanish Conquistadors' annihilation of the native Americans in Latin America; the mass-murdering Croatian priests; the slaughter of the Slovakian Jews by priestly president Tiso; the Rwandan Catholic priests' and nuns' involvement in the Hutu genocide of hundreds of thousands of Tutsis; or clerical complicity with the European Holocaust. Or possibly he felt bad about the harmonious communities that had been split and set against each other by the activities of his missionaries.

Conceivably he had in mind the discriminatory teaching by senior clerics condemning Jews, women, homosexuals, Atheists, Humanists, Protestants and non-Christians in general. Or he might have been thinking of his fellow clerics' opposition to most scientific and philosophical learning, and to virtually all progress in medicine, politics and sociology – their opposition to medical regenerative research, their censorship and destruction of important works of science, philosophy and literature, and their promotion of ignorance. Perhaps he was thinking of his predecessors' opposition to human rights and freedom of speech and thought for the masses. Or maybe he was apologising for the psychological damage that his clerics' teaching had done to so many of the faithful by conditioning them to believe that they were miserable sinners who should spend their lives grovelling on their knees, begging forgiveness.

Perhaps he had in mind the hundreds of thousands of young lives his paedophile priests had destroyed with the connivance and protection of his bishops; or it could have been the cant and hypocrisy of much of his Church's moral teaching that had upset him. Perhaps he was apologising for his clerics' unwarranted disruption of national and international political affairs, and their demands to national governments for special tax concessions, grants and costly privileges; or could it be that he was feeling a little guilty about the contribution of Catholic dogma to global overpopulation and the serious trouble it was causing in terms of poverty, starvation, disease (especially AIDS), pollution, water stress and global warming? We'll never know, because he didn't actually mention any of these things. As a Vatican spokesman pithily explained, 'Given the number of sins committed in the course of twenty centuries, it must necessarily be rather summary.' (See AC Grayling's essay on 'Repentance' in *The Meaning of Things,* Phoenix Paperbacks, London, 2002)

The Pope's apology was an implied admission that these atrocities were committed not by God, but by devout Christians under the guidance and encouragement of Christian clerics. However, the clerics reserved the most sadistic behaviour for themselves; US agnostic Robert Ingersoll (in his 1892 essay on Thomas Paine) summarised their achievements thus:

You have imprisoned the human mind; you have been the enemy of liberty; you have burned us at the stake – wasted us upon slow fires – torn our flesh with iron; you have covered us with chains – treated us as outcasts; you have filled the world with fear; you have taken our wives and children from our arms; you have confiscated our property; you have denied us the right to testify in courts of justice; you have branded us with infamy; you have torn out our tongues; you have refused us burial. In the name of your religion, you have robbed us of every right; and after having inflicted on us every evil that can be inflicted in the world, you have fallen on your knees and with clasped hands you have implored your God to torment us for ever.

CHAPTER 2

PROMOTE IGNORANCE, OPPOSE PROGRESS

[The Christians'] *injunctions are like this. 'Let no one educated, no one wise, no one sensible draw near. For their abilities are thought to be evils. But for anyone ignorant, anyone stupid, anyone uneducated, anyone who is a child, let him come boldly.'*
Origen in 'Against Celsus' 3.44. (third century)

Reason must be deluded, blinded and destroyed. Faith must trample underfoot all reason, sense and understanding.
Martin Luther (1483–1546)

When the facts change, I change my mind. What do you do?
Maynard Keynes

We tend to fear those things we don't understand – ignorance therefore breeds fear, and fear breeds credulousness and a tendency to clutch at straws. Ignorance is therefore good for the religion business, because fearful people will follow a leader who claims to know the right path, and a religious congregation that is conscious of its ignorance of God's wishes will respond to a cleric who claims special knowledge and total rightness in everything. But he must keep his congregation ignorant. The cleric must not tolerate doubters or freethinkers – he must instantly denounce them as agents of Satan, asserting that free thought is the path to perdition.

Accordingly, Christians are taught that in the Garden of Eden, Eve committed the Original Sin when she tasted the apple of knowledge, and this was such a heinous crime that God vehemently cursed all humankind to the extent that every human being must bear the guilt for Eve's action, now and forever more. That's how serious it is.

The gospels confirm that knowledge is taboo: 'I will destroy the wisdom of the wise' (1 Corinthians 1:19); 'God chose what is foolish in the world to shame the wise' (1 Corinthians 1:27); 'For the wisdom of the world is folly with God' (1 Corinthians 3:18–19). Jesus said, 'I praise you Father ... because you have hidden these things from the wise and learned, and have revealed them to little children' (Matthew 11:25). When asked why he talked in riddles, Jesus exposed his racist side when he explained that it was in order to deceive non-Jews, lest they too achieve salvation (Matthew 13:10–17, Mark 4:11–12 and Luke 8:9–10). He chose disciples who were uneducated peasants, and from them he demanded uncritical acceptance of his teaching: '...unless you change and become like little children, you will never enter the kingdom of heaven' (Matthew 18:3). Significantly, little children don't ask for evidence the way Pharisees (i.e. senior clerics) did, and Jesus clearly feared intellectuals. Hence, 'Blessed are those that have not seen and have believed.' As we will see, about the only thing that modern clerics still have in common with Jesus is their dislike of people who ask for evidence.

The clergy ... have in most modern countries been the avowed enemies of the diffusion of knowledge, the danger of which to their own profession they, by a certain instinct, seem always to have perceived.

Henry Thomas Buckle (1821–62)

It is ominous, then, that these outspoken advocates for ignorance should have managed to gain for themselves so much influence in the running of our schools and seats of learning, and to have maintained that authority even into the third millennium CE.

Censorship

Two thousand years ago, mature adults understood less of the workings of nature than a typical eight-year-old knows today. Scientific findings have shown virtually all early 'knowledge' to be factually wrong, yet modern Christians still cling to the 'truths' revealed by superstitious goatherds. For a thousand years, clerics were so politically powerful that they could solemnly and with great ceremony kill anybody who produced evidence contradicting their dogma. This would certainly silence the troublemaker, and provide an object lesson to anyone else who might be thinking of thinking. Going with the crowd was always the easiest way to survive.

The early Christian clerics energetically set about their task of destroying knowledge: in 391 CE, for example, 700,000 ancient rolls in the library of Alexandria were burned on the orders of Archbishop Theophilus, including 270,000 ancient documents assembled by Ptolemy Philadelphus (king of Egypt). In 529 CE, Justinian, builder of the inaptly-named 'Church of the Holy Wisdom' in Constantinople, suppressed the Academies of Plato, Aristotle and the Stoics because they taught 'pagan' ideas. In the fifth century, the pope produced a list of 'heretical' books which he forbade the faithful from reading. The masses were thus kept ignorant of inconvenient truths for a thousand years, until Gutenberg's invention of the printing press in 1450 enabled multiple copies of dissenting tracts to be made public. Clerical censors were left spluttering with frustration, which they vented on the authors: in 1520, Leo X issued a papal bull calling for the burning of the works of the heretic Martin Luther. In 1552, Spanish theologian Michael Servetus' treatise *Christianity Restored* (which questioned the Holy Trinity) hit the fan, and the clerics hunted Servetus across Europe. When they caught him in France he was sentenced to death; he escaped and was finally caught by Calvinists in Switzerland, where he and his book were burned for having 'tried to infect the world with stinking heretical poison'. A convincing defence of the Holy Trinity?

In 1559, Pope Paul IV formalised the *Index Librorum Prohibitorum* (The Index of Prohibited Books, known as the 'Roman Index') in an effort to suppress knowledge of anything that deviated from Church dogma. This included much of the Church's actual history and similar unwelcome truths. The pope sought to 'expunge from human memory the names of heretics'

23

such as Rabelais, Erasmus and Machiavelli. Later editions of the Index naturally went on to host Galileo's *Dialogue* and Darwin's *Origin of Species*, as well as works by, among others, Bacon, Berkeley, Copernicus, Defoe, Descartes, Diderot, Gibbon, Goldsmith, Hobbes, Hume, Kant, Leibniz, Locke, Mill, Paine, Pascal, Rousseau, Sartre, Spinoza, Sterne, Voltaire and Zola. Descartes' *Meditations* was added in 1948, just three years after the end of World War II, though significantly Hitler's *Mein Kampf* was never listed. The clerics finally abandoned their Index in 1966 (when it still listed more than four thousand forbidden books), and in 1992 they even forgave Galileo for his wicked heresy.

The Bible is probably the most censored book of all. It was banned originally because clerics didn't want their flocks corrupted by 'incorrectly interpreting' the script, instead of blindly following their dogma. In particular they were unimpressed by Tyndale's translation of the Bible into English in 1525; so they strangled him at the stake and then burned him with his bibles. Even in the 1990s there were various legal attempts at suppression in the USA, generally on the grounds that the 'lewd, indecent and violent contents of that book are unsuitable for young children'! (quote from a legal action taken in 1992 in the township of Brooklyn Center, Minnesota).

Other sacred scriptures have fared little better: the Koran's text was supposedly brought by the Angel Gabriel directly from God to the prophet Mohammed, and is therefore 'the Scripture whereof there is no doubt'. Naturally, therefore, successive popes deemed it heretical and started burning it as soon as the first printed copies appeared in Europe. The Mayan holy book *Popol Vuh* similarly fell foul of the Spanish missionaries, who burned it to destroy evidence of a superior civilisation (though they said it was because they reckoned that the Devil had written it). It was also decided that the Jewish Talmud was blasphemous. Clerics started burning it in 1144, and these particular flames were not extinguished until the Second Vatican Council in 1965.

Religious censorship and self-censorship continues to the present day. Many publishers and libraries around the world refuse to handle material which might attract the wrath of the likes of Ayatollah Khomeni, who issued his infamous edict in 1989 sentencing to death 'the author of the book entitled The Satanic Verses ... and all those involved in its publication who were aware of its contents'. Many innocents were killed as a result of this intervention, and publishers are now naturally reluctant to handle anything that Muslim clerics might arbitrarily deem to be 'grossly offensive' ... such as the children's story of the *Three Little Pigs*. Islamic clerics are even more sensitive than Christians, and unfortunately the divinely ordained laws of Islam (as laid down in Sharia, the Koran and Hadith) are quite incompatible with free speech, critical thought and universal human rights.

Many US Protestant clerics tell us to throw away our schoolbooks because, they claim, the Holy Scriptures (written, remember, by early Catholic clerics) contain all the knowledge humankind will ever need. They are particularly hostile to Darwin's observations about evolution. As a measure of their success in suppressing them, an ABC news poll dated February 2004 found that more than a hundred million Americans claimed to believe that God created fully developed humans and placed them on Earth at some time in the last ten thousand years (actually at 9am on 23 October 4004BCE, according to Archbishop Ussher, Primate of All Ireland 1625–56).

So bitter have the creationists been toward Darwin's ideas about evolution that they accuse researchers worldwide (including biologists, geologists, astronomers, geneticists, nuclear physicists, cosmologists, archaeologists, climatologists, palaeontologists, microbiologists and virologists) of conspiring together to produce fake evidence to support evolutionist 'lies'. Creationist Henry Morris (in *The Remarkable Birth of the Planet Earth*, Dimension Books, Minneapolis, 1978) declared that '[e]volution is the root of atheism, of communism, nazism, anarchism, behaviourism, racism, economic imperialism, militarism, anarchism, libertinism, and all manner of anti-

Christian systems of belief and practice'. According to *Creation* magazine, these also included apartheid (26:2 March 2004), Stalinism (10:4 Sept 1998) and even the Rwandan genocide (21:2 March 1999). Poor Darwin, a messenger blamed for somewhat more than his elegantly simple message.

Propaganda

Christian clerics suppressed learning practically from the start, in Nicaea in 325CE, and it was not until the Renaissance in the sixteenth century that the first stirrings of a non-papal intellectual movement in the western world began to appear. Based on ancient Greek philosophy, there was guarded talk of human rights and reason, and a questioning of divine revelation and miracles. Such heresy raised serious challenges, which Pope Gregory XV dealt with not only by force, but also in 1622 by establishing the *Sacra Congregatio de Propaganda Fide*, the Sacred Ministry of Propaganda. This was intended to spread Catholic dogma by more subtle means, as it had become apparent that mass slaughter wasn't conveying quite the right message about their loving God. 'Propaganda' originally meant 'education', but the pope's stuff was so manipulative that the word soon gained negative connotations. Sure enough, within ten years the propagandists were suppressing Galileo's discoveries about our solar system.

Hitler was particularly impressed by the effectiveness of propaganda as a weapon. He wrote in *Mein Kampf* what clerics had long known:

> *The driving force which has brought about the most tremendous revolutions has never been a body of scientific knowledge which has gained force over the masses but … devotion … and hysteria which has urged them into action. We must avoid excessive intellectual demands on the public … The propagandist should exploit the primitiveness of sentiment in the mass of the people.*

Just as the clerics did.

ClericSpeak and Obscurantism

When clerics talk of transubstantiation, they claim that 'the whole substance of the wine is literally converted into the blood of Christ', and they justify this by redefining 'literally' to mean just the opposite. Clerics tell us that God sends natural disasters that torment mankind because he 'greatly loves and cares for us' – it's a 'hatred' kind of love and an 'uninterested' kind of care. They claim that human love is undependable and inferior to a love for God, which somehow involves unquestioning obedience to his clerics. They tell us that ignorance is 'wisdom'; their 'freedom' excludes freedom of speech or thought; and 'life' to them means 'life in Jesus', which takes place after physical death. For clerics, suffering is a blessing, and pain is desirable.

Such Orwellian ClericSpeak is intended to confuse our thinking, and Sir Leslie Stephen (English author, 1832–1904) knew well the reasoning when he asked rhetorically: 'Would it not be easier to say "the doctrine is not true" than to say "the doctrine is true, but it means just the reverse of what it is taken to mean"?' (from 'The Aims of Ethical Societies', in *Social Rights and Duties*, 1900) ClericSpeak is deliberately incoherent and unintelligible, making most religious claims either so ambiguous, or else such complete gibberish, that they are incapable of being discussed rationally, let alone of being shown logically to be false. It is sham profundity, legerdemain that is deliberately obscure so that simple mortals will assume that it must contain deep truths too profound for their humble intellects.

> *Public language that defies normal understanding is an ancient repressive artifice known to all the churches.*
> Primo Levi, Italian writer and Auschwitz survivor (1919–87)

An opportunist can speak with authority on any topic of which his audience knows less, or thinks that it knows less, than he does. A cleric can therefore claim expertise in the matter of God's Will. His audience, conscious that it knows nothing of God or his will, can only accept his self-proclaimed authority, especially as they are already impressed by his pallium, alb, mitre and crosier. The ritual of the sacrament, and especially the ClericSpeak, will be assumed to be very wise and deep – too deep, as we have already noted, for ordinary men to understand, its lack of substance shrouded inside a cloud of mysticism and incense.

In the November 2009 report on clerical child abuse in Dublin, Ireland, we were introduced by Cardinal Desmond Connell to a pathetically juvenile ploy known as 'mental reservation', which permits a cleric to convey a 'misleading impression' without being guilty of lying. The Cardinal insisted that he had not been lying, for example, when he said that he had cooperated with the police because 'we never said we cooperated *fully*'. He had not misled journalists when he told them, 'diocesan funds are not used to compensate victims,' because he never said that they were *never* used for such a purpose. According to Dr Connell, this childish ploy 'has been developed and much discussed over the centuries' by senior Catholic clerics.

Another deceptive trick popular with clerics is to switch definitions in mid-argument. 'The Catholic Church', for example, has several possible meanings: the pope; the Vatican; the Curia; Catholic policy and dogma; the agglomeration of all the national churches and their clergy; or the 1.1 billion lay members of the Catholic Church around the world. So the statement 'Catholics abhor socialism' may be spoken as if on behalf of all Catholics when in fact it may apply only to the Curia. In a discussion, the Vatican may present itself as anything between an independent secular State and a humble mouthpiece for God, depending on the circumstances, and without indicating that the subject has been changed. And as we have seen, bland impersonal references to 'the Church' or 'Mother Church' distract attention from the clerics who actually pull the strings and operate the levers behind the reverential façade.

Until recently, Catholic services were conducted in Latin, which was gibberish to most of those present, and great stress was placed on the exact performance of mumbo jumbo incantations, ritual gestures, chants, candles, incense and theatrical presentation. The dogma tells us, for example, that baptism doesn't 'work' if, in the absence of water, the priest uses unmelted snow, saliva, wine, tears, sweat, milk, beer or soup. The Mass wine will not turn into blood if it is of the 'wrong' kind, if it is diluted or if the form of words (i.e. the magic spell) is not exactly correct. The wizards who perform this sorcery are nevertheless highly critical of the 'superstitions' of other faiths. They seem not to notice that their petitionary prayers, no matter how accurately phrased and performed, simply don't work – God ignored his chosen people in Auschwitz and Belsen, he was heedless of the innocents in Dresden and Hiroshima, and he studiously ignores the pope's prayers for peace every Easter. To my way of thinking, clerics who depend for their authority on talking Godswallop, uttering mumbo-jumbo incantations and dressing up like the cast of the *Mikado* deserve ridicule rather than respect.

Freedom of Speech and Thought

In 2002, the British Broadcasting Standards Authority (BSA) reprimanded broadcaster James Whale after a radio discussion with Bishop Sean Manchester about exorcising evil spirits. His offence? James had 'unjustly and unfairly' addressed Sean by his Christian name, where he should of course have been more unctuously respectful of someone claiming the inside track with evil spirits. The BSA required all broadcast media to show obsequious respect to clerics who had done nothing to deserve it.

'Respect' is a word robbed of its meaning – good manners reasonably require that we should respect (in the sense of 'be considerate of') people's religious beliefs, and that we should respect (in the sense of 'uphold') their right to express them. However, respect in the sense of 'admiration' must be earned, and there should be no duty to admire a naïve or cynical person, as a self-proclaimed exorcist must be, when scorn for his disclosures about evil spirits would be more appropriate. We have a moral duty to be considerate of all of our fellow humans, and to uphold their rights regardless of their ethnicity, sex or ability, which are beyond their control. There is, however, no duty to admire a person's political or religious affiliations, or their opinions on supernatural matters, about which they know as little as we do, even when their public displays of religious affiliation in the form of special clothing or ornament clearly show that they expect sycophantic treatment. Barbara Smoker points out (in *Freethinker*, July 2006) that claiming to be deeply wounded by constructive criticism is a way of gaining privilege; but that political correctness now requires that we *pretend* to esteem dogma that actually offends our intellects, making us complicit in the harm being done.

Early clerics conceived the offences of blasphemy, sacrilege and heresy to protect themselves from reasoned criticism while compelling everyone to show reverence for whatever they chose to call 'sacred'. Historian David Christie-Murray explains (in *A History of Heresy*, Oxford University Press, 1989) that heresy is 'the opinion held by a minority of men which the majority declares unacceptable and is strong enough to punish'. So it is really just a word describing the superior power of intolerant majorities. As Galileo's case showed, heresy hurts most when it's true, and though John (8:32) tells us that 'the truth shall set men free', in clerical circles, the truth is what really pisses them off the most. Heresy (they got Jesus for it) is about challenges to authoritarian clerical power, and until quite recently the punishment for it varied from confiscation and exile to torture, imprisonment and death. As Michael Nugent of Atheism Ireland points out: 'The reason religious beliefs need protection from ridicule is that they are ridiculous.'

The absence of *autos-da-fé* today has more to do with the clerics' loss of political power than with any realisation that their ways of expressing God's great love were sending out the wrong sort of vibes. However, we are still legally required to avoid offending oversensitive clerical feelings, especially Muslim ones, by using our limited freedom of speech 'responsibly'. As novelist Philip Hensher asks in his essay 'Free Speech Responsibly' (in *Free Expression is no Offence*, Penguin, London, 2005): Who decides when speech is being used 'responsibly' ... the police? The Vatican? The tabloids? The Taliban? ... the very organisations which currently use free speech most irresponsibly. Yes, we should tolerate other people's harmless superstitions as a matter of courtesy, just as they should respect ours, but '[t]he history of special pleading, special whining, sacrilege laws, blasphemy laws and censorship is a history of licensed bigotry, sometimes murderous, at best moralistic.' (*Observer*: Jonathan Mendos' criticism of Michael Burleigh's book *Earthly Powers*)·

A big problem with blasphemy legislation in a multicultural society is that one religion's truth is another religion's blasphemy. The Attorney General of India (Soli Sorabjee SC, in the UK House of Lords Select Committee on Religious Offences, HL Paper 95-1, 10 April 2003, para 52) explains:

> ... *experience shows that criminal laws prohibiting hate speech and expression will encourage intolerance, divisiveness and unreasonable interference in freedom of expression. Fundamentalist Christians, religious Muslims and devout Hindus would then seek to invoke the criminal machinery against each other's religion, tenets and practices. That is what is increasingly happening today in India. We need not more repressive laws but more free speech to combat bigotry and to promote tolerance.*

Which is to say that individual human rights should not extend to freedom from fair criticism.

In 2008, sixty years after the 1948 UN Universal Declaration of Human Rights, the United Nations Human Rights Council (UNHRC) took a big step backwards when the Organisation of the Islamic Conference (OIC), representing 57 Islamic states, managed to change the mandate of those special rapporteurs who had previously been responsible for protecting freedom of expression ('Art 19: Everyone has the right to freedom of opinion and expression'). They would now be required 'to report on instances in which the abuse of the right of freedom of expression constitutes an act of racial or religious discrimination'. Happily, the resolution was non-binding. In 2011 the concept of 'defamation of religion' lost traction in the world of human rights, to be replaced with a more reasonable resolution concerned with incitement to violence.

The True Price of Ignorance

In matters of science, clerics have been consistently wrong. They have opposed medical research from the beginning (they forbade the dissection of a human corpse, calling it 'a desecration of the temple of the Holy Ghost'), and have continued through to their current condemnation of genetic research. They have presided over fifteen hundred years of wilfully blocked opportunities for the human race to better itself socially, medically and technically. They were absolutely wrong when they told us that disease was caused by 'demon possession', and that it was 'God's punishment for sin'. Clerics even condemned Franklin's invention of the lightning conductor as an attempt to defeat God's will. Unabashed, they are still lecturing the medical profession about the sinfulness of 'playing God', declaring now that it is immoral to investigate genetic modification, or to work on embryonic stem cells. It is wrong, they say, to undertake in-vitro fertilisation, surrogate motherhood, medically assisted reproduction or therapeutic cloning, or even to tackle the spread of AIDS with condoms (though since 2010, this restraint no longer applies to male prostitutes, according to Pope Benedict).

Science only began to address natural phenomena a few hundred years ago. Its achievements have been impressive, and the more so when compared with Christianity, which has been around for a couple of thousand years. During this time its clerics first suppressed and defiled the knowledge that we had inherited from the ancient Greeks, and then dogmatically obstructed practically all scientific, social and economic progress. Such deliberate ignorance has cost our race dearly – it has been suggested by a number of writers that but for clerical opposition, education would have flourished and man might have landed on the moon and conquered cancer a couple of hundred years ago. The Irish historian John Bury has noted:

> *History shows that knowledge grew when speculation was perfectly free in Greece, and that in modern times, since restrictions on enquiry have been removed, it has advanced with a velocity which would have seemed diabolical to the slaves of the mediaeval church.*

It is the same with Islam. Mathematics, especially algebra (*al-jabr*), and medicine flourished during the Golden Age of Islam (ninth to twelfth centuries) while the western world languished in the Dark Ages, and some of that legacy is to be found today in beautiful and intricate Islamic architecture. However, around 900CE, the Sunni community in Arabia decided that they had resolved all the questions pertaining to right belief and that there was no further scope for discussion. The gates of reason were henceforth closed. Then, in the twelfth century, Persian theologian Imam Al-Ghazali (1058–1111) proclaimed that revelation was superior to reason and that mathematics weakened the faith. Religious orthodoxy now came to dominate, and the scholars who had made Islam great were persecuted. In 2002, according to the UN *Arab Human Development Report*, half of all Arab women were illiterate and the entire Arab world translated only around 330 books per year. Pervez Hoodbhoy, Professor of Physics at Quaid-r-Azam University, Islamabad, described their universities in *Science and Islam* as 'intellectual rubble'. In this era of nuclear energy and instant communications, more than a billion Muslims still allow every aspect of their daily lives (how to wash, how to defecate, and so on) to be dictated by instructions purportedly revealed to an illiterate merchant 1,400 years ago. A Muslim renaissance is long overdue.

Sociologist Max Weber (1864–1920) noted a hundred years ago in his essay 'The Protestant Ethic' that nineteenth-century industrial and social development had taken place mainly in those countries that encouraged hard work and Spartan living. It did not flourish in those other countries, otherwise equally equipped for industrial 'take off', where religious cultures were resistant to change; where free thought, rights, liberty and individualism were discouraged; where unthinking, blind subservience was enforced and the *status quo* was vigorously defended. Weber's thesis is that religious dogma and clerical political pressure had stifled major social advances. The 2005 UN Human Development Report found that the most developed countries in the world, in terms of life expectancy, literacy, income, education and gender equality (countries such as Norway, Iceland, Australia, Canada and Sweden), happened to be the least religious countries, places where clerics had little power. The fifty least developed nations were also found to be the most devoutly religious, ruled largely by clerics. Is this a coincidence?

It is worth considering how much love, time and effort have been devoted by believers to their ungrateful God, who has never once acknowledged them. Consider the lifetimes committed by the world's greatest stonemasons to building enormous and unimaginably beautiful cathedrals and mosques; the financial resources and artistic skills devoted to producing religious treasures and works of art; the lifetimes devoted by some of the world's greatest thinkers to theological questions for which there are no answers; and, finally, the billions of man-hours collectively spent each year by the devout in grovelling on their knees. Such commitment surely deserves a more appreciative god.

Who do we blame for our ignorance – God or clerics? Surely no god would have endowed us with the power to think and then forbidden us from using it. But clerics interested in power would have every reason to keep us ignorant in order to protect their elevated positions. Is anyone else to blame? Yes, the Emperor Constantine, for giving the clerics political power in the first place, because whenever clerics have held untrammelled power, they have ruled pretty much as the Taliban does today. God, though, is clearly innocent.

CHAPTER 3

SIN AND MORALITY

... Christian too is a certain cruelty toward one's self and toward others: hatred of unbelievers; the will to persecute ... Christian is all hatred of the intellect, of pride, of courage, of freedom, of intellectual libertinage; Christian is hatred of the senses, of joy in general.

Nietzsche (1844–1900)

All national institutions of religion, whether Jewish, Christian or Turkish, appear to me no other than human inventions set up to terrify and enslave mankind, and monopolize power and profit.

Thomas Paine in *The Age of Reason* (1794)

It is no accident that the symbol of a bishop is a crook, and the sign of an archbishop is a double cross.

Dom Dix, Anglican Benedictine monk (1901–52)

Origins of Secular Morality

Carl Sagan (in 'The God Hypothesis' in Christopher Hitchens' *The Portable Atheist*, Da Capo Press, Philadelphia, 2007, p.233) tells of Nile crocodiles that carry their eggs in their mouths over prodigious distances in order to protect their young. Despite the obvious temptation, eating the eggs is not an option – those crocodiles with a taste for egg leave no offspring. After a few generations, therefore, all you have are crocodiles that are genetically predisposed not to eat their eggs. Self-evidently, this seemingly 'moral' behaviour owes more to evolution than to ethics.

We humans find ourselves in a cold, unsympathetic universe that ignores our prayers; a universe where, if we are to survive and flourish, we must live harmoniously and constructively with each other. Fortunately, like the crocodiles, we have an inherited predisposition to do just that. In human pre-history, anti-social individuals would have failed to breed successfully and their genes would die away, while altruistic, collaborative types would flourish, breed successfully and hand on their genetic predispositions toward co-operative behaviour to subsequent generations. This has left our race with an inherited tendency to socialise and to cooperate with each other, and it is on this basis that humankind has risen to the top of the animal kingdom.

Clearly, behaviour that lubricates the functioning of human society and helps its members to lead useful and happy lives is necessary to human survival. It is 'good' behaviour, and can be deemed to be 'moral' behaviour. Again, it is a consequence of evolution, and it is the origin of that inbuilt moral knowledge of right and wrong that we call 'conscience'. Social morality is a natural evolutionary characteristic among all behaviour-acquiring social creatures. This does not just apply to humankind – we can see such behaviour in many social animals, in the form of restrained behaviour and even altruism and self-sacrifice, especially among the higher primates.

Ongoing harmonious relations within human societies are mainly facilitated by informal moral norms designed to make it easier to live and work fearlessly together. These norms consist of voluntary personal constraints and guidelines about peoples' relationships and their obligations towards all those whose wellbeing and happiness they might influence. Good manners, honesty and trustworthiness are essential, because, in spite of our diverse languages and cultures, all humans share the same basic values and concerns: we all know what it means to feel fear, desire, sadness and pleasure, and we all suffer if we are imprisoned, victimised or humiliated. It is in everyone's interest that we should seek for others all that we wish for ourselves.

Moral philosopher Adam Smith (1723–70), in his 1759 book *The Theory of Moral Sentiments*, points out that individuals who act so as to further the interests of others ultimately serve their own interests – he calls it 'enlightened self-interest'. This is the origin of morality and conscience: acts of theft, false testimony, rape and killing are immoral simply because they hurt other people, not because God says so. Belief in an all-seeing God might once have promoted superficially 'moral' behaviour, but only in the sense that having a policeman watching you promotes good behaviour. Significantly, most authorities now place more trust in CCTV than in God to keep the peace.

There are no absolute rights and wrongs in secular morality, just as there are no unconditional values or dogmatic commandments. There are merely flexible guidelines, such as:

- The Golden Rule (treat your neighbour as you would wish him to treat you);
- The Universalisation Test (what if everyone behaved like this?);
- The Model Test (what would a wise and virtuous person do in these circumstances?);
- Rawls' 'veil of ignorance' test (design a society without knowing in advance what your own role in it will be); and
- The Universal Declaration of Human Rights.

Secular morality involves a duty of care: stepping forward to help those in need; and a duty of respect: stepping back to leave them free to lead fulfilled lives. As Confucius said, 'Concern for humanity is the root of all morality.' The great moral questions of the twenty-first century are about the human rights of the victims of oppression; the vast inequalities between rich and poor; overpopulation; the effects of unregulated globalisation; and the trillion dollars spent annually training and equipping military forces to rain death, disfigurement and destruction on innocent civilians around the world. They are not about gay bishops or re-married divorcees, or the other trivialities that seem to obsess clerical ethicists.

The Origins of 'Revealed' Morality

Christian clerics have proclaimed themselves the true arbiters of morality, and they are widely acknowledged in this role. They claim that God has given them 'the gift of moral discernment and certainty'. This means that clerical morality is 'revealed' morality, supposedly revealed to clerics by God. It follows that it is arbitrary and quite unrelated to human welfare – clerical morality is whatever God tells his clerics it is, and they then report it to us in the form of a litany of commandments, prescriptions, constraints and taboos. Most of these, it turns out, have very little to do with concern for humanity.

Clerics state emphatically that without God there can be no morality. To illustrate this point they often cite the 'godless' regimes of Stalin and Hitler as examples of what happens when nations abandon God. This is a rhetorical ploy, a distraction, and it should be observed that Stalin and Hitler presided over totalitarian organisations that demanded unthinking obedience on pain of punishment. They denounced independent thought and demanded absolute conformity with their dogmas. They were the very antithesis of free thought and had much more in common with the authoritarian religions upon which they were modelled. As Hitler admitted (Mein Kampf, Vol.2, chapter 5):

So far there has been nothing more imposing on earth than the hierarchical organisation of the Catholic Church. A good part of that organisation I have transported directly to my own party.

Far from abandoning God, as Jesuit Archbishop Thomas Roberts acknowledged, 'The factual evidence seems overwhelming that German Catholics generally – bishops, clergy, people – supported the Hitler war effort.' Protestants too – Lutherans, Calvinists and the rest. As for the Holocaust, it was conceived and conducted by Christians with '*Gott mit uns*' ('God with us') on their belt buckles. As Peter de Rosa confirmed (in *Vicars of Christ*, Poolbeg Press, Dublin, 2000):

There is, tragically, an undeniable link between the fires, the crosses, the papal legislation, the pogroms – and the gas chambers and crematoria of the Nazi death camps.

While the pope was busily excommunicating communists wholesale, he never even hinted to any of those responsible for the Holocaust that what they were doing might be wrong.

It is disingenuous, therefore, to cite the Holocaust as an example of what happens when men abandon their faith; rather it is another fine example, along with the Crusades, the Inquisition and the witch burnings, of what happens when they heed it.

With or without religion, good people will do good and evil people will do evil, but for good people to do evil, that takes religion.

Stephen Weinberg, physicist

The Holocaust showed clearly that unthinking acceptance of inflexible political doctrine leaves no room for sympathy or thoughtfulness. It is the very antithesis of morality, just as blind obedience to rigid religious dogma eradicates all that is good in the human breast: the ability to love, to care and to empathise with others; to know when to step forward and when to step back.

Incredibly, those clerics who quote Dostoyevsky's dictum, 'If God does not exist, then everything is permitted,' seem to be taking him as saying that if they had no belief in God, then they would feel perfectly free to rape, kill and pillage whenever they felt so inclined, since it is only God's embargo that makes such behaviour immoral. Humanists argue that it is precisely *because* God exists in men's minds that everything is permitted. For many soldiers, for example, it is God who allows them to kill, and who will anyway exonerate them if they confess and ask for forgiveness. The worst evil has been done at the behest of clerics, who have persuaded their followers that God's instructions always trump inner conscience and social morality. Plato (in his dialogue *Euthyphro*) long ago disposed of the fallacy that there can be no morality without God, simply by asking:

Does God say that something is wrong because it is wrong, or is it wrong just because God says so? If the former, then God is simply passing on existing information and his authority is irrelevant; if the latter, right and wrong are arbitrary since God might equally have decreed that murder is virtuous.

Today, Catholic clerics excommunicate women who wish to become priests, whilst supporting priests who torture and rape young children. There is clearly a vast chasm between 'revealed' morality, as it is revealed to these clerics at any rate, and secular morality. To most decent people, revealed morality can be seriously immoral – at best it is amoral. This is not confined just to Christianity; other religions fare no better, inciting the forced marriage of children, obligatory wearing of the burqua, genital mutilation, bride burning and similar horrors.

Many clerics insist that, because they preach God's Word, their moral norms should be forcibly imposed on all society – believers, other-believers and unbelievers alike. Naturally, this dogmatic attitude is a source of societal friction. It is significant that terrorism and oppression are usually justified by the wishes of God, as supposedly conveyed to clerics. Obedience to God in the hope of reward in the next world trumps happiness and the wellbeing of humankind in this world. But it is worse than that because, by distracting attention away from the truly serious moral issues of human rights, warfare, inequality and so on, and by concentrating on relatively petty matters such as women priests and divorcees, these clerics are allowing the major injustices to flourish unnoticed, thereby serving those promoting the gravest immorality in the world.

Beware of the Dogma: Sin

The Bible contains very few useful moral injunctions (the Exodus ones aren't useful), and anyway Christians consciously ignore the ethical requirements found in Jesus' teachings. These include: give away all you own and make no provision for the future; disown your family; accept all suffering and injustice passively; and love your persecutors and enemies. As for sexual taboos, Christ himself didn't seem to have any hang-ups about sex. What, then, is Christian morality founded on?

Clerical morality isn't really about care or respect for other people at all – it is mostly about sins. Sins are mostly victimless taboos, concerned mainly with private thoughts (such as failing to admire the priesthood or doubting God's existence); private emotions (pride, avarice, lust, envy, gluttony, anger and sloth are deadly); and consensual private sexual thoughts and behaviour. Sinful behaviour involves usually pleasurable aspects of normal everyday human behaviour that are unavoidable – after all, who can refrain from coveting his neighbour's wife's ass? But if sins are unavoidable, then everybody is a sinner!

'Sins' give rise to terrible guilt and remorse in the minds of the sinners, who have been conditioned from an early age to grovel and beg forgiveness from clerics. Thus clerics are clearly placed in positions of power over the sinners, which is to say that they gain authority over everybody who believes in sin. Neat! It is certainly hard to imagine how the otherwise largely pointless concept of sin came about, if not for this sole purpose. It certainly didn't come from God.

Sin is founded on the notion of free will and of consequent moral responsibility for our thoughts and behaviour. But psychologists have shown that most human behaviour is not freely chosen; rather it is consequent on subconscious needs and drives of which we are not aware and over which we have no control. Clerics know that free will is an illusion and that we cannot therefore be held morally responsible for all of our behaviour. Yet in devising sin and promoting the notion that God gave us all free will, clerics have deliberately set up unrealisable goals. These inevitably lead to feelings of helplessness and unworthiness among the sinners (everyone), making them dependent on clerics whilst promoting clerical authority.

Nietzsche decided that 'the priest rules through the invention of sin', but the device is itself immoral partly because, as

Thomas Paine points out: 'Morality is injured by prescribing to it duties that, in the first place, are impossible to be performed.' It also harms others and injures their wellbeing. Paul denounced any man who even looks at a woman lustfully for having already committed adultery with her in his heart; and the cleric still points contemptuously at the sinner. 'You had free will!' he chides, knowing well that he didn't. To compound the misery, James (2:10) adds, 'For whoever keeps the whole law and yet stumbles at just one point is guilty of breaking all of it.'

> *Those who set themselves up as the deity's interpreters form institutions that develop their own strategies, which are designed to expand and consolidate their power over the believer. In the case of Christianity, these god-talking shepherds have been able to convince the sheep that they are innately evil …*
>
> Wendell Watters in *Deadly Doctrine*, Prometheus Books, New York (1992)

Clearly, sin has little relevance to the topic of 'morality', which concerns our dealings with other people. However, by deliberately confusing 'sin' with 'immorality' (sin is wrong; immoral behaviour is wrong; therefore sin equals immorality), clerics have used their exclusive 'divine gift of moral discernment and certainty' to establish themselves as the arbiters of morality.

> *It is not God that is worshipped but the group or authority that claims to speak in His name. Sin becomes disobedience to authority, not violation of integrity.*
>
> Sir Sarvepalli Radhakrishnan, Indian statesman and philosopher (1888–1975)

It was never integrity or love that those teachers sought to instil; rather it was guilt and fear, intended to keep the faithful on their knees. John Carroll, writing about Lutheran teaching, explained the procedure:

... His message is that I shall so bury you under your own guilt, your own pitiable weakness, your total dependency on the Lord God that I shall have you living on your knees in prayer. You are nothing. You are nobody. I shall fling you back into the spiritual dungeon where your thinking facility has no chance of creating the illusion that you have some control over your own destiny. It is down there in the dark, where the light of neither reason nor law shines, where only God can help you, that you may find grace.

J Carroll, *Humanism: The Wreck of Western Culture*, London: Fontana (1993, p.54)

Most clerical notions of morality are downright immoral, for it is not just the deliberate invention of sin, but also the fact that:

Every single bit of progress in humane feeling, every improvement in the criminal law, every step toward the diminution of war, every step toward the better treatment of coloured races, or every mitigation of slavery, every moral progress in this world, has been consistently opposed by the organised Churches of the world.

Bertrand Russell (1872–1970)

For centuries the mystics of spirit had existed by running a protection racket – by making life on earth unbearable, then charging for consolation and relief ... by declaring production and joy to be sins, and then collecting blackmail from the sinners.

Ayn Rand (1905–82)

Sin is designed to have us all grovelling on our knees in musty churches and mosques, pleading for forgiveness. Meanwhile, the Humanists are out in the sunshine smelling the flowers; for, as Boris Pasternak said, 'Man is born to live, not to prepare for life.'

44

The Immorality of Blind Obedience

According to clerics, 'good' flocks are sheep-like because religious morality is a simple matter of following God's (i.e. their) instructions to the letter. 'When you submit to the bishop as to Jesus Christ, I see you no longer living like men but like Jesus Christ', said St Ignatius of Antioch (ignoring Jesus' antipathy to bishops). This is to say that lay believers can avoid responsibility for their own actions by blindly obeying their cleric's instructions, even when he wants them to do something immoral such as opposing women's rights or killing an abortionist. As we saw in Auschwitz, those who yield to an authoritarian regime are encouraged to feel no responsibility for their behaviour – 'I was only obeying orders' – so the perpetrators can feel quite virtuous when obeying a clerical instruction for a crusade or a suicide bombing (as long as they remember to love the people they're killing).

On the other hand, when a cleric calls for behaviour that just happens to be moral in secular terms, well, there's nothing particularly virtuous about obeying a tyrant. A dog can be trained to be obedient, and the atheist who doesn't steal even though he is unlikely to be caught is surely more virtuous than the believer who resists temptation only because he thinks that God is watching.

Clerics present themselves as responsible to none save God himself, and claim that God's Will trumps all secular law. On this basis they even oppose democracy, demanding that everybody, including the State, must obey God's (i.e. their) wishes. In 1907, Pope Pius X issued *Lamentabile, Syllabus Condemning the Errors of the Modernists*, which describes as 'madness' the notion that individuals should be free to exercise freedom of conscience: 'Only the college of pastors have the right and authority to lead and govern; the masses have no right or authority except that of being governed, like an obedient flock that follows its shepherd.' In 1954, the Church declared Pius X to be a saint.

The Ten Commandments

There are six hundred and thirteen commandments in the Book of Exodus alone, so I'm told. They include, for example (21:20): 'If a man beats his male or female slave with a rod ... he is not to be punished if the slave gets up after a day or two, since the slave is his property'; and (21:32): 'If a bull gores a male or female slave, the owner [of the bull] must pay thirty shekels of silver to the master of the slave, and the bull must be stoned.' They also include detailed specifications for the construction of arks, lampstands and tabernacles. Christians completely ignore these Commandments.

However, Protestant clerics generally place special emphasis on the obligations posed by the Ten Commandments listed in Deut. 5:6–21. The first four ('No other gods'; 'No graven images'; 'Don't take God's name in vain'; and 'No work on the Sabbath') have nothing at all to do with relations with other people, and of the remainder only three forbid hurting others: 6, Murder; 8, Theft; and 9, False Testimony. So the Commandments aren't primarily about 'morality' as we understand it. Rather they were intended as a guide to Jews' relationships with their God (Yahweh) and each other. They were sexist and racist: the seventh Commandment, for example, prohibits a Jew from seducing a fellow Jew's wife, but only because she is his property; the eighth requires a Jew to refrain from stealing from fellow Jews, but gentiles are fair game. God himself contradicted the sixth, 'You shall not kill' (Deut 5:17) when, a few short verses later (Deut 7:1), he instructs the Jews: '... you must destroy them totally, make no treaty with them, and show them no mercy'. So clearly this Commandment similarly applies only to killing Jews, and it's open season on the rest of us.

The penalties for breaking any of the Commandments are pretty steep: death for taking the Lord's name in vain (Leviticus 24:16 specifies stoning to death); death for cursing your father and mother (Exodus 21:17); and death again for working on the Sabbath day (Exodus 31:15).

Much more significant is what the Commandments omit: there is no mention of fairness or human rights, nor are there any commandments supporting democracy, sexual equality, freedom of speech or social inclusion. As we have seen, most clerical ideas of morality show little respect for humanity in general, especially if the zealots in Jewish Israel, Christian USA or Muslim Afghanistan are anything to go by.

The Psychological Damage to the Sinner

Clerics claim that sound mental health demands a good relationship with God, which 'neatly places atheists in the class of the mentally sick'. (Thomas S Szasz in *Ideology and Insanity: Essays on the Psychiatric Dehumanisation of Man*, Doubleday & Co., New York, 1970) On the other hand, we may wonder about the mental health of those whose self esteem is founded on an abject dependence on an invisible, unresponsive God. Surely clerical exploitation of human weaknesses such as dependency, anxiety, fear, guilt and sexuality must damage the stability of the true believers. Nathanial Branden confirms that:

> [a]*nyone who engages in the practice of psychotherapy confronts every day the devastation wrought by the teachings of religion.*
>
> The Six Pillars of Self-Esteem

Atheists find it difficult to accept that believers in an afterlife can enjoy inner peace, when their whole belief system has been so obviously designed to turn them into shivering wrecks. Only recently, I was handed a note that informed me: '... we have broken God's law by our wrong-doing. The Bible says that we "have all sinned", and that we continually fall short of what God wants us to be (Romans 3:33) ... Our wrong-doing has serious consequences, for God is holy and will not tolerate sin. The Bible says "The wages of sin is death" (Romans 6:23). Sin is spoiling our present life. It will also keep us out of heaven, cut us off from God forever, and cause us eternal grief, pain and loss. This is the wage sin pays – "death" of the worst possible kind ...' and so on. This anachronistic leaflet clearly sought to puncture its recipients' self esteem by making them feel frightened and guilty, and guilt (whether real or merely imagined) is a major cause of psychological breakdown.

Frightened people are pliable. 'Obey these Commandments or burn forever in Hell' is a well-calculated way to create anxiety and mental stress among loyal flocks; and the trauma caused by clerics indoctrinating small children with vivid descriptions of the flames of Hell engulfing wretched sinners was very real. A hundred years ago, the fire and the chains of darkness could seem quite tangible to susceptible victims of such manipulation. In the school that the author attended (Anglican, mid-twentieth century), we were entertained by John Bunyan's story of *The Pilgrims Progress*, which in one passage tells how the Interpreter took the pilgrims to see a butcher killing a sheep. He tells them:

> *You must learn of this sheep to suffer, to put up with wrongs without murmurings or complaints. Behold how quietly she takes her death, and, without objecting, she suffereth her skin to be pulled over her ears. Your King doth call you his sheep.*

We got the message ... but lost the will to live.

It can be worse for the priests who must teach this stuff:

> *At the seminary, the constant effort I expended to censor my thoughts and feelings began to exhaust me – a real self-induced neurosis ... Devoutness had brought out some of my worst tendencies. I had grown not in righteousness but in rigidness, not in purity but in priggishness, not in holiness but in ass-holiness!*
>
> Edmund D Cohen

Some believers are so fearful of having a sinful thought that they suppress *all* emotion, becoming as frigid, humourless, dogmatic and intolerant as the senior clerics themselves. Nathaniel Brandon was shocked:

> *It is impossible to compute the magnitude of the disaster, the wreckage of human lives, produced by the belief that desires and emotions can be commanded in and out of existence by an act of will ... teachings are clearly an injunction to practice repression.*

The poor 'sinner' is eviscerated, his self-esteem punctured, his independence gone, for such is his horror of accidentally having 'sinful' thoughts that he begins to see his own mind as a potential traitor, a threat to his salvation ... he is now on a well-worn path to mental breakdown.

In times past, gullible victims used to starve and torture themselves in the frantic hope that they might avoid worse in the next life. Hermits lived desolate and hungry, wearing sackcloth and horsehair, regularly scourging themselves, but happy because in their delirium they thought they would avoid Hell. Saint Catherine of Siena flagellated herself with a chain three times daily, each session lasting ninety minutes, until her whole body was pouring blood. On one occasion when dressing the cancerous wounds of a patient she collected all the pus, and drank it! She died at the age of thirty, after starving herself. Psychologically balanced?

Ultimately, in *Viruses of the Mind* (1992), Richard Dawkins equates *all* religious conviction with mental illness. His argument is that anyone who argues that belief is all the more virtuous *because* there is no evidence to support it must be deranged. We will see in Chapter 10 that such reasoning is not unusual.

Moral Relativism

Religious taboos evolve within cultures. Like law and language, they vary in detail between different eras and places. Conflicting taboos can be equally valid, being neither morally 'right' or 'wrong' in a secular sense, providing that no one is hurt. It is none of my business if a Muslim drinks alcohol, and I will happily tolerate a Catholic who uses condoms, because drinking alcohol and using condoms aren't immoral in my book. Of course, if you want to be a Muslim or a Catholic, you must abide by their taboos; otherwise you sin and must beg for forgiveness.

However, we should all be absolutely intolerant of taboos and rituals which adversely affect the wellbeing of others, and which are therefore absolutely immoral. There should be no room for relativism where stoning a woman to death for having fallen victim to rape may accord with some cleric's ideas of justice. Such a ritual is absolutely immoral, wherever and whenever it is undertaken, and those relativists who tell us that we should be tolerant of other people's primitive beliefs, 'because nothing is absolutely right or wrong', are themselves absolutely wrong. Within Christianity the intolerance, anti-feminism, homophobia and anti-Semitism; the passive support for violence and sadism; and the opposition to democracy, learning and free thought are all areas where Christian teaching is absolutely immoral, because it harms other people.

No one can accuse Pope Pius XI of relativism: 'The fool who hath said in his heart, there is no God, will walk the ways of corruption. The number of such fools, who today attempt to separate morality and religion, has become legion.' He too was absolutely wrong – morality has nothing at all to do with religion. Nor has it anything to do with calling people who choose to think for themselves 'fools'.

Low Standards in High Places

We have seen how St Paul condemned sex. In 391CE, St Augustine decided that even lust was mortally sinful unless it was accompanied by a desire to procreate, and he convinced the Church that only by celibacy could a man really be sure of salvation. However, by publicly professing celibacy, clerics had made a rod for their own backs. The stench of hypocrisy rose up every time one of them was discovered up to his neck in what he so sanctimoniously denounced. This was especially true in the early days of the Church, when the priesthood was so steeped in testosterone that it was seriously suggested that the ordination ceremony ought to include castration! In modern times, priestly passions merely provide the Sunday papers with ribald headlines such as 'The Knicker Vicar' or 'The Bonking Bishop'.

The Vatican claims that the papacy forms an unbroken chain all the way from Jesus, via his disciple Peter, to the present pope. There are, however, a few kinks in the chain, as Nigel Cawthorne describes in his book *Sex Lives of the Popes* (Prion Books, London, 1996):

> *Many* [popes] *have been married. More, while making a show of celibacy, have installed their mistresses in the Vatican and promoted their illegitimate sons – or 'nephews' as they are known in the Church – to high office. There have been gay popes who have made their catamites cardinals. There have been grossly promiscuous popes of both persuasions. Orgies were not unknown in the papal palaces.*

Pope John XII worshipped Satan and ran a brothel out of the Lateran Palace while Gregory VII canonised himself and then set up a school of forgers to create and amend documents redefining the role and power of the Church, thus effectively reinventing Roman Catholicism. Some popes were atheists; some were heretics. Several supplemented their incomes by taxing the Roman prostitutes, while others sold indulgences to the clergy in the form of a 'sin tax' that allowed them to keep their mistresses. Boniface IX charged a fee to 'authenticate' Jesus' supposed foreskin as well as the bones of various saints (Peter De Rosa noted that the catacombs must have provided a veritable El Dorado for unscrupulous popes).

In those days, the Church was (and it probably still is) by far the wealthiest multinational corporation in the world. Its CEO, the pope, could give free rein to his most perverted desires – he was answerable only to God, who of course never objected. The rot spread downwards – in the thirteenth and fourteenth centuries, most bishops kept harems and convents were more like brothels.

Naturally, the Church has since done its best to conceal these scandals. For example, John XXIII was an ex-pirate, and noted as a pope-poisoner, a mass-murderer, a mass-fornicator with a taste for nuns, a simoniac, a blackmailer and a pimp. So, when another Pope John XXIII was elected in 1958, several Catholic cathedrals had to hastily excise the ex-pirate from their list of popes. John XXIII was interesting also in that he was elected by a special council called to resolve the schism brought about by the existence of two concurrent pretender popes, one in Avignon and the other in Rome. For a while, therefore, there were three rival popes, all part of the 'unbroken line of teaching and holiness that goes back to the first apostles who knew Christ'.

Nigel Cawthorne also tells of a pamphleteer who 'blithely lists which popes were poisoners, murderers, fornicators, whoremongers, drunkards, lechers, gamblers, necromancers, devil worshippers, and atheists, and includes a special section for those who had committed incest'. These would have included popes Alexander VI (Rodrigo Borgia), Sergius III, John X, Benedict VIII, Clement V, Clement VI, Sixtus IV, Pius II, Innocent VIII, Julius II, Gregory XIII and Urban VIII.

History explodes the myth of a papacy lily-white in the matter of truth. In an age of barbarism, the popes led the pack; in an age of enlightenment, they trailed the field.

> Peter de Rosa, *Vicars of Christ*, Poolbeg Press, Dublin (2000)

After all this, Pope Pius XI (1922–29) piously told the world that his Church would 'stand erect in the midst of the moral ruin which surrounds her, in order that she may preserve the chastity of the nuptial union from being defiled by this foul stain' (meaning not murder, or incest, but contraception).

According to Peter de Rosa, the present successor to Jesus (the poor homeless lay preacher who so heartily despised wealth and pretentious clerics, i.e. Pharisees), lives in an eleven-thousand-roomed palace (the Vatican). An army of purple Excellencies, Graces, Eminences and Most Reverends, all living in palaces and seated on thrones, supports him and his lieutenants, the thirty-strong Congregation for the Doctrine of the Faith (a.k.a. the Inquisition). There is much bowing, scraping, genuflecting, ring-kissing and reverent whispering, and an air of self-proclaimed sanctity as Their Eminences and Their Graces vie for a share of the papal pomp, perks, prerogatives, panoply, prestige and power. Yet if David Yallop's book *In God's Name* (Jonathan Cape, London, 1984) is anything to go by – and its detailed revelations were never refuted – these most illustrious clerics appear to be quite tolerant of murder (including the murder of Pope John Paul I in 1978), fraud, cover-up and corruption. They protected one of their number ('God's banker', Marcinkus) from the authorities who wanted to question him about his alleged ties with the Mafia, the 'P2' Masonic Lodge, the theft of hundreds of millions of dollars, arms smuggling and murder.

Ostentatious displays of the Church's wealth are everywhere you look. In Seville, for example (according to Richard Girling in *Greed*, Corgi Books, London 2010):

The altarpiece in the Cathedral's High Chapel is a floor-to-ceiling cascade of pure gold. Even a waterfall this big would be a crowd-puller in the Lake District ... And an account of the Cathedral's treasures is like a court inventory – tonnages of gold and silver, circumferences of pearl, roll calls of precious stones, monstrances, tabernacles, crowns ... if greed is a virtue, then here, surely, is the nearest we will ever get to heaven on earth.

This greed is not confined to Roman Catholicism. Consider the antics of the Greek Orthodox clerics (reported in the *Observer* on 20 March 2005):

... Almost daily, men once revered as paragons of virtue have been exposed as lascivious money-grabbers. Recorded

conversations of eminent clerics engaging in 'love-talk' have been broadcast on television, secret bank accounts revealed, and malfeasance unearthed, with priests emerging as central players in activities as disparate as trial-fixing, antiquities smuggling and election rigging.

According to Nikos Dimou (in his book *The Misery of being Greek*), 'In many ways, the Greek Orthodox Church has been revealed for what it is: a completely amoral and unethical multinational company.'

Muslim clerics too can be incredibly hypocritical in devising ingenious ways to facilitate sinners, while complying with the letter of Islamic teaching – for example, with regard to the rules against charging interest on loans, or visiting brothels. Iranian mullahs sell temporary marriage licences and wedding certificates to those indulging in forbidden sexual antics. When the 'business' has been satisfactorily concluded, for a fee, they witness formal divorce declarations.

But the whole question of clerical morality becomes farcical when we look at American Protestant televangelists. Jesus preached to, at most, 30,000 people in his whole life, but in the 1980s, between 10 and 45 million Americans subscribed to televangelists. These included Jim and Tammy Faye Bakker, who raised $150 million a year for their PTL (Praise The Lord, a.k.a. Pass The Loot) business, using their daily television shows to weep copiously whilst begging their 2½ million viewers for money. Their lifestyle included private jets, pet giraffes and his'n'hers Rolls Royces. In 1980, when Jim was alleged to have spent a night with Jessica Hahn, a secretary of the Full Gospel Tabernacle, he suppressed the story using $265,000 PTL hush money.

Meanwhile, clean-living hellfire preacher Jimmy Swaggart headed a rival $60 million-a-year ministry. When he heard the Hahn story, he confronted Jim's Assembly of God church, and the nearby *Charlotte Observer* happily printed the story. Overnight it became international news, as Swaggart vindictively denounced Bakker as an adulterer and 'a cancer on the body of Christ'. Shortly thereafter, Bakker was indicted for fraud in connection with a $200 million Christian theme park (Heritage USA), and he was sent to jail for five years. Then one of Swaggart's rivals surfaced with a dossier of incriminating photographs showing him with a prostitute in a cheap motel. Even though he warned his congregation, 'God says it's none of your business!' he too became history.

PTL fell into the hands of yet another rival televangelist, the Rev. Jerry Fallwell (founder of the 'Moral Majority'). The Bakkers sued him, and Falwell responded with allegations that, despite the Jessica Hahn affair, Jim Bakker was in fact a homosexual. By the time Bakker came out of jail in 1993, PTL had folded.

Meanwhile, On 4 January 1987, televangelist Oral Williams had threatened that unless his followers gave him $8 million before the end of March, 'God will call me home,' and he would jump off his sixty-metre-high church tower. He was on his way up when a dog-track owner from Sarasota offered him $1.3 million not to do it, and as this brought his total receipts for the stunt up to $9.1 million, he didn't.

After the terrorist attack on the World Trade Centre in 2001, Jerry Fallwell was back in the headlines, announcing that the destruction was God's punishment for the US government's toleration of homosexuality and women's rights. By now, however, a new breed of televangelists had arrived on America's screens: Pat Robertson's Christian Broadcasting Network was bringing in $240 million a year, and James Dobson's 'Focus on the Family' collected $150 million a year. Meanwhile, the salvation shows of Juanita Bynum, Creflo Dollar and Benny Hinn were bigger and brassier than ever, though the message was still the same: 'Praise the Lord and give us as much as you can afford. God loves generous givers, and he will see to it that whatever you give, you will receive back many-fold [though not until after you're safely dead, of course].' Altogether, Americans give almost $100 billion per annum. (James Haught in 'Fading Faith', *Free Inquiry*, February 2010)

That is around $11 million every hour, 24 hours every day, and all of it tax-free.

Televangelist Joyce Meyer, whose turnover in 2004 was around $100 million, claims that those preachers (like Jesus?) who say that it is virtuous to be poor are quite wrong. In fact, she says, the Devil is using them to keep people from wanting to serve God, who 'wants His people to prosper ... those who give generously to His ministries can have anything they want ...' she says, which has prompted a rival to complain that, 'Meyer treats God like a slot machine.'

It would be unfair to blame God for the moral mess that is 'revealed morality', because it is readily apparent that clerics know nothing about morality. Their notion of 'sin' is clearly designed solely to make the faithful subservient to, and dependent on, them. But the faithful are not the only ones who are losing out: clerical notions of morality are costing the whole human race dearly, non-believers and other believers included, as we will see in Chapter 4.

Chapter 4

Some Sample Sins

If lightning is the anger of the gods, then the gods are concerned mostly with trees!

Lao Tse

I believe the spreading of Catholicism to be the most horrible means of political and social degradation left in the world.

Charles Dickens

Sinful Condoms

According to the World Health Organisation, more than three billion people are malnourished, almost a billion of them 'chronically hungry', and 30,000 children die every day just from lack of food. That's one every three seconds. This is obscene, grinding poverty. It is the daily struggle to survive, a constant obsession with getting food and water, any food and any water, and is often suffered in the face of war, drought, disease, corruption and global overheating. For us in the developed world, where an untimely death is a tragedy, ten million such deaths in a distant foreign land can only be a meaningless statistic. Yet it is ongoing, the equivalent of a 9/11 terrorist attack every couple of hours of every day of every year ... and they told us that 9/11 would change the world for ever.

Starvation is merely one symptom of the underlying problem of global overpopulation. Too many people means a scarcity of resources, and in the competition for those resources the strong and powerful always win; the weak and poor inevitably lose out and receive an ever-smaller share. Scientists estimate that without farming and technology, the world could sustain at most 40 million people (hunter-gatherers). We now have 175 times that number, and the fertiliser and good farming land are long since fully exploited. There are no new lands to colonise;

nowhere left to emigrate to. Marginal land is over-cultivated and over-grazed, forests are disappearing, soil is eroding, land is turning to desert and species are becoming extinct as natural habitat disappears. Water tables are sinking and what is left is increasingly polluted – the World Commission on Water reckons that by 2025, four billion of us will be living in conditions of 'water stress'.

Overpopulation is an underlying cause of poverty, starvation, epidemics, global overheating, pollution, environmental devastation, mass extinction, infrastructural overload and wars over dwindling resources. It is probably the most serious threat facing humankind. Some argue that disease and starvation are caused not so much by overpopulation as by corruption, war, AIDS, Western consumerism and inequitable distribution of resources – even so, there is surely no-one who seriously believes that the world's population can continue to grow for ever?

Well, no one except for certain Christian and Muslim clerics, who apparently foresee no limit to the spread of humankind, ever. Motivated by a blind desire to maximise their flocks, they are engaged in a war of what psychiatrist Dr Rebecca Wendell Watters calls 'demographic aggression' (in *Deadly Doctrine*, Prometheus Books, NY, 1992). The objective of this is to swamp the opposition by sheer weight of numbers, based on the simple observation that propagation of the faith depends on propagation of the faithful. This is why, in 1994, Pope John Paul II complained about couples who kept their families 'below the morally correct level of births' (whatever that might be). Meanwhile, the Muslims were already claiming that 'The wombs of our women will give us victory' (Algerian President Boumedienne at the UN in 1974). More chillingly: 'Thanks to your democratic laws we will invade you – thanks to our Islamic laws we will conquer you' (Muslim cleric at an interfaith meeting in Turkey).

For the record, the Muslims are winning, with 1,200 million versus the Catholics' claimed 1,100 million. Birth rates among nominal Christians are declining in secularised Western Europe (leaving young people wondering who will pay their pensions), though the total population is still rising due to immigration, mainly by Muslims. The Muslim percentage of the total population in Europe is therefore increasing and, if present trends continue, states such as France and Germany will be predominantly Muslim within forty years.

This slow-down in Western Europe is overcompensated for in most of the poorer countries of the world. In some cases, populations have tripled in the past fifty years, and large families (6.1 children per family in Rwanda) are the norm despite the horrific attrition rates from starvation and AIDS. The result is that the world's net population is still growing, by more than 200,000 people per day.

The main clerical weapon in their war of demographic aggression is a piece of dogma that deems that all artificial means of birth control are sinful. This is ostensibly because they are not natural, though it is also claimed that condoms promote promiscuity (similar reasoning leads to the notion that confession promotes sin). The predictable result is a population explosion in those countries that can least afford it, which is to say, those countries that have the most religious, and hence the least educated, populations.

It is clearly impossible for a country with an excessive birth rate ever to become self-sustaining. The government must concentrate all its resources on feeding its people in the short term, postponing long-term objectives like building hospitals and universities. This drastically discourages foreign investors – would you willingly invest your money in a hostile, unstable environment where internal migration of uneducated masses from rural areas to big cities already riddled with unemployment has created vast and ungovernable shanty towns? Practically all concerned agencies agree that for a poor country to prosper, economic growth must outpace population growth. Development of family-planning services, together with education to change attitudes to the role of women, would be by far the most cost-effective investment a government or aid agency could make in a poor country. Yet ever since efforts were first made to address the overpopulation problem, religious interests have consistently and very successfully blocked all such moves at government level and in the United Nations.

Back in 1962, the consequences of global overpopulation were first becoming apparent. Catholic congregations demanded to be allowed to use artificial means to regulate their own families. Pope John XXIII set up a Papal Commission on Population and Birth Control, to consider whether the Church should revise its dogma. After six years of deliberation, the lay commissioners voted 60 to 4 (and the clerical commissioners voted 9 to 6) in favour of a change in Church teaching on birth control. But John had died in 1963. His successor, Paul VI, was mindful of the biblical injunction: 'increase in number; fill the earth and subdue it' (Gen. 1:28). He told the farmers of the world at the UN in 1965: 'You must strive to multiply bread so that it suffices for the tables of mankind, not rather favour an artificial control of birth ...' He blithely ignored the Papal Commission's considered vote, and unilaterally reinforced the absolute papal ban on artificial contraception with the publication of *Humanae Vitae* in July 1968.

Humanae Vitae raised a question in US President Nixon's mind: might global overpopulation threaten US security? At a time when it was thought that planet Earth could sustain at most four or five billion people, he drew urgent attention to it:

> *Today, 1969, the world stands at 3½ billion persons. One of the most serious challenges to human destiny in the last third of this century will be growth of population. Whether man's response to that challenge will be a cause of pride or despair in the year 2000 will depend very much on what we do today.*

Nixon initiated an investigation that culminated in the National Security Study Memorandum 200, concluding that there was indeed a need for urgent action to tackle overpopulation. NSSM 200 presented a workable plan of action for increasing the availability of artificial means for family planning, together with greater educational opportunities for women. Alas! The Vatican had already intervened behind closed doors and, long before it became publicly available, NSSM 200 had itself been aborted by the Reagan administration. At the World Conference on Population in Mexico City in 1984, the US even withdrew its funding from two of the world's largest family-planning organisations: the International Planned Parenthood Federation and the UN Fund for Population Activities, among others. In 1994 in Cairo, and again in 1999 in the UN General Assembly, the Holy See colluded with the OIC (a bloc of 57 Islamic States) and US Protestant leaders to form a blockbuster force opposing any attempt to control world population.

By 2012, the world's population has reached seven billion ... and counting. As predicted, water, food, land, oil and other resources are drying up, resource wars are breaking out (mainly for oil and water), our world is increasingly polluted, there are threats to security worldwide and we are already experiencing climate change. As William Laurance, biologist at Smithsonian Tropical Research Institute, Panama, wrote in *New Scientist*, 1 September 2007, '... it is inconceivable that efforts to slow global warming will succeed as long as the population keeps expanding'.

There is also the AIDS crisis. Globally, 35 million people are currently living with HIV, and the figure is growing at a rate of five every minute. Together, there are 300 million new cases of sexually transmitted infections (STIs) annually, causing indignity, pain and 230,000 deaths. Condoms would provide the most dependable protection against STIs and unwanted pregnancy. However, in poor countries where condoms are most needed, clerics distribute disinformation instead: Cardinal Tujillo, as President of the Vatican's Pontifical Council for the Family, claimed that condoms actually *cause* AIDS and promiscuity, and lead to broken families. It was not until November 2010 that Pope Benedict indirectly admitted that condoms do prevent STIs, though he amazed all by denying that this represented a change in Church teaching.

Meanwhile, a certain unpronounceable Nigerian state suspended its UN polio vaccination programme because

Muslim clerics declared that the vaccine was 'un-Islamic'. By the following year, nine previously polio-free neighbouring countries had been re-infected by the virus as it spread from that one Nigerian state. Then, when the US sent grain to a drought-stricken part of Africa, the local Mullah decided that it had been genetically modified, and forbade his congregation from touching it … so they starved. Clerics have even intervened physically, as when the Archbishop of Nairobi, Cardinal Maurice Otunga, burned boxes of condoms and safe-sex pamphlets in front of a crowd in Uhuru Park, Nairobi, in 1966.

It seems that the only dependable form of population control acceptable to these clerics is painful and premature death caused by starvation, disease, amateur abortion, civil war or AIDS. But then, as Pope John Paul II pointed out, the sick and starving are 'poor only in the economic and material sense. In a moral sense, poverty means wealth,' so lucky old them. These clerics claim to be guarding the world's morals, but just how moral is it to oblige a poor woman to have children she doesn't want and can't afford, only to see them starve slowly in the stinking streets of some squalid slum?

Some Christians break this mould. Martin Luther King Jr commented:

Unlike plagues of the dark ages or contemporary diseases we do not understand, the modern plague of overpopulation is soluble by means we have discovered with the resources we possess. What is lacking is not sufficient knowledge of the solution but universal consciousness of the gravity of the problem and education of the billions who are its victim.

On 24 February 2004, Bishop Desmond Tutu issued a statement condemning the Catholic edict that bans the use of condoms. He cited a report from the Christian Aid organisation, which dismisses Vatican claims that condoms cause promiscuity, and he begged the Church to be 'realistic'. The UN Population Fund (UNFPA) believes that family planning is the most effective means of tackling the problem. Werner Fornos, president of the

UNFPA, criticised the Holy See for 'interfering in the lives of people throughout the world because of religious dogmas'.

The Vatican was unmoved. A report in 1994 by the Pontifical Council for the Family, titled 'Ethical and Pastoral Dimensions of Population Trends', amazed those concerned by announcing, 'There is no present population explosion and no world overpopulation crisis.' At a meeting with African bishops in Rome on 10 June 2005, Pope Benedict XVI reaffirmed his Church's ban on the use of condoms to tackle AIDS, cynically claiming, 'The Catholic Church has always been at the forefront both in prevention and treatment of this illness.' Under the circumstances, that's not even funny – his Church (in collaboration with the Mullahs and the born-again Protestant leaders) has been at the root of both the pandemic and the overpopulation crisis. Pious hand-wringing and prayer haven't worked.

Rome has managed to alienate not only the famine-relief agencies and those fighting to control the spread of AIDS, but also tens of millions of ordinary Catholics who have lapsed from active membership of the Church. They can rationalise that if they are already condemned for using a condom on Saturday night, there is nothing further to fear if they fail to turn up for Mass on Sunday morning.

Sinful Abortion

Clerical opposition to abortion is ostensibly about the fate of unbaptised souls. The trouble with souls, though, is that there is no way of knowing even if such things exist (and many people don't think they do), and, if they do, the exact moment when we each receive our soul. All clerics agree that animals don't get one at all; Muslims get theirs 120 days after conception; and Jehovah's Witnesses carry their souls in their blood. Catholics used to be ensouled between forty and ninety days after conception, but in 1780, clerics decided that it actually occurs at the very moment of conception. Now they must teach that a single fertilised cell, an egg three-hundredths of a millimetre in diameter, is guilty of original sin and will go straight to Hell if aborted without first being baptised. Alas! Fifty to eighty percent of all fertilised embryos spontaneously abort within fourteen days, without the mother even being aware that she was pregnant. Clerics are silent on the misfortune of these billions of souls doomed to eternal punishment in Hell as they are unwittingly flushed down the toilet ... unless the flushing counts as baptism?

It is perhaps nit-picking to observe that a human brain alone contains 100 billion cells (*Economist*, 23 December 2006), and Hooper *et al* (1998) reckon that a human body is assembled from ten trillion cells, while these clerics and 'pro-life' campaigners regard a single cell as a living person. This cell is guilty of sin, and is capable of being murdered, on the basis that it has the 'potential' to become a living person. Given the reality of cloning, any human cell now has the *potential* to become a living person, so by this reasoning, scratching your bum is murder. Philosopher Peter Cave also noted that all living persons have the *potential* to become corpses! Nevertheless, it is still a mortal sin for a twelve-year-old girl to take a 'morning-after' pill after her father has raped her, and a mother must similarly bring to term a damaged foetus that has no central nervous system. Otherwise, according to Catholic dogma, she sins mortally, and her soul goes to Hell. Such is Christian compassion.

I imagine that most reasonable people would agree that abortion is highly distasteful and should never be undertaken lightly. But prohibition only ever drives distasteful problems underground, as it did with alcohol, gambling, prostitution and religion itself. Without properly run, officially sanctioned clinics, women seeking abortions must resort to back-street butchers wielding coat hangers, meat-skewers, purgatives and poisons, and operating in insanitary conditions. Those who pontificate loudest about abortion rarely have to live with the consequences, and amateur abortion is still the foremost method of birth control in those countries where condoms aren't readily unavailable, thanks to the clerics.

In 1973, the US Supreme Court, knowing nothing of souls, ruled that life begins at birth, and that an unborn foetus does not therefore have the legal status of a living person. This ruling (*Roe v Wade*) made possible the provision of properly regulated abortion clinics with qualified medical staff. It also turned abortion into a political issue – clerics now urged Christians to kill medical staff working in abortion clinics. One such killer explained, 'I have talked to my pastor and this is what God wants us to do.' (Charles Selengut in *Sacred Fury*, Alta Mira Press, Walnut Creek, 2003). Poor old ScapeGod! Clerics applied so much political pressure to close the clinics that, by 2004:

> *87% of US states have no legal abortion clinics, public funding for family planning services has been cut back or eliminated, laws defining 'personhood' as beginning at the moment of fertilisation have been passed, anti-Choice judges are filling the federal courts, and … ideologues are now appointed as 'experts' on scientific advisory committees.*
>
> Gloria Feldt in *The War on Choice: The Right Wing Attack on Women's Rights and How to Fight Back*, Bantam Books (2004)

The inevitable consequence, according to Whoopi Goldberg, is that, 'One woman dies of an ILLEGAL [abortion] procedure every six minutes. They die because they got pregnant in the wrong country.' (Whoopi Goldberg at the March for Women's Lives in Washington, 25 March 2004)

American clerics are unmoved, insisting that to destroy a fertilised egg is murder, and God's commandments expressly say, 'Thou shalt not kill.' Well, okay, napalming civilian targets and enforcing sanctions that result in the lingering deaths of a hundred thousand Iraqi children are okay if they help to unseat a political opponent. But terminating a pregnancy merely because the mother might die and the baby will starve is not a just cause, according to those claiming the inside track with God. Why, even the Spanish Conquistadors scrupulously baptised the native Indian babies before smashing their skulls in, so that they would go straight to Heaven.

When the UN defined forced pregnancy (rape followed by unlawful confinement for the purpose of affecting ethnic composition) as a crime, the clerics of the Holy See objected that there was nothing criminal about such behaviour. But when the Genocide Convention was being drafted, they insisted that obligatory birth control be classed as genocide, no less.

Sinful Genetic Regeneration

One day after fertilisation, an egg will have split into four cells; the next day, into eight cells. After five days the egg will have developed into a 150-cell blastocyst, containing stem cells that have the potential to reproduce themselves or to become any of 230 different kinds of specialised cells (brain, skin, etc.) as required. The body also uses stem cells to repair damage – a cut finger or broken bone, for example. This property is of great interest to medical researchers, who see the possibility of using leftover stem cells produced *in vitro* (discovered in 1998) to replace damaged or lost cells. This process could potentially provide cures for millions of humans who variously suffer from brain and spine injuries, Parkinson's and Alzheimer's diseases, diabetes, stroke and heart disease, arthritis, burns, muscular dystrophy, blindness and deafness, and even leukaemia.

Stem cells offer a potential cure for all these, but unfortunately, harvesting embryonic stem cells involves dismantling blastocysts and, you guessed it – clerics claim that this is mass murder! They oppose all stem-cell research. In 2003, clerics pressurised the US House of Representatives into all but banning embryonic stem-cell research – in the USA, the 'rights' of blastocysts trump those of the victims of agonising injury, disease and disability.

It is right that we should be considerate of people's private religious views; freedom to manifest one's belief is a Human Right, after all. But if human rights mean anything at all, then the real possibilities of properly feeding the world's population;

of providing elementary protection against AIDS for everyone; and of curing killer diseases like diabetes and Alzheimer's should trump medieval superstition every time. They should, but they don't, and this is part of the true price that our human race is paying for its religious freedoms.

Sinful Psychiatry

At the beginning of the twentieth century, psychologists studying normal human motivation and behaviour began to discover all sorts of phenomena: conditioning, reflexive behaviour, the subconscious, denial and suppression, and so on. They started to lay out the foundations of elementary psychiatry that would lead to means of treating neuroses and mental disorders. Unfortunately, the notion that we are motivated by subconscious urges, of which we are unaware and over which we have little control, rather contradicts the concept of free will that underlies the notion of 'sin'. If we are deemed not to be completely responsible for our thoughts and behaviour, then there is no longer any need to beg forgiveness for our 'sins', and, as we have seen, forgiving sins is a large part of the basis of clerical power. The whole mystery of religious belief is threatened as consciousness and the workings of the brain come increasingly to be understood by scientists, geneticists and psychologists. Clerics have therefore decreed that psychiatry is 'dangerous', and they deny the discoveries of psychiatric researchers.

The cleric and the psychotherapist are at cross-purposes in other ways, too. For example, while clerics are busily promoting self-loathing and humility and stressing the worthlessness of their congregations, psychotherapists are actively encouraging self-esteem and self-love. Each is constantly contradicting and trying to undo the work of the other. Perhaps there's an element of retaliation too: Sigmund Freud pondered the question of how religion had such a grip on human minds, and announced in 1927 that it derived from 'an obsessional neurosis not unlike hallucinatory psychosis' – a mental illness. Naturally, clerics

67

didn't like that. They publicly discredited Freud and the whole business of psychotherapy (whilst privately exploiting several of its discoveries).

Sinful Medicine

The Bible reports that Jesus cured lepers and cripples by driving out the evil spirits that 'possessed' them. Until a couple of hundred years ago, clerics similarly claimed for themselves the power to cast out evil spirits. If they did enjoy any success, we may suppose that it was due to the placebo effect. The common people of pre-Reformation Europe relied more on 'wise women' to cure their ills. These were intelligent women who had learned about the curative powers of medicines extracted from plants, herbs and drugs found in nature – medicines that actually worked! While male physicians were killing their patients with mercury and blood-letting and purging, wise women were curing them with real medicines. This didn't suit the clerics. They insisted that good health comes only from God, and certainly not from the efforts of mere women!

Clerics solved the problem neatly by accusing those who cured the sick of witchcraft, declaring that those who used herbs for cures did so only through a pact with the Devil. Witchcraft was a capital offence. And so we read that the 'ailing archbishop of St Andrews called upon Alison Peirsoun of Byrehill and then, after she had successfully cured him, not only refused to pay her but had her arrested for witchcraft and burned to death' (Julio Baroja, *The World of Witches*, University of Chicago Press, 1961). This clerical move steadily led to the virtual eradication of effective medicine in Europe.

Nor did clerics like it when modern medicine started to evolve, and it was discovered that cleanliness was actually better than godliness in preventing plagues. Treating unhealthy children by simply washing them was enough reason to have a Scottish woman convicted of witchcraft (Helen Ellerbe, *The Dark Side of Christian History*, Morningstar and Lark, Florida, 1995). In 1722, the Rev. Edmund Massey denounced inoculation against smallpox, claiming that 'diseases are sent, if not for the trial of our faith, for the punishment of our sins'. He continued that if cures for diseases were found,

> ... there would be no fear of punishment in this life nor belief of any in the next ... Let us not sinfully alter the course of nature by any presumptuous imposition. Let us bless God for the afflictions which he sends upon us, and the chastisements wherewith he intends to try or amend us.

Even after they had conceded that altering the course of nature wasn't always sinful, clerics never admitted that they had been wrong about the evil spirits. They just stopped praying for people's physical bodies (because everyone could see that it wasn't working), and started praying for their souls (because nobody could see that it wasn't working). Tending to the dying still provides opportunities for putting themselves in the way of generous legacies.

Clerics used to teach that venereal diseases were God's retribution for lust, and that victims of syphilis (painful sores that erode flesh and bone, eating away noses and lips, deforming bones and leading ultimately to insanity and death) must not be helped medically, since their souls could only be saved if they were left to face agonising deaths alone. Scientific and medical discovery cannot be forced back into the box, but there are still Christians who reject proven medicine in favour of prayer. The Christian Scientists of Boston, for example, denounce conventional medicine as an attempt to 'play God'. They still regard disease as God's punishment for sin, and they leave AIDS victims to die in agony, as punishment for their presumed lust – the only 'treatment' permitted is prayer to beg forgiveness of the patient's sins.

These self-righteous Christians readily condemn their own children to pain and suffering, for example by forbidding immunisation against infectious diseases and blood transfusions (because blood contains souls). Several states in the USA protect the parents' rights in such cases. Even when they have abused their children, parents have only to show that they prayed for the child's soul to be free of criminal responsibility. As Gerald Witt, mayor of Lake City, Florida, explained in April 2008:

It may be necessary for some babies to die to maintain our religious freedoms. It may be the price you have to pay, everything has a price.

But what a price!

Incredibly Sinful Sex

For 1,200 years before the Reformation, married men had been welcomed into the priesthood. Several popes were, in fact, the sons of priests. However, the clerics at the Council of Trent (1545–63) were concerned that wives and families sometimes distracted priests from their duties to the Church, some priests even bequeathing their possessions to their families (shock!) instead of to the Church's coffers, and showing loyalty to their wives and families (horror!) instead of to the bishop. They wanted their priests to be totally dependent on the senior clerics, and so at Trent (in northern Italy) the bishops deemed that, thenceforth, all priests were to remain celibate and the wives and families had to go. With hindsight, we can see that love and compassion went with them, because strict celibacy and sympathetic ministry are generally incompatible, celibates of both sexes tending towards assertiveness and estrangement, coldness and cruelty.

Celibate clerics are fully aware that their diktats concerning sex cause stress and psychological harm to susceptible believers: inhibitions, frustration, anxiety and guilt are generated, lasting from childhood to old age, yet they are unyielding. Worst affected are the priests themselves, for how can a celibate young priest, with no personal knowledge of sexual relationships or the emotional make-up of women, make judgements and advise women about this most intimate aspect of their lives? And how can a priest ever become a mature person if he is denied experience of this fundamental component of life? 'Why should we take advice on sex from the pope?' asked Irish dramatist George Bernard Shaw (1856–1950). 'If he knows anything about it, he shouldn't.'

Catholic teaching informs us that the only legitimate purpose of sex is to beget children, and that masturbation and homosexuality are therefore much more serious sins than rape, because rape can result in pregnancy (and another little Catholic).

Glorious Misery

The Christian logo, a desolate Jesus bleeding to death on a gallows, is calculated to inspire wretchedness and misery in all who contemplate it, except for sado-masochists. This is because clerics have a vested interest in human misery.

> *Christianity has glorified weakness and suffering and held them up as necessary elements in an ideal character. It has taught people to be patient under wrong and oppression ... From thousands of pulpits Christianity has preached that pain develops the character and that suffering sweetens and ennobles life. They do nothing of the kind. They deaden and degrade.*
>
> Chapman Cohen, *Christianity and Ethics* (1945)

In deference to their paymasters – the powerful and wealthy monarchs and landlords – Christian clerics have treated their flocks as 'sheep'. They have fleeced them, patronisingly preaching the virtues of meekness, servile humility and self-sacrifice (i.e. misery), and strongly warning against those balanced individuals, the free-thinkers, who live happy, self-actualised lives without unnecessary pain and suffering.

Pope Gregory IX (he who formalised the Inquisition in 1231) decided that mankind could only achieve salvation through suffering and pain. He reasoned that, since the soul and the body are separate entities, and since the soul is all-important while the body is the source of all sinful passions, then clearly the body needs to be punished regularly. Even today, members of cults such as Opus Dei are required periodically to use a five-thonged lash – called a 'discipline' – on themselves. They take down their pants and beat themselves on the backside with it. They also wear a 'cilice', a steel chain wrapped tightly around the thigh with sharp spikes sticking into the flesh, which they believe will make them pure and virtuous, though some might consider it halfway to madness.

From the Dark Ages, Catholic clerics disparaged all bodily comfort and physical wellbeing. They taught that we should treat our bodies as sworn enemies, subduing them through hard work, fasting, hair shirts, flagellation and other mortifications. Meanwhile, Protestant clerics were teaching that any sort of pleasure was to be rejected – dancing in particular, but also singing, storytelling, romance, public entertainment and even bathing and washing were to be avoided, especially on the Sabbath. In fact, Protestants and Counter-reformed Catholics competed in the neglect of their own bodily hygiene – the stench in their respective churches must have added gloriously to their sufferings. From the clerical point of view, the most praiseworthy thing that Jesus ever did was to suffer and die in agony. They canonised saints by virtue of their martyrdom and torment, because true Christians consider themselves fortunate if they must suffer and die in agony – suffering and agonising death are the badge of honour of true Christians.

Puritan clerics hijacked traditional seasonal festivals and celebrations, such as the harvest and the winter solstice, and turned them into occasions of religious misery: 'Holidays are not for the pleasure of the body but for the salvation of the soul; not for laughter and frolic but for weeping' (Jean Delumeau, *Sin and Fear*, NY, St Martin's Press, 1990). Fun and merrymaking were inappropriate for people who should have been concentrating on defeating the Devil. Musical instruments, and even drinking toasts to bridal couples, were deemed to be abominations – so much for 'Merrie England'.

Needless to say, the equation of worldly pleasure with sin and guilt didn't stop people from seeking pleasure. But the memory of Luke's gospel (6:25), 'Woe to you that laugh now, for you shall mourn and weep,' was sure to spoil their enjoyment of the only life they could be sure of. Today, clerics are beginning to accept that happiness might not necessarily be all sinful, and that for some it might indeed be a symptom of spiritual fulfilment – but too late. We might wonder if this bunch of sad, embittered old men would recognise true happiness, even if it jumped up and bit them.

Worthless Hope

It is said that a major virtue of Christianity is that its followers can live in the hope that their beliefs will come true in the supposed afterlife, whereas non-believers can hope for nothing. But what value has hope? It is the negation of happiness and peace of mind, since to hope is to be fearful and anxious that the hope will not be fulfilled. To hope for happiness in the future is to lack happiness in the present because, when you have happiness, you can only hope that it won't stop, and such hoping destroys your peace of mind and brings you back to a state of anxiety. Thus hope and anxiety are tied to each other – if you hope for tomorrow's happiness you cannot experience today's. 'There is no hope without fear, no fear without hope' (Spinoza). We are cut off from happiness by the very hope that urges us to pursue it; cut off from the real world by the imaginary, hoped-for world of life after death. As Paschal put it, 'Instead of living, we hope to live.' Andre Comte-Sponville adds the Humanist dictum that, 'It is not hope that helps us to live ... it is love.'

Even if hope really did equate with happiness, Shaw points out: 'The fact that a believer is happier than a sceptic is no more to the point than the fact that a drunken man is happier than a sober one.' He adds that if religion provides solace, then so too do tobacco, alcohol and recreational drugs. Indeed, alcohol may be preferable to the psychological and emotional devastation wrought by the bitter realisation at some late stage in life that the promises that the priest conditioned into you as a young child, and that have sustained your whole life, are now seen to be false. The missed opportunities, the false loyalties – what a waste!

A Crazy World – The Rightness of Majorities

Around ninety percent of the population tend to be 'belongers'. They get reassurance from belonging to the majority, and tend towards right-wing beliefs – blind loyalty to the nation and its leaders, right or wrong; tribal attitudes to outsiders; and unthinking belief in the established religion. They are upholders of law and order, and readers of right-wing newspapers, which reflect their views and guide them on matters of popular opinion. They trust each other and they mistrust the ten percent minority of 'oddball' freethinkers who judge for themselves what is right and what is wrong. Such is life – the majority can enforce their views and the freethinkers must concede, regardless of the merits of their opinions.

Psychiatrist Thomas Szasz famously observed:

> *If you talk to God, you are praying; if God talks to you, you have schizophrenia. If the dead talk to you, you are a spiritualist; if God talks to you, you are a schizophrenic.*
> Thoms Szasz, *The Second Sin: Schizophrenia* (1973)

This is not the case, however, if you are a cleric and enough people believe your incredible claims. Individuals who hold ridiculous beliefs are generally deemed to be crazy, but when such a belief is held by a lot of people, the crazies are reclassified as 'religious'. A man who believes that the Martians are coming is considered mad, but a suicide bomber who believes that he will be rewarded with seventy-two virgins in another world is not only sane, but heroic. It is a fine line, defined by how many people are thought to share the belief. Anatole France (French novelist, 1844–1924) argues that even 'if fifty million people believe a foolish thing, it is still a foolish thing'. Cardinal Ratzinger agrees (at least, in the context of his opposition to democracy): 'Truth is not determined by a majority vote.' In the real world, though, there is sanity in numbers – it is not considered madness when enough people believe that a priest can turn a biscuit into Jesus' living flesh (which he then eats!). So Christians are not crazy, but only because there are a lot of them!

Viewed objectively from outer space, the human race does indeed appear to be crazy. We terrorise each other because we have been conditioned with different notions about the wishes of some supernatural thing-in-the-sky. The human race should be declared insane, and all sharp objects should be withheld. Instead we are, at incredible cost, stockpiling arsenals of the most sophisticated weaponry, which some of the world's most powerful political leaders assure us will be righteously used to fulfil God's (i.e. ScapeGod's) will. Unfortunately, when five hundred million people purport to believe a religious absurdity, they can enforce that belief militarily.

> *The cause of all this misery, mayhem, violence, terror and ignorance is of course religion itself, and if it seems ludicrous to have to state such an obvious reality, the fact is that the government and the media are doing a pretty good job of pretending it isn't so.*
> Muriel Gray in the *Glasgow Herald*, 24 Jan 2005

This is not quite correct. The misery, mayhem, violence, terror and ignorance all need clerics to make them happen. But God is clearly innocent.

CHAPTER 5

DIVISIVENESS

If the characteristic mark of a healthy Christianity is to unite members by a bond of fraternity and love, then there is no country where Christianity has more completely failed than Ireland.

WEH Lecky

It is said that a shared religion unites people. It is meant to reinforce communion of thought and adherence to the community spirit, helping to make for a coherent, easily governed society. A shared religion is therefore *a good thing*. Indeed, group psychologists confirm that any randomly segregated group of people, such as a group of people with blue eyes, do indeed enjoy a clannish sense of 'belonging' – they will be predisposed to like each other and will tend to agree amongst themselves over a range of topics. Unfortunately though, they will also be united in their distaste, hostility even, toward members of other groups (say, those with brown eyes), and this is a *bad thing*.

The group effect is powerful. Hesitant and shrinking individuals become confident and arrogant when they join a group. They enjoy feelings of superiority over other groups, and the effect is magnified when a passive group becomes an active crowd – the members of a crowd become suggestible, imitating and escalating the behaviour of those around them, and scorning outsiders. Crowd psychology is most apparent among adolescent football fans, but we saw it clearly among mature adults on either side of the religious divide in Northern Ireland. Here the two dominant brands of Christianity had become reactionary and intolerant of each other by virtue of their respective tribal religious upbringings, and the sectarian division manifested itself in politicised violence.

Denominations and Sects

We shall see later that the Christian Gospels are ambiguous. Differences in their interpretation have led to the formation of hundreds of different denominations and sects, dividing groups of Christians against each other, often in the most uncompromising ways. It is more than mere academic disagreement over the meanings of biblical passages – it is part of a war of demographic aggression between the clerics of the various denominations. Each is trying to maximise his respective power base, and it can get quite nasty: some Presbyterians denounce the pope as the 'Antichrist'; and Catholic clerics teach that Anglican Holy Orders are 'absolutely null and utterly void' (*Aposticae Curae*, 1896). While Catholic clerics consider that 'concelebration of the Eucharistic sacrifice with ministers of ecclesiastic communities which do not have apostolic succession' is a sin every bit as grave as the rape of a small child, Anglicans tell us that Catholic Masses are 'blasphemous fables and dangerous deceits' (Anglican 39 Articles).

Even within denominations, there can be bitter differences of opinion regarding taboos, such as those relating to female or homosexual bishops, or liberation theology, for example. Minorities can become so isolated that they cut themselves off from the outside world by retreating into convents, monasteries, the Waco compound, the Guyanan jungle, or the mountains of Afghanistan, rather than expose themselves to the contrary and more moderate opinions of the majority. So much for coherence and ease of governance – and so much for Christian love and tolerance.

Differences of opinion should provide opportunities for discussion and compromise, but religious differences inevitably close minds. There are similar divisions within Islam (e.g. between Shi'ite and Sunni), and Muslim clerics can be equally intolerant of each other. Of course, the bitter divisions between Christianity and Islam cost lives practically every day. Sam Harris put it this way:

[M]ost of the people in this world believe that the Creator of the universe has written a book. We have the misfortune of having many such books on hand, each making an exclusive claim as to its infallibility ... Each of these texts urges its readers to adopt a variety of beliefs and practices, some of which are benign, many of which are not. All are in perverse agreement on one point of fundamental importance, however: 'respect' for other faiths, or the views of unbelievers, is not an attitude that God endorses.

'Why Religion is a Dangerous Myth', reprinted in the *Dubliner* magazine, January 2005

As we can see, coexistence in multicultural societies with large religious minorities can be pretty stressful.

Social Division

The headline shouted, 'Segregated Schools Not Socially Divisive, Say Bishops'. (*Irish Times*, 31 December 1983) It was eye-catching, because most people would reckon that 'to segregate' means 'to divide socially'. However, readers who persevered through more than fifty column inches eventually read that, 'The research ... gives no support to the claim that separate Catholic education is socially divisive in the sense that it is associated with rigid, intolerant attitudes and lower levels of social consciousness.' By slyly redefining 'socially divisive' in this unique way, clerics gained support for their socially divisive schools, without which Northern Ireland would by now have been a more cohesive and altogether happier place. Once a society has been split by segregated religious education, the rigid, intolerant attitudes and ghetto mentality follow by themselves. Those clerics would have served their flocks better had they heeded the words of Dr Doyle, another Irish bishop, who said in 1826:

I do not see how any man ... can think that peace can ever be permanently established ... if the children are separated at the commencement of life, on account of their religious opinion.

The Ulster Humanist Association's handbook adds that '... schools in a divided society are totally failing in their moral duty if they themselves remain a microcosm of that division'.

Despite the patent failure of segregated education in Northern Ireland, many governments, including those of the UK and Southern Ireland, actively continue to subsidise religiously segregated schools. They thereby collaborate in the indoctrination of gullible children into uncritical acceptance of mutually contradictory dogmas, and hence into active intolerance of all those of other faiths and those of no faith, in the full awareness that 'faith' is no more than a strong belief in something for which there is absolutely no evidence.

Sociologists claim that cultural diversity within a community is mutually stimulating for those who live there, but only for those with open minds, and only for so long as the minority cultures remain picturesque and unthreatening. This must also only be against the best efforts of the respective clerics, who will necessarily be hostile to the 'godless' followers of other faiths and none. Muslim clerics denounce Christians who sunbathe topless and drink alcohol; while Christians regard veiled Muslim women as backward and repressed.

Christians have a poor record in the matter of toleration. The religious freedom granted by the Edict of Toleration in 313CE was reversed only twelve years later at the Council of Nicaea, which prohibited and thenceforth persecuted all those still practicing non-Christian rites. In a similar vein, Pope Clement VIII condemned the Edict of Nantes (1598) for granting equal citizenship to all regardless of religion. Pope Innocent X denounced the Peace of Westphalia (1648) for advocating toleration of other religions. Finally, Pope Gregory XVI (1831–46) went the rest of the way when he condemned as 'heretical vomit' freedoms of religion, worship, the press, assembly and education.

The current Pope's spirit of toleration was glimpsed in 2007, when Benedict XVI proclaimed that the Church of England was 'not a proper Church', and that Protestant denominations in general had not even the right to call themselves 'churches'. 'In a sea of bigotry, the voice of reason tends to get drowned,' say the Humanists of Northern Ireland, where Church and Hate still refuse to be separated and where, until very recently, the public domain was 'commanded by people with loud mouths, Armalites, bombs, baseball bats or dog collars'.

Philip Pullman, in his essay 'Against Identity', speaks of the 'sharp and intoxicating tastes' experienced by zealous believers: 'Those inclined to it can become addicted to the gamy tang of the absolute, the pungency of righteousness, the furtive sexiness of intolerance.' And when there are enough believers in positions of political power, they may feel obliged to exercise their moral judgement by removing the freedom of minorities to manifest contrary beliefs. They may even claim virtuously that they're doing them a favour. Then again, some freethinkers find the notion of being 'tolerated' by clerics even more offensive than being the subject of their intolerance.

Another aspect of the ongoing demographic war between sects is that clerics firmly denounce anybody who leaves the faith. Some Muslim apostates face death; the Jew who marries outside the faith is deemed to have 'died'; and where one marriage partner is a Catholic, then the Catholic Church demands that the children be brought up as Catholics.

There is one thing on which the clerics of every stripe are united, however: their distaste for those freethinkers who subscribe to no religion at all. Atheists and Humanists are denounced at every opportunity, lest the example of their ability to lead happy and fulfilled lives without religion be seen by the faithful as a realistic alternative to grovelling obedience to an invisible God. The existence of cheerful unbelief is an open challenge to clerics, and they have come to regard unbelievers with such loathing that they have infected our language with their venom. A visit to *Roget's Thesaurus* illustrates this. Here we find the modest word 'agnosticism' associated with: heresy, dissent, mistrust, casuistry, unreliable, graceless, materialist, infidel, alien, heathen and mundane; whereas the word 'religious' conjures up: spiritual, devoted, virtuous, inspired, pure, saintly, just, scrupulous, good, righteous, conscientious and faithful. For hundreds of years, clerics have so castigated freethinkers that, to the present day, many atheists prefer to use euphemisms rather than admit to their lack of religion – they seem to be ashamed of their ability to think for themselves.

Sexism

It will yet be the proud boast of woman that she never contributed a line to the Bible.

GW Foote, founder of the *Freethinker* in 1881

You expect it [the holy trinity] to be like the story of the three bears – the Daddy God called God, the baby God called Jesus and the mummy God called … there is no mummy god, only a holy fucking ghost.

Jeanne Rathbone in *Humanism Ireland*, May/June 2010

It might seem that a God who created us and gave us life and who is always there to look after us and comfort us like a mother must be female. However, clerics assure us that God is, in fact, male! They explain that women are inferior beings, drudges and child-bearers. For most churches, it would be out of the question for a woman even to be a cleric. Prominent Catholics, who outwardly show great respect for Mary, the Mother of Jesus, have always displayed an arrogant distaste for all other women. Saint Paul was a misogynist, who admonished, 'If they want to enquire about something, they should ask their husbands at home; for it is disgraceful for a woman to speak in church.' (1 Corinthians 14:34–35) Nor were women permitted to sing in church choirs – when soprano voices were needed they used boys or older men specially castrated for the purpose.

I don't permit a woman to teach or have authority over a man; she must be silent. For Adam was formed first, then Eve. And Adam was not the one deceived; it was the woman who was deceived and became a sinner.

1 Timothy 2:11–14

No wickedness comes anywhere near the wickedness of a woman ... sin began with a woman [Eve] and thanks to her we all must die.

Catholic Bible, *Ecclesiastes* 25:19–24

The Council of Macon (585CE) even considered a book by Alcidalus Valeus entitled *Paradoxical Dissertation in Which We Attempt to Prove that Women are not Human Creatures*, and then went on to debate whether or not women had souls. Saint Thomas Aquinas considered that '... woman is defective and misbegotten ...' and, as far as Martin Luther was concerned, 'If they become tired or even die, that does not matter. Let them die in childbirth, that's why they are there.' (according to 'Women in Islam', by Dr Sherif Abdel Azeem). Saint Augustine wrote to a friend, 'I fail to see what use a woman can be to a man, if one excludes the function of bearing children.' The Bishop of Arles took it one step further: 'Any woman who acts in such a way that she cannot give birth to as many children as she is capable makes herself guilty of that many murders.'

The Bible tells us that because of Eve's sin, God himself ordained that all women should be punished by drudgery, subservience and pain during childbirth. Indeed, long after anaesthetics had been discovered, clerics ensured that they were withheld during childbirth because of God's supposed ordinance – it took Queen Victoria to knock that one on the head.

It wasn't until the Married Women's Property Act of 1882 that a woman in the UK was permitted to own property in her own right:

It has taken nearly 2000 years for the married woman to get back that personal independence which she enjoyed under the later Roman law, but lost through the influence which Christianity exercised on European legislation. And it may be truly said that she has regained it, not by the aid of the Churches, but despite their opposition.

E Westermarck, *Christianity and Morals* (1939)

The world has moved on, but the Vatican has not. As recently as July 2004, a 37-page 'Letter to the Bishops of the Catholic Church on the Collaboration of Men and Women in the Church and in the World' cites feminism as the cause of all social ills. Claiming 'expertise in humanity', senior clerics remind their bishops that 'the liberation of women entails criticism of the holy scriptures', and that 'the Son of God assumed human nature in its male form'. They sternly remind women that, 'Your husband shall rule over you.' The document calls for the urgent repeal of any rights that women had gained in recent years. At the UN, the clerics of the Holy See pressed for the words 'respect for women's rights' to be replaced by 'respect for women's status'. Pope John Paul II refused to grant an audience with anyone who advocated the ordination of women priests, apparently because a menstruating woman would 'pollute' the altar. So much for 'Mary, full of grace'.

Islamism goes further: Muslim women are instructed to protect themselves from the gaze of men – and they really mean it: in Nigeria, two hundred people were butchered in riots intended to prevent women from exposing their limbs during the 2002 Miss World competition. In the same year in Mecca, fourteen girls were burned to death when police prevented the fire brigade from rescuing them from a blazing building because they didn't have their heads adequately covered. Much ado about some unimportant bits of clothing ... though Maryam Namazie disagrees:

> *The veil is anything but a piece of cloth or clothing. Just as the straightjacket or body bag are anything but pieces of clothing. Just as the chastity belt was not a piece of clothing. Just as the Star of David pinned to Jews during the Holocaust was not a bit of cloth ... [The veil] is meant to segregate. It is representative of how women are viewed in Islam: sub-human, 'deficient', 'inferior', without rights, and despised.*
>
> Maryam Namazie, 'The Veil and Violence Against Women in Islamist Societies', *International Humanist News*, August 2007

The cleric Sheik Taj Aldin al-Hilali explains (during an address to 500 worshippers in Sydney in September 2008) that uncovered women invite assault:

If you take out uncovered meat and place it outside ... without cover, and the cats come and eat it ... whose fault is it, the cats' or the uncovered meat's? The uncovered meat is the problem. If she was in her room, in her home, in her hijab, no problem would have occurred.

So that settles it, at least for those who regard women as 'meat'.

In this context, six thousand young girls *every day* may look forward to genital mutilation. According to the World Health Organisation Chronicle 51 (1986), the circumcision of female children,

... involves amputation of the clitoris, the whole of the labia minora, and at least the interior two thirds and often the whole of the labia majora. The two sides of the vulva are stitched together with silk, catgut or thorns, and a tiny sliver of weed or reed is inserted to provide an opening for urine and menstrual blood. The girl's ankles are usually bound together from ankle to knee until the wound has healed, which may take anything up to forty days.

There are around 100 million women alive who have suffered this butchery. Girls also face acid attacks, rape, forced pregnancy, infanticide and dowry killing (in India, around 15,000 young brides are burned to death each year by their new in-laws because the dowry money is inadequate). Based on birth statistics, the UN reckons there are between 113 and 200 million missing women in the world due to unequal medical care and sustenance, and deliberate infanticide – that is between 4,000 and 8,000 women 'lost' every day. Thirteen million female foetuses were aborted in India in the past twenty years as a result of pre-natal gender tests. 'One in seven girls are killed in the womb in Delhi, and the situation goes on in Britain,' according to Dr Sabu George, a New Delhi gender rights specialist. He adds that they say in the Punjab that rearing a girl is 'like watering a neighbour's garden'.

The Jewish view of a woman, as expressed in the Talmud, is that she is costly baggage, like a lame animal. She is the property of her father until she marries, when she immediately becomes her husband's property, together with her dowry and everything she owns. As the Talmud reasons:

> *How can a woman have anything; whatever is hers belongs to her husband? What is his is his and what is hers is also his ... Should she invite a guest to her house and feed him, she would be stealing from her husband ...*
>
> (San. 71a, Git 62a)

Since a wife is a mere item of property, a husband is free to be unfaithful – but never with a married woman, because she is another man's property. No woman may sign contracts on her own behalf; nor is religious education available to her: 'Let the words of the Torah be destroyed rather than imparted to women'; 'Whosoever teaches his daughter Torah is as though he taught her obscenity.' (Denise L Carmody, 'Judaism', in Arvind Sharma (ed.), *Women in World Religions*, 1995) Little wonder that every day, Orthodox Jews recite '... praised be to God that he has not created me a woman'. (Talmud, Menahot 43b)

We cannot leave it at that. Let us reconsider Eve in the Garden of Eden: she risked death and opted for knowledge and wisdom in preference to blind obedience and submission. For that, all freethinkers should be grateful ... so let's hear it for Eve!

God's Chosen People

There should be hundreds of millions of Jewish people in the world, but in 2011, after centuries of forced conversions, pogroms, violence and extermination at the hands of Christians and Muslims, they number fewer than twenty million worldwide. Christians have persistently persecuted Jews for

1,700 years, ever since Constantine's initial anti-Jewish legislation gave them the power to do so. But even before that, St Paul stirred up trouble for them when he claimed that the Jews had 'killed the Lord Jesus and the prophets'. (1 Thess. 2:15) The New Testament contains several viciously anti-Semitic passages – according to Daniel Goldhagen ("A Moral Reckoning" 2002 Vintage Books, USA), there are 80 in Matthew, 40 in Mark, 60 in Luke, 130 in John and 140 in Acts. Jesus himself told the Jews (in John 8:44), 'You belong to your father, the devil.' Saint John Chrysostom maintained the tone: 'Let anyone call it [the synagogue] brothel, home of vice, refuge of the devil, citadel of Satan, corruption of souls, abyss of corruption and all mischief – whatever he may say it will be less than it has deserved.' (St John Chrysostom of Antioch, 347–407CE, from his 'Eight Homilies Against the Jews', as quoted in Werner Keller's *Diaspora*, 1971)

As a result, the ostensibly anti-Muslim Crusades incidentally saw the massacre of whole Jewish communities in the Rhine and Danube regions, in France and elsewhere. Over a hundred thousand Jews were subsequently expelled from England and France. The Dark Ages saw Jewish people forced to wear distinctive jackets and live in locked ghettoes, permitted to earn money only through pawn-broking and money lending, for which they were then castigated as usurers. They were the whipping boys of Europe, and pogroms (mass murders of Jews) became commonplace. Christian clerics spread rumours that Jews drank the blood of Christian babies and were responsible for the Black Death. They forbade Jews from contact with Christians, even blaming them for precipitating the Reformation, though Luther was no lover of Jews either:

> *Beware then of the Jews, and know that a Jewish school is nothing other than a nest of the devil ... when you see or hear a Jew teaching, then realise that you are hearing a venomous basilisk that can poison or kill people with the sight of its face.*
>
> Quote from his treatise 'On the Jews and their Lies', published in 1543

He also advised: 'Burn their synagogues!' It was only the secular influence of the French Revolution that led to an easing of official hostility toward Jews. But they were increasingly reviled in central Europe, and pogroms became epidemic in Russia between 1881 and 1917, in the Ukraine in 1918–20 (where 60,000 were murdered, according to M Gilbert in *The Holocaust: A History of the Jews in Europe during the Second World War*, Henry Holt, New York, 1985) and in Romania, Poland, Hungary, Austria and elsewhere. But the Nazi pogroms and extermination camps of the early 1940s were worse than anything they had ever suffered before, when Christians systematically and cold-bloodedly murdered six million Jews whilst their clerics silently acquiesced. Even after the war, in 1946, forty more Jews were killed in a pogrom in Kielce, Poland.

On a wave of sympathy and guilt over the Holocaust, the Allies saw to it that the independent Jewish state of Israel was proclaimed in 1948. Predictably, Catholic clerics refused to recognise Israel, despite the tasteless fact that they had earlier signed a concordat implying support for Nazi Germany. In 1965, Vatican clerics eventually withdrew the charge that the Jews bore responsibility for killing Jesus, but it was not until 2005 that Pope John Paul II finally repealed Catholic dogma denouncing Judaism.

Homophobia

Providing that both parties agree, private homosexual relationships can hardly be called immoral, insofar as they don't affect outsiders and there are no victims, even if homosexuality isn't everyone's cup of tea. But it is proscribed in the Bible, both in the Old Testament (Kings 14:4; Leviticus 18:22 and 23, and 20:13; and Deuteronomy 22:5) and by Paul in the New Testament (Romans 1:24–27; and Corinthians 6:9). Christian clerics have consistently denounced homosexuality as 'sinful', even though some of the most outspoken of them have shown themselves to be surprisingly tolerant of the widespread homosexuality, not to mention paedophilia and buggery, within their own ranks. Even the easy-going Anglican Church is seriously divided over the question of gay bishops.

In the UN, reactionary clerics seek to force their homophobia on the whole of society by having homosexuals excluded from such basic human rights as protection from discrimination (Article 7 of UDHR) and employment (Article 23 of UDHR). The Vatican has instructed Catholic politicians around the world to vote against any legislation aimed at giving legal recognition to gay couples, even vindictively ordering Catholic institutions such as state-funded Church schools and hospitals to dismiss all homosexual employees. In 2006, Catholic clerics stirred up further hatred by publicly labelling homosexuals 'immoral, unnatural, objectively disordered sinners', inciting bullying in schools and 'gay-bashing', and causing untold sadness and mental stress, and even suicide in extreme cases, among vulnerable homosexuals. This is God's love, as expressed by 'His' clerics, whose claim about gays' 'unnatural, objectively disordered' sex lives is a bit rich, coming from a group of self-proclaimed celibates.

Slavery and colonialism

In 2006, the clerics of the Church of England formally apologised for their Church's role in the slave trade, even though slaving had flourished with the full endorsement of the Bible:

> *Your male and female slaves are to come from the nations around you; from them you may buy slaves ... You can will them to your children as inherited property and can make them slaves for life ...*
>
> Leviticus 25:44–46

> *All who are under the yoke of slavery should consider their masters worthy of full respect, so that God's name and our teaching may not be slandered.*
>
> 1 Timothy 6:1

Slaves submit yourselves to your masters with all respect, not only to those who are good and considerate but also to those who are harsh.

1 Peter 2:18

In fact, the only constraints appear in Leviticus (25:42): 'Because the Israelites are my servants, whom I brought out of Egypt, they must not be sold as slaves ...' and Christian clerics added the further proviso that Jews were forbidden from owning Christian slaves. The Quakers alone were consistent in their opposition to slavery, despite being castigated and denounced as 'atheists' for their stance by Christian clerics. Slavery flourished throughout Christendom in the Dark Ages – in the eighth century, for example, the monastery of Saint-Germain de Pres exploited 8,000 slaves. Altogether, the Christian slave trade saw the abduction and enslavement of probably forty million humans, and the Muslim slave trade accounted for a further ten million men, as well as animals and women, taken in slave-hunting raids.

Colonialism began with missionaries proselytising in foreign lands. In their efforts to enforce Christian doctrine on humankind around the globe, they used coercion, including starvation and physical and mental violence. Their limited success soon fragmented previously coherent communities, turning tribe against tribe, and children against parents.

Missionary interference was so resented by the 'savages' that God's messengers soon needed the protection of military garrisons. European soldiers (assisted by mercenaries and petty criminals) violently suppressed and ethnically cleansed vast areas of the world (consider Africa and North and Central America) to make way for Christian clerics. Once the 'brutes' had been tamed, commercial exploitation of their lands could begin, and to the present day, many Eastern and African people still equate Christianity with forced imperial exploitation.

These are a few examples of the divisive effects of the Christian teaching both within Christianity and also between Christians and those of other religions. Once again, it is obvious that the trouble is caused not by God, but by those religious (and political) leaders who dishonestly claim to speak on His behalf. And it gets much worse – as we shall see in the next chapter.

CHAPTER 6

GOD IS ON OUR SIDE

This is the concentration camp and crematorium at Auschwitz. This is where people were turned into numbers. Into this pond were flushed the ashes of some four million people. And that was not done by gas. It was done by arrogance. It was done by dogma. When people believe that they have absolute knowledge, with no test in reality, this is how they behave.

Jacob Bronowski, *The Ascent of Man* (1973)

Faith is a negation of reason ... when people can doggedly choose to believe that black is white, and can, in their utter certainty, go so far as to shoot you because you do not agree, there is little room for debate.

AC Grayling, *The Meaning of Things*, Phoenix Paperback (2003)

Faith is what I die for, dogma is what I kill for.

Anon

Having noted how effectively Charlemagne (crowned Emperor of the Romans by Pope Leo III in 800 CE) had spread the faith across Europe using military force, senior Christians realised that slaughter, fear and terror were perhaps the most effective means for sharing Jesus' message of love and peace, and certainly for maximising their own power and influence. As Archbishop of Canterbury Rowan Williams confirmed in 2008, 'Despite Jesus's words in John's gospel, Christianity has been promoted at the point of a sword.' However, if you complain that historically, Christians and their clerics have often behaved like psychopathic butchers, you will often be told that these weren't 'real' Christians – a 'real' Christian could never be guilty of harming another, because 'real' Christians are, by (selective) definition, tolerant and charitable.

But consider how 'real' Christian clerics piously persuaded simple people to admit, for example, that they were witches: stretching on a rack, optionally with an iron cauldron of mice placed upside-down on the bare abdomen so that when the iron is heated the mice will burrow down to escape; toe and thumb screws; having a tapered screwed device inserted unto the mouth, anus or vagina and forced open; being pulled off the ground by hands tied behind the back in order to dislocate the shoulders (*strappado*); being clamped into a Spanish Chair and having the feet slowly roasted over a brazier, the flesh being well larded to prevent it from burning too quickly; or being burned to death at the stake (though if the accused repented, he or she was mercifully strangled before they lit the fire). The approved method for interrogating suspected sodomites was the *chamber chauffee*, which involved lowering the naked suspect on to a red-hot spike. 'Real' Christians crushed bones in iron boots; tore off flesh with hooks and pincers; cut off lips and eyelids; pulled out fingernails and pushed needles into the bleeding quicks; tore out tongues and hammered nails into eyes. They mocked their victims as they stole their property and prayed to God to bless their handiwork. Catholics, Lutherans, Presbyterians, Episcopalians – each strove to out-brutalise the other.

It is the self-righteousness of religious belief that clerical pretenders have used to justify their stomach-churning sadism. This is vindicated by reference to the Bible or the Koran, the former of which instructs without any qualms that you must mercilessly kill a man and all his children if he doesn't share your religious beliefs. Even gentle Jesus wanted unbelievers 'thrown into the fire and burned' (John 15:6), presumably based on the manipulative reasoning that 'he who is not with me is against me' (Luke 11:23). Self-evidently, terror was a particularly effective persuader, good for the business of spreading 'God's bounteous love'. Montaigne missed the point when he wrote, 'It is putting a very high price on one's conjectures to have a man roasted alive because of them,' because we can be pretty sure that it wasn't really about conjecture or belief; it was about securing clerical power.

Religious Sadism

It was not always so. For the first couple of centuries CE, Christians debated whether or not Roman soldiers who had converted to Christianity should be obliged to disarm, since they were now required to love their enemies and turn the other cheek. It was Augustine, in his efforts to square the Sermon on the Mount with the butchery of the Old Testament, who reasoned that Jesus' constraints on violence must apply only to the soul, and not to physical behaviour. After all, Jesus had commended the Centurion for his faith and never criticised his profession, so obviously a man could be a soldier and still please God. Next, he figured that since any war initiated by God must be good, 'because God is good', and since the authority of the State came from God, then a war initiated by the State was effectively a war initiated by God and, therefore, a soldier was doing God's Will whenever he killed enemies of the State. And so, by 400AD, Augustine had managed to take a key sentiment of Jesus' teaching, and stand it on its head.

In-fighting among Christian sects became worse and worse, so that in 1027 the Council of Elne adopted a law permitting fighting only from sunrise on Monday to sunset on Wednesday each week, excepting feast days. This led to frustration and pent-up violence, which Pope Urban II unleashed in 1095 when he launched an unprovoked attack on the Muslims in Palestine. He promised the belligerents remission for all their sins on arrival in Jerusalem, thereby giving the holy warriors *carte blanche* to indulge in wholesale rape, murder and mutilation of women and children, plunder, burning and general destruction. These 'real' Christians made their way through Hungary and across Europe towards their devout objective of 'wiping these impurities [Muslims] from the face of the earth'. The Crusades witnessed the slaughter of twenty million Muslims, Christians, Jews and anyone else who happened to get in the way – all justified by Augustine's notion of a righteous war and the clerical equation of holiness with wanton butchery. Priests blessed flags and weapons; knights who had murdered and raped were now revered as chivalrous. Raymond of Aguilers was an eye-witness:

> *Wonderful things were to be seen. Numbers of the Saracens [Muslims] were beheaded ... Others were shot with arrows, or forced to jump from towers: others were tortured for several days, then burned with flames. In the streets were seen piles of heads and hands and feet. It was a just and marvellous judgement of God, that the place should be filled with the blood of unbelievers.*

All violence was sanctified that was committed by the forces of the Church against external opposition. But equal violence soon came to be used internally, against voices of dissent within the Church, as clerics redirected the nauseating momentum of the Crusades against the Cathars. These were a popular, well-educated Christian group living in Southern France who were critical of the regal lifestyle of Pope Innocent III (he who modestly called himself 'King of Kings and Lord of Lords'). For thirty years he had them methodically butchered until they stopped criticising, by which time the so-called Albigensian, or Cathar Crusade had seen the slaughter of around half a million people.

The sadism continued through the Inquisition, which began in 1229, marking the start of a Reign of Terror which was to last for six centuries, taking in the anti-Hussite Crusades and the Anabaptist persecution. The Inquisition was formalised by Pope Gregory IX. Its purpose was to put the fear of Rome into the masses. The Inquisitors were answerable only to the pope himself, and the assumption was to be 'guilty until proven innocent'. In Southern Europe, clerical inquisitors solemnly tortured alleged heretics, confiscated their property, and burned them at the stake (*auto-da-fé*): Voltaire (in his *Treatise on Toleration*, 1763) explained the procedure:

94

... it is a question of your eternal salvation. It is for your good that the heads of the Inquisition direct that you shall be seized on the information of any one person, however infamous or criminal; that you shall have no advocate to defend you; that the name of your accuser shall not be made known to you; that the inquisitor shall promise you pardon and then condemn you; and that you shall then be subjected to five kinds of torture, and afterwards either flogged or sent to the galleys or ceremoniously burned ... and this pious practice admits of no exceptions.

If a condemned man relented and kissed a crucifix, he was strangled before being burned (they preferred strangling and burning because of a biblical injunction against spilling blood). Thomas of Torquemada, a Dominican friar, ceremoniously fried 10,220 victims during his fifteen-year stint as Grand Inquisitor – two per day! How, one wonders, would Torquemada have dealt with Jesus, the anti-authoritarian, anti-clerical troublemaker who regularly broke the Sabbath and caused a riot in the temple?

William Lecky wrote: 'A bishop in Geneva is said to have burned five hundred within three months, a bishop of Bamburg six hundred, a bishop of Warzburg nine hundred.' (in *A History of the Rise and Influence of Rationalism in Europe*, 1865, Part II) 'Canon Llorente who was secretary to the Inquisition from 1790 – 2 and had access to the archives of all the tribunals, estimated that in Spain alone, the number of condemned exceeded 3 million, with about 300,000 burned at the stake' (in *A Woman Rides the Beast* 1994 by Dave Hunt). All of these torturers, informers and inquisitors were 'real' Christians, formally ordained officers of the Church who gravely and solemnly inflicted their atrocities – the instruments of torture, for example, were inscribed with the motto 'Glory be only to God' and they had to be first blessed by a priest before they could be used.

The Inquisition greatly encouraged belief in witches to spread, and throughout the fourteenth and fifteenth centuries, every calamity from storm damage to potato blight was deemed to be the work of a witch. In accordance with the decree 'You shall not permit a sorceress to live' (Exodus 22:18), thousands of confused old women (and men) were tortured and burned by 'real' Christians, for having sold their souls to the devil – a large, hairy sprite with horns, a long tail, cloven feet and dragon's wings according to the clerics of the day.

Charges of witchcraft were 'proven' with the aid of torture. There was no defence and, once proven, the witch's property was confiscated and the witch was burned to death. It was all too easy for an amorous priest whose advances had been rejected, or a neighbour intent upon a widow's property, or a cleric jealous of a wise woman's success with medicine, to lay charges of witchcraft.

In 1492, Columbus discovered the Indies. Here, in the 1530s, in the name of God and in pursuance of his avowed aim of 'converting the heathen Indians to our Holy Faith', the Spanish massacred the native Indians by the hundreds of thousands. Their methods perhaps 'failed to respect the religious sensitivities of the Aztecs in Mexico, the Incas of Peru and the Mayas of Yucatan'. (Gerald O'Collins, *Catholicism: A Very Short Introduction*, OUP, 2008) A well-known Cuban had this to say about what happened:

When Columbus arrived here with his Church – the Catholic Church – he came bearing a sword and a cross ... the conquistadors were mainly concerned with gold. They criticised the others for worshipping stones, while they themselves worshipped gold ... they made thousands of human sacrifices to the god of wealth and gold, for they killed millions of Indians by making them work in the mines ... The colonisers wiped out 90% of the Indian population ... who should have been considered God's children too ... When nearly all the Indians had been exterminated, hundreds of thousands of Africans were torn from their land and turned into slaves to work in the mines, in the cane-fields, and on the coffee plantations.

Fidel Castro in *Fidel and Religion* by Frei Betto, Havana, 1985

At least 28 million Africans were forcibly taken by 'real' Christians as slaves between 1650 and 1900. As we have seen, the Good Book decreed that it was the slaves' place in life to obey their masters without protest – it was all part of (Scape)God's plan. Similar missionary zeal was seen around the world – in Goa (India), in Japan, in China and throughout the Americas.

Kevin Annett (Canadian rights campaigner and ex-minister of the United Church of Canada) tells of a silent campaign of genocide against the native Indians by settlers in Canada in the drive to take over their land and mineral assets. The State worked hand-in-hand with clerics (65% Protestant, 35% Catholic), who ran schools which the Indian children were obliged to attend. A death rate of 50% among the Indian children was not uncommon: the children were seriously mistreated, and one tactic was deliberately to mix healthy kids with children dying of diseases like TB, so that whole classes would be wiped out. We may assume that similar genocides of natives took place in Christian schools in Australia, India and throughout Asia.

Meanwhile, Rome had become so corrupt that in 1517 Martin Luther challenged the pope's legitimacy ... and Protestantism was born, leading to yet more bloodshed among Christians in the Counter Reformation. So bitter was the battle for domination that in Paris on Saint Bartholomew's Night 1572, during one of the more successful Catholic attempts at ethnic cleansing, the Seine was reportedly choked with the corpses of 'up to a hundred thousand Huguenots (i.e. protestants) killed'. It is said that when the news reached Pope Gregory XIII, he 'cried with joy and retired to St Peter's to sing a Te Deum to the glorious deed'. (Cali Ruchala in *Black Magic Woman: The Life of Catherine de Medici*, Chaps 16 and 17, *Degenerate* Magazine, Diacritica Press)

The Protestants were little better, with Luther claiming, 'The pacifism of Jesus is no more binding on his followers than his celibacy or his carpentry.' (Ferguson, *War and Peace in the World's Religions*, pp. 108–9) Catholic forces wrought havoc on their critics in the bloody Wars of Religion which culminated in the Thirty Years War, when Protestants and Catholics sadistically slaughtered each other by the million until the Peace of Westphalia in 1648 ended it. Except of course in Ireland, where, one day in 1649, Oliver Cromwell happily butchered around two thousand Catholic men in Drogheda. He attributed the slaughter to 'the Spirit of God ... and therefore it is right that God alone should have all the glory.' (Robert Kee's *Ireland: A History*, Abacus Books, 2006) All of these atrocities were committed by 'real' Christians.

Fanatical religious faith is incompatible with tolerance – tolerance can survive only in the absence of religious certainty. There can be no logical basis for such certainty, but men will eagerly kill and maim each other when they have it. Christian clerics throughout the ages have always been quite certain that any degree of cruelty towards heretics was justified.

> *Thus, during seven centuries, in the name of the religion of love, hundreds of thousands of people were not merely killed but atrociously tortured in ways that make the gas chambers of Belsen seem humane.*
>
> Margaret Knight, *Honest to Man*, Elek Books, London (1974)

Any pacifist who mentioned the Sermon on the Mount stood condemned of heresy – clerics in the Vatican proclaimed that the gospels' teaching now applied only to private thoughts, not to physical behaviour. In any case the faithful should now heed only what the gospels forbade, not what they commanded. The Curia went on to divide the contents of gospels into 'precepts' (obligatory) and 'counsels' (advisory). These distortions are still part of today's 'beloved tradition' of Catholicism, though they very clearly contradict the 'rock' upon which the papacy claims to be founded.

In China in 1850–64, the Christian followers of Hong Xiuquan (who thought that he was the Messiah) fought against the government in the Taiping rebellion. This war cost between twenty million and thirty million lives. Then World War I (1914–18), promoted by Christians in the British Cabinet and the three deeply religious emperors, saw the slaughter of almost ten million young men. The atrocities of the Christian Iron Guard in Romania were eclipsed by Franco's fascist forces with enthusiastic Vatican support in the Spanish Civil War, which introduced the mass killing of undefended women and children into warfare. Vatican clerics subsequently cooperated with fascist dictatorships around the world: France's Vichy government; the Ustache in Croatia; Mussolini's Italian fascists; Petain; Pinochet; Salazar; and Hitler's Nazis (in exchange for their lucrative 1933 concordat).

World War II (1939–45) witnessed the slaughter of a further 55 million mostly uninvolved human beings. These included six million Jews and half a million Eastern Orthodox Christians, as well as the civilian victims of aerial fire bombings, in which up to 100,000 innocents were killed at a time. These were planned and executed by people who called themselves 'real' Christians. 'Real' Christian padres blessed and prayed for the bomber squadrons, in the full knowledge that whenever bombs were dropped from a great height, many uninvolved innocents would be killed, blinded, crippled, disembowelled, paralysed, orphaned, made mad, or just made homeless. These are the same padres who now so vociferously condemn abortion because of 'the sanctity of life'. Father George Zabelka solemnly blessed the endeavours of the crew of the bomber *Enola Gay* (USAF motto: 'Peace is our business') before they dropped the first atomic bomb on Hiroshima in 1945, blithely killing a hundred thousand more Japanese civilians just to impress Stalin. Then, a couple of days later, they dropped another on Nagasaki while clerics stood silently by. David Eller (in *Natural Atheism*, American Atheist Press, NJ, 2004) noted that if condoms had been dropped on Hiroshima, the Vatican would have been apoplectic.

As for the Germans, all the Nazi leaders had Christian upbringings, and were united with clerics in their revulsion and fear of Judaism and 'atheistic' communism. Membership of

Himmler's feared SS was confined to Christians: 'Be in no doubt that we would not be able to be this body of men [i.e. the SS] bound by a solemn oath if we did not have a profound belief in a Lord God ...' (*Hier spricht Deutschland*, Wolfram Kaiser, 2011). Hitler claimed of the Holocaust that 'by defending myself against the Jews I am fighting for the work of the Lord'. He was clearly anxious to placate the clerics – he feared their disapproval, and their potential to use their political influence and the propaganda machine to attack Nazism from within.

Luckily for Hitler, neither Pope Pius XII nor any other cleric uttered a word of condemnation. Though many communists and theologians were excommunicated during this period, Hitler himself was never criticised by the Vatican. Jesuit Archbishop TD Roberts, among many others, has confirmed that, 'The factual evidence seems overwhelming that the German Catholics generally – bishops, clergy, people – supported the Hitler war effort.' (Archbishop TD Roberts SJ, *Objections to Roman Catholicism*, 1964) In a radio broadcast, Pius XII described the German attack on Moscow as 'magnanimous acts of valour which now defend the foundations of Christian culture'.

In Yugoslavia the Vatican made no secret of its support for the extermination of 487,000 Eastern Orthodox Christians (Serbs) and 30,000 Jews and 27,000 Gypsies. A further 240,000 Serbs were forced to convert to Catholicism, by 'methods that managed to shock even the Nazis, who considered them too sadistic'. (David Rannan in *Double Cross: The Code of the Catholic Church*, Theo Press, London, 2006). This was an attempt to create a 'pure' Catholic Croatia. (Vladimar Dedijer, *The Yugoslav Auschwitz and the Vatican*, Anriman-Verlag, Freiberg, 1988). Those responsible for killing over 200,000 people in the death camp at Jasenovac received the papal blessing. And after the war, Church officials (notably Bishop Alois Hudal) actively helped Holocaust mastermind Adolf Eichmann and Auschwitz's 'Angel of Death' Joseph Mengele, as well as Martin Bormann and Franz Stangl, to escape to Argentina. These were 'real' Christians.

In 1947, a million Muslims, Sikhs and Hindus were killed for religious reasons during the creation of Pakistan, and in 1948 more Muslims died when Israel was created in the middle of Palestine, again for religious reasons. The Vietnam War of the 1960s saw more bombs dropped by pious Christians – who presumably subscribed to the notion of the sanctity of life – than were dropped by all sides in the whole of the Second World War, resulting in the mutilation and killing of more millions of innocents. The Cold War (1946–early 1990s) saw the pinnacle of pious hysteria, as the US was reported to have built a Doomsday bomb with which to destroy all human life if it ever seemed that atheistic communism might prevail. 'Better dead than red,' they chanted, 250 million citizens of the most devoutly Christian country in the world, and they really meant it.

More recently, in 1994, the Vatican supported the Catholic Hutus in Rwanda in their attempted genocide of Tutsis. 800,000 Tutsis were killed, and stories have circulated that Hutu nuns provided the petrol used to incinerate 5,000 Tutsis they had lured into the 'sanctuary' of their church, while Father Athanese Seromba bulldozed his church to crush the 2,000 Tutsis he had sheltering inside. The Vatican subsequently protected Seromba and gave him a new identity, while the pope distracted attention from the butchery by announcing that 'the greatest genocide of all time' was in fact the contraceptive pill. (Mother Teresa similarly reckoned that, 'The greatest threat to peace is abortion'!) Concurrently in Uganda, The Lord's Resistance Army was busy with God's work, slaughtering 120,000; displacing 1.5 million; and enlisting 25,000 children.

Altogether, the twentieth century saw 187,000,000 human lives wasted by war, and at least a billion more orphaned, maimed, crippled, blinded or made insane or homeless. '… it is the scale and the deliberate, systematic character of the destruction of human beings in the twentieth century which stuns the imagination'. (A Bullock, *The Humanist Tradition in the West*, London, Thames and Hudson, 1985) We can do it even better in the twenty-first: the 2008 military budget in the US for stockpiling ever more sophisticated means of killing and mutilating people was $716,500,000,000.

Today there is a new evangelical crusade dubbed 'evangelical capitalism' or the Gospel according to Halliburton, promoting uncontrolled capitalism, it sees the hand of God in economic freedom of the big corporations to dominate and control all national and global economic activity.
> Paul Kurtz, 'The Free Market with the Human Face', *Free Inquiry* Magazine, Vol. 24, No. 2

Today's soldiers still kill for 'Peace', in 'Wars to End Wars', but given the availability of nuclear weapons to the fundamentalist Christians of America, the Muslims of Pakistan and the Jews of Israel, it is easy to conceive of a religious war in which the belligerents will happily seek martyrdom in their respective quests for everlasting glory. Such a war could indeed end all wars ... as well as all human life on Earth.

Since Auschwitz, we know what man is capable of. Since Hiroshima, we know what is at stake.
> Christopher Hitchens in *God is not Great*, Atlantic Books, London (2007)

Terrorism

The impact of unregulated globalisation and arrogant Western imperialism on ancient cultures has seriously affected the self-esteem of those poorly educated and insecure societies at the receiving end. Western businessmen have systematically exploited their homelands and scorned their cherished cultures and beliefs. Ever more forced relationships are being imposed by the dictates of uncontrolled speculators whose sole concern is money, and ordinary people can only stand helpless while their culture is crushed under a flood of Burger Kings, foreign mining companies, sweatshops, puppet politicians and helicopter gunships. It is no wonder that they are clinging tighter than ever, and more fundamentally than ever, to the comfort of their cultural religious beliefs, especially since the collapse of communism has left the Christian, Jewish and Islamic communities openly glaring hatefully at each other. Some have turned to terrorism.

Terrorism is rarely born out of poverty or ignorance. The billion or so really poor people on this planet are too weak and too busy finding their next meal to fight un-winnable battles. The Islamic terrorists responsible for the 9/11 attacks on the New York World Trade Center were well educated and well fed and their mentor Osama bin Laden was a multi-millionaire. UN relief worker Nasra Hassan observed after interviewing hundreds of aspiring Palestinian would-be suicide bombers that their motivation came from frustration at years of humiliation at the hands of the Israelis who have, without a shred of compassion or understanding, taken over their land and rewritten their history. The invasion of foreign cultures into ancient lands has reawakened memories of the Crusades and created the general hardening of Muslim attitudes

This is helped along by more than two hundred verses in the Koran that variously legitimise jihad (holy war). The extremist religious fundamentalism which this encourages is exploited by hate-filled clerics, preaching the imaginary virtues of martyrdom. Many would-be Islamic suicide bombers just want religious martyrdom. Maybe they believe the literal truth of the passage in the Koran that promises a hero's welcome in heaven for those who have died for the faith – according to Gibbon's *Decline and Fall*, there will be seventy-two black-eyed girls of resplendent beauty, blooming youth, virgin purity and exquisite sensitivity created for the use of the meanest believer, a moment of pleasure will be prolonged to a thousand years, and his facilities will be increased a hundred-fold to render him worthy. Sam Harris tells of a failed Palestinian suicide bomber whose professed motive was 'the love of martyrdom … I didn't want revenge for anything. I just wanted to be a martyr.' If he really believed the seventy-two-virgins stuff, then we can see why!

It must be said that the overwhelming majority of Muslims are peace-loving and less interested in world domination than, say, evangelical Christians. The notion that Islamic terrorists are fighting for Islamic supremacy is fuelled by the activities of certain fundamentalist sects such as the Wahhabists, which require their adherents to swear total loyalty to their religious teachers. These clerics instruct them to engage in jihad against all unbelievers, apostates and blasphemers (which by their extreme standards covers just about everyone else, including many Muslims).

Like the Bible, the Koran is packed with contradictions. Though its generally accepted central theme is about mercy, charity and tolerance, it is possible, by focussing on particular passages and ignoring others, to legitimise obsessive intolerance and merciless terrorism. This is what the Wahhabists do – selective reading out of context, whether of the Talmud, the Koran or the Bible, is at the root of all religious fundamentalism. Of course, such negativism tends to stifle all social, technical and political progress, and indeed, until 1973, Wahhabism languished ineffectually in poverty and ignorance. But in 1973, after the Arab–Israeli war and the formation of OPEC, the price of crude oil rocketed. The Wahhabists in Saudi Arabia suddenly found themselves in a position to fund the building and operation of the finest mosques, madrassahs (faith schools) and social centres for their followers, mostly in the Indian sub-continent. According to Charles Allen (*God's Terrorists*, Little Browne, London, 2006), it is estimated that since 1978, Saudi Wahhabists have spent seventy billion dollars on such projects, including 10,000 madrassahs in Pakistan alone. Mullah Omar's Taliban deny any links with Wahhabism, but in 1996, while Osama Bin Laden was trying to impose a Wahhabi-style Islamic state in the Sudan, they took Kabul and immediately introduced a strictly Wahhabist version of Sharia law.

The documents left by Mohammed Atta, the alleged leader of the 9/11 terrorists, show that they were acting on deeply-held religious convictions: shortly before he flew a fully-laden plane into the World Trade Centre in New York, Atta prayed: 'God I lay myself in your hands. I ask with the light of your faith that has lit the whole world and lightened all darkness on this earth, to guide me ...' (Greg Austin, Todd Cranock and Thorn Oommien, *God and War: An Audit and Exploration*) In reply, US President Bush said, 'God told me to strike at Al Qaeda and I struck them, and then he instructed me to strike at Saddam [i.e. at Iraq], which I did.'

Unfortunately, people who believe that God is talking to them are immune to reason or compromise. Unfortunately also, as Voltaire observed, 'Those who can make you believe absurdities can make you commit atrocities.' Any society that defends the legitimacy of the cold-blooded cluster-bombing of undefended civilian targets is surely in no position to criticise the morality of isolated acts of terrorism by frustrated Muslims.

'Either you are with us or against us in our war of good against evil,' said President George W Bush in December 2001. He equated Islam with evil and, as a believer in the redemptive powers of destruction, presumably saw the demolition of ancient Mesopotamia (Iraq) as some sort of virtuous crusade. Such divisive rhetoric can only provoke militant Muslims, and it must also stir the baser instincts of devout Christians in positions of power in the Pentagon. If you couple their obsession with making ancient prophesies come true with their access to vast nuclear stockpiles, then it is not a little disturbing to reflect that they actually have the capacity to bring about the horrors prophesied in the Book of Revelations. The Iranian President, a devout Shi'ite, also believes in the imminent end of the world and the coming of the Twelfth Imam (the messiah of Shi'ite theology). He too showed impatience in a speech to the UN in 2005, when he pleaded, 'O mighty Lord, hasten the emergence of your last repository, the promised one ...' Armageddon happens to be in northern Israel.

And Islam is not unique, for as Charles Selengut noted (in *Sacred Fury – Understanding Religious Violence* 2004 Altamira Press):

Nearly all religions offer over and above rewards in heaven for martyrs who are killed fighting for their religion. Religion does more than justify violence, the God of each side orders it.

Christian clerics also teach that their martyred saints were all heroes, who now justly reside in Heaven. Modern Christian saints will include the US Protestants who murder abortion doctors, and the Serbian leader Radovan Karadzic, who was allegedly responsible for atrocities against Muslim civilians in the Balkans conflict. He is honoured by the Greek Orthodox Church as 'one of the most prominent sons of our Lord Jesus Christ working for peace'. (Mitja Veliconja, 'In Hoc Signo Vinces: Religious Symbolism in the Balkan Wars 1991–95', a paper presented at the conference 'Nationality and Citizenship in Post Communist Europe', July 2001)

Predictably, Richard Dawkins feels that the problem is not so much religious extremism as religion *per se* – the notion conditioned into children by clerics during their formative years that it is virtuous to believe absurdities; that believers must be respected *because* they believe absurdities. If we accept this, then,

It is hard to withhold respect for Osama bin Laden and the suicide bombers ... who do what they do because they really believe what they were taught in their religious schools: that duty to God exceeds all other priorities.

Richard Dawkins in *The God Delusion*, Bantam Press, London, 2006

Differences of dogma are rarely the issue, but very few acts of terrorism could take place without clerical provocation and assurances. As new weapons are being developed apace, it is disturbing to reflect that, 'We are entering an era where a single person can, by one clandestine act, cause millions of deaths, or render a city uninhabitable for years.' (Martin Rees)

Apocalyptism

Jesus expected the world to end at any minute, and he devoted his life as a preacher to trying to panic the Jews (he didn't care what happened to the rest of us) into preparing for it: Forget your short-term interests and concentrate on getting into long-term Heaven, and woe betide anyone who doesn't heed the call, because the gates of Hell are swinging open and there's going to be the mother of all teeth-gnashings any day now. He was, of course, absolutely wrong.

An obsession with the imminent end of the world goes back to the Persian prophet Zoroaster, some time between 1500 and 1200BCE. He first predicted the long-term triumph of good over evil, when 'all things would be made perfect once and for all'. Today, improbable beliefs about the end of the world are features of Islam, Bah'ai, Rastafarianism and all the various versions of Christianity. Rather than admitting the finality of death, or at least ignorance of what happens next, these believers have done away with it altogether. They have persuaded themselves that at the end of time a redeemer will lead all oppressed people into a better future.

Christians expect that evil will be defeated in a cataclysmic battle, graphically described in the Book of Revelation (16:16–21). This refers to 'flashes of lightning, rumblings, peals of thunder and an earthquake so tremendous that its like has never before occurred since man came on earth', and predicts 'the collapse of the cities of the nations'. Some Christian groups claim that this is a prophesy of an all-out nuclear war, and that the onset of global overheating and the exhaustion of natural reserves are welcome signs of the imminent Second Coming. It looks as if there won't be much left for the meek to inherit, but Jesus will then gather all the good Christians and carry them up to Heaven, where they can enjoy a grandstand view of those left behind perishing in overwhelming wars, fires, plagues and earthquakes. At some stage, the armies of the Antichrist will attack, leading to a final showdown in the valley of

Armageddon, where all the Jews (except Jesus, presumably) will be killed.

However, none of this can take place until the Biblical conditions have been fulfilled. Israel must occupy the so-called promised lands, since this is somehow a necessary precursor to Christ's return. The myth says that God promised Abraham: 'To your descendants I give this land, from the river of Egypt [Nile] to the great river, the Euphrates' (Genesis 15:8). This is, of course, a source of much friction – it is a large area, covering Palestine, half of Egypt, half of Iraq, and Sinai, Jordan, Syria and Lebanon. The claim to this territory has absolutely no historical validity, regardless of all the propaganda, media hype and political incitement that has gone into promoting it. But in their dealings with their Palestinian neighbours, Israelis appear nevertheless to have operated in accordance with the biblical injunction: '... you shall make no covenant with them and show them no mercy.' (Torah, Deut. 7:1–2; see also Isiah 60, or Jeremiah 30)

Meanwhile, some fifty million US apocalyptists were overjoyed when the US and UK invaded Mesopotamia (Iraq), hoping that this was the start of a war to the death between Christianity and Islam. For these Christians, the establishment of the state of Israel in 1948 had been a significant sign of the End Times, and this was reinforced by the 1967 six-day war, when Israel extended her territories. An article in *Christianity Today* said:

> *For the first time in 2000 years, Jerusalem is now completely in the hands of the Jews. It gives the student of the Bible a thrill and a renewed faith in the accuracy and validity of the Bible.*

In the US, politically influential evangelical clerics press the US government to support the Israelis and provide them with military and financial aid. The churches themselves donate $1 billion each year to Zionist causes.

Nicolas Guyatt, in his book "Have a Nice Doomsday" (Ebury Press 2007), tells us that US apocalyptists are worried about another prophesy – that just before the apocalypse, 'the Antichrist' will rule the world, and that no one will realise it's the Antichrist until it is too late. Now, to rule the world, you would need some sort of world government, and so, in order to thwart the Antichrist, evangelical clerics are urging their followers to do all in their political power to derail any move in the direction of world unity. They even oppose the pathetic United Nations Organisation in order to make it impossible for anybody ever to 'rule the world'.

Apocalyptic belief is far from harmless. This is especially true in the USA, where believers reason that there is no point in preparing for the future when there is hardly any future left. There is no need to worry about global warming, or pollution, or the using up of limited natural resources, because the Lord will provide right up to the end. They quote Matthew (6:26): 'Look at the birds of the air, they do not sow or reap or store away in barns but your heavenly father feeds them.' Americans are similarly taught that, whereas 'the secular or socialist has a limited resources mentality and views the world as a pie ... that needs to be cut so that everyone can have a piece', and whereas 'many secularists view the world as overpopulated ... Christians know that God has made the earth sufficiently large with plenty of resources to accommodate all the people.' (US High School textbook *America's Providential History*) This teaching is backed up by many of the 1,600 Christian radio stations and 250 TV stations that are spread across the USA, which tell listeners that tsunamis, droughts, tornadoes and floods are certain signs that, at last, the longed-for Apocalypse is on its way.

There are even those who reason that the faster we can exhaust the world's resources, the sooner we can expect the Joyous Day. Unfortunately, the people behind this argument just happen to be supporters of the same politicians who are funded by the big oil and mining companies, who also have an interest in exhausting resources as fast as they can. These politicians include James Watt, who, as President Reagan's Secretary of the Interior, told the US Congress that protecting natural resources was unimportant in the light of the imminent Second Coming:

'... after the last tree is felled, Christ will come back'. While we're waiting, the US government has been busily repealing the Clean Air Act, the Clean Water Act, the Endangered Species Act, the National Environmental Policy Act and the regulations on ozone and other pollutants. They have opened up the rainforests and national parklands for logging and mining, opened the Arctic to mining and oil extraction companies, and generally pursued short-sighted, short-termist policies. They have poured scorn on the international Kyoto Agreement, which seeks merely to limit emissions of greenhouse gases. America is militarily the most powerful country in the world, so there's absolutely nothing anyone can do, either about the stockpiles of nuclear weapons awaiting Armageddon, or about the acid rain, wasted resources, decimated rain forests, spreading deserts, melting glaciers and polluted air that go with the wait.

Mind you, doomsayers have announced the imminent end of the world many times before. Each time there has been a craze for fasting and self-flagellation in eager anticipation, and each time ... nothing happened. The Seventh Day Adventist sect was created when Jesus failed to turn up in 1844, and Jehovah's Witnesses lived through nine promised apocalypses, between 1874 and 1973, without a blush. It must have been a great disappointment to the 200,000 Americans who expected 2001 to herald the Apocalypse when 2 January dawned, and we were still here. The effect of so many Great Disappointments has been to make millions of Christians ever more certain that *this time*, surely, the end really is nigh. According to Sam Harris, 66 million Americans are certain that Jesus will return to Earth sometime in the next 50 years, and a further 66 million believe that he is likely to – he is currently scheduled for 2012, when the rogue planet Nibiru is going to collide with Earth. If humanity does survive the twenty-first century, ours will surely be the most despised and hated generation in all history, for the irredeemable damage we have done to our planet and for our total disregard for future generations.

Yet again we find sadism, slaughter and suffering perpetrated in the name of God by clerics and politicians, secure in the knowledge that God will not contradict them. We can only blame the perverted, and surely psychopathic, clerics for the physical and mental torture and the present dangers they have inflicted on our race at every opportunity, in their pursuit of temporal power and wealth. Once again, however, God is clearly innocent. The next chapter offers a final demonstration of the cold depravity of certain clerics and the depths to which they are prepared to sink in order to hold on to their power and wealth.

CHAPTER 7

SUFFER, LITTLE CHILDREN

Parents who imagine themselves to be 'Jehovah's Witnesses' have refused permission for their children to receive blood transfusions. Parents who imagine that a man named Joseph Smith was led to a set of buried golden tablets have married their underage 'Mormon' daughters to favoured uncles and brothers-in-law, who sometimes have older wives already. The Shia fundamentalists in Iran lowered the age of 'consent' to nine, perhaps in admiring emulation of the age of the youngest 'wife' of the 'Prophet' Mohammed.

Christopher Hitchens, *God Is Not Great*

... the footsteps in the night that heralded yet another horrific rape of a terrified crying child.

Jimmy Boyle

As the scale of the paedophilia outrage in the catholic church started to emerge in 1992, senior clerics' responses were astonishing. Instead of showing contrition, abjectly apologising, recompensing the victims and attempting to ensure that such things could never happen again, Cardinal Law of Boston arrogantly called down 'the Power of God' – not on the abusers, however, but on those newspapers that had reported the activities of a certain Father Porter. This man had sexually assaulted many hundreds of children, including an eleven-year-old girl who had heard someone crying in the school bathroom, and found Father Porter raping a six-year-old girl: 'I tried to stop him but he grabbed me and sodomised me ... he told me that ... he had the power of God', and '... that God would punish me if I told anyone'.

The Cardinal wasn't particularly concerned about Father Porter, or the six-year-old girl, or even the vain use of God's name. What bothered him was that the media had found out about it, and had the temerity to publish it. There are two outrages to consider: firstly, that so many Catholic priests should have been so psychopathically depraved as to routinely treat innocent children in this sickening way; and secondly, that *all* of the senior Catholic clerics regarded such bestial behaviour as a trivial, private matter, a minor sin to be confessed secretly and then forgotten, with the victim sworn to secrecy and then also forgotten.

Priestly Depravity

When we see televised news reports of droughts in sub-Saharan Africa, the stark horror of the situation is brought home to us by close-up pictures of starving children, too weak to wave away the flies that crawl over them. When there is a devastating flood or an earthquake, it is the newsreel shots of orphaned children sobbing uncontrollably that sicken us most. All of humankind feels compassion for innocent children, yet clerics teach that their loving God, who could have prevented them, inflicted these sufferings. Perhaps it is God's apparent indifference to the plight of these little children that has rubbed off on clerics, as they continue to demand (and receive) the right to take wide-eyed innocents who still believe in Father Christmas, and put the fear of God into them. Terrifying threats of Hell and punishment, along with the repeated affirmation of superstitious dogma, so indoctrinate small children that they thenceforth 'belong' to the Church, unable ever again to think clearly for themselves.

Richard Dawkins (in *The God Delusion*) argues that the process of indoctrinating and labelling young children as 'Catholics' or 'Anglicans', and then segregating them in different schools, amounts to child abuse. Maryam Namazie similarly considers that the Muslim practice of segregating nine-year-old girls from boys, teaching them that they are inferior, putting veils on them and restricting them from playing and swimming and doing the things kids do, is also child abuse. One can only feel compassion for the victims of such indoctrination, but equally one experiences a burning sense of outrage and frustration toward those clerics responsible for the deception – sympathy for those on their knees, disgust for those who put them there.

But consider a young priest, recruited from school before he knows what life is about and sworn to celibacy. The task of controlling his thoughts must be next to impossible. He must repress his emotions and struggle against his natural desires throughout his entire life. He will learn to hate his own body, and may develop very depraved views of sexuality along the way. Many priests cope with the help of alcohol, and others by taking a less literal view of the dogma, but the consequence (as shown by various studies in the US and Europe) is that only around ten percent of celibates are deemed to be 'emotionally mature'. Many (e.g. David Yallop in his book *The Power and the Glory*, Constable & Robinson, London, 2007) claim that the whole Catholic Church, including many bishops and cardinals, is riddled with sexual perversion: there are those with secret concubines; and sexual abusers of boys, men and women, including nuns and novices.

However, the secret children of the more than twenty percent of Catholic priests who have illicit heterosexual relationships ('Errant priests' secret children sue church', Irish *Sunday Times*, 18 April 2010, quoting Austrian theologian Paul Zuhlener, who put the figure at 22%) have little to look forward to. Of those who have survived the abortion option, most are sent to orphanages or for adoption. Those mothers who insist on keeping their children are sworn to secrecy, and the children are raised in single-parent families, not knowing, and usually denied by, their fathers. They are thus denied the basic right of a normal family life, while Mother Church treats them, not as children or as victims, but as legal threats, to be 'dealt with'.

'He told me it was God's will to have sex with me and when I turned him down I wasn't being obedient to God.' In 1979, a priest told sixteen-year-old Rita Milla, 'God wants you to do all you can to keep His priests happy … it's your duty' (LA Times

5th December 2007). She ended up keeping seven priests happy, until she became pregnant the following year.

When clerics go bad, they can go very bad indeed, committing acts of sexual depravity that would sicken even the most grievous sinner. The spate of paedophile scandals, which started to break into the news in the 1980s, testify that repressed sexuality has an unfortunate habit of finding devious expression. Even the Vatican, with its notorious inability to face reality, acknowledged that 'lapses are unavoidable'. Carl Sagan nevertheless spotted one redeeming feature of celibacy: 'It tends to suppress any hereditary propensity toward fanaticism.'

Christianity was host to adulterers and paedophiles long before celibacy became mandatory – since as early as 177CE, when Bishop Athenagoras formally anathematised them. They were still around in the eighth century, when the Penitential of Bede felt the need to recommend severe penances for priests who sodomised children. Later, in 1051, the Book of Gomorrah denounced the widespread sodomy (intercourse with animals and sexual abuse of children) still practised by the clergy of the day. It particularly criticized 'priests who defile men or boys who have come to them for confession' – still a popular ploy, apparently. There is abundant evidence that paedophilia continued unabated within the priesthood for the next 900 years, and all the more so after obligatory celibacy was introduced, around 1560. As we saw in Chapter 4, strict celibacy and sympathetic ministry are generally incompatible, as celibates of both sexes tend towards assertiveness and estrangement, coldness and cruelty.

Clerical Depravity

The official policy toward such 'unavoidable lapses' among their priests is that they 'should be kept from the knowledge of the faithful'. The 1962 Holy Office instructions demand total secrecy – the abuser would be quietly transferred to another assignment; the victim and any parent or witness would be sworn to eternal secrecy, on pain of summary excommunication. This is the so-called 'secret system'. It had worked to the Church's satisfaction for hundreds of years, with no priest ever exposed in open criminal proceedings, until the outrage started to boil over in the USA in the 1980s. Even then, in order to preserve the status quo, clerics urged victims' families to sweep the sickening business out of sight, in order 'to avoid scandal and harm to Mother Church'. If they wouldn't buy that, they were encouraged to hush it up for the children's sake, 'to avoid further injury or trauma to the young victims by requiring them to testify in a public Courtroom'. The majority of families, not wishing to distress their children further, accepted modest out-of-court settlements in return for total secrecy.

Catholic clerics, whose dogma informs them that masturbation is a greater sin than rape, maintain to the present day that paedophilia is a mere personal 'sin', to be dealt with secretly in the confessional. They fiercely oppose the notion that it is a serious criminal matter, best dealt with in an open court of law. A case eventually went to court in the USA in October 1984, and a Grand Jury publicly indicted Father Gilbert Gauthe, who had been abusing a total of 100 boys, some of them several hundreds of times each. The defence managed to plea-bargain for twenty years in jail. This was in order that there would be no need for witnesses to describe lurid details in court; details that the media might pick up and disseminate. So the evidence was never presented, though Faye Gastal, the mother of one nine-year-old victim, was nevertheless invited to share her thoughts with the court: 'I think of Gauthe sticking his penis in my son's mouth, ejaculating in his mouth, putting his penis in his rectum. That's what I think about.' The clerics' compassionate response was to pressurise advertisers to boycott all newspapers that publicised the case.

As the scandal gained momentum, bishops routinely exploited plea-bargaining to keep details out of the public arena. For example in 1985, a Father Baltazar plea-bargained for seven years for 'lewd behaviour with a minor' after a twenty-year binge of sexual abuse of children, including a critically ill boy on a kidney dialysis machine, and another boy in double leg traction in hospital.

Despite the pope's insistence that it was confined to the USA, the paedophilia outrage quickly became apparent in twenty-seven countries outside America, including Belgium, Malta and the Philippines, but especially in Canada, Australia and Ireland. Here the Order of Christian Brothers was exposed as a sadistic sect who physically and sexually abused children in their care as a matter of routine. Their sadism was equalled only by orders of nuns with euphemistic names like the Sisters of Charity and the Sisters of Mercy. Their 'Nazareth Homes' in four continents provided a cover for regimes of physical abuse and degradation of thousands of young children that would scar them for life. In Ireland during the 1950s and 1960s, nuns 'tortured children as young as eleven months (flogging and scalding them as well as subjecting them to astonishing acts of psychological cruelty) "for the sins of their parents" (i.e. the sin of their own illegitimacy) ... thousands of these infants were forcibly separated from the care of their unwed mothers and sent overseas for adoption'. (Sam Harris, *The End of Faith*, The Free Press, London, 2004)

In Ireland in 1987, when it looked as if the lid was about to blow, the various dioceses even took out insurance against exposure to claims arising from abuse. They told the insurers that they had heard of problems in the USA, and that they just wanted to cover themselves in case a similar problem arose in Ireland – they did not reveal that they already knew of at least twenty Irish priests against whom allegations had been made. Irish dioceses subsequently received insurance payouts of €12.9 million, in return for premiums of only €50,800.

Clerics in the orders responsible for these crimes deviously obstructed attempts by the government to investigate reports of child slave labour in the Magdelene laundries, even as they were quietly making hundreds of millions of euros in property deals and cynically shifting the money and the land deeds to offshore trust funds, beyond the reach of the victims' redress courts or the Irish authorities. In one such deal, the Sisters of Our Lady of Charity sold about four hectares at High Park in suburban

Dublin for €61.8 million. Construction workers later found a mass grave on the site, containing the bodies of 133 women.

Little has changed despite the exposures. As recently as December 2008, Cardinal Brady publicly supported John Magee, the Bishop of Cloyne, as he deliberately misled investigators looking into a series of allegations of sexual abuse of children against two priests in his diocese. Magee had concealed these even though the Church had previously agreed that every single case of 'alleged abuse of a child' was to be brought immediately to the attention of the police. In the *Irish Times* of 27 November 2009, reports of the cover-up uncharacteristically described the Catholic Church and its officers as 'revulsive', 'malign' and 'traitors'.

For, despite claiming that they had changed their ways and would henceforth deal openly with any allegation of abuse, clerics had secretly redefined 'alleged abuse'. For them, it now required 'material evidence or a credible witness to the abuse to come forward and make a statement within seven days of the alleged abuse'. In such a case, the police were to be notified as agreed; otherwise, the matter was to be dealt with secretly, as before. In the overwhelming majority of cases, of course, there can be no material evidence or witness. The clerics' promise was deliberately spurious. Victim support group One-in-Four understated the situation when it declared in December 2008: 'The Catholic Church cannot be trusted to put the safety of children first.'

Despite the Church's enormous wealth, the clerics have also refused to accept responsibility for the financial compensation of their victims. They reluctantly agreed to hand over €128 million 'worth' of unsellable property, such as the deeds of operating schools, leaving Irish taxpayers (atheists and all) with a bill of over €1,200 million in compensation to the clerics' victims.

Meanwhile, in Rome, Vatican clerics ignored requests from the Irish Government for help with their inquiry, until the matter became a diplomatic issue. Then they resentfully replied – in Latin. The provocative and arrogant approach of the Vatican eventually led the Irish Prime Minister, Enda Kenny, to make a speech in the Irish Parliament on 20 July 2011, in which he spoke of the:

> ... *dysfunction, disconnection and elitism, and narcissism which dominates the culture of the Vatican to this day ... The rape and torture of children were downplayed or 'managed' to uphold instead the primacy of the institution, its power, standing and reputation* ... [not to mention its wealth]

Irish Catholics generally applauded this politically courageous speech, and the Vatican promptly withdrew its Papal Nuncio. The Irish government subsequently closed its embassy to the Vatican in 2012, on grounds of economy.

The perverted nature of some priests is a serious matter, but the real scandal is the scale of the abuse, and that it is aided and abetted by senior clerics. These clerics have methodically facilitated and encouraged these crimes. They have routinely concealed the perpetrators, protecting them from the consequences of their perversions, and even providing them with fresh hunting grounds whenever their destructive activities have become known in their old ones.

Clerical Justification for Abusing Children

US theology professor Mary Ann Parker makes the following argument:

> *God required his son to suffer in order to save the world. That is an image of God as child abuser, and Jesus is imagined as the perfect victim – he accepts the abuse and does it silently. He is praised by his religious community for accepting the abuse as the highest form of love ... So ... how is the victim of the priests' abuse going to find a justification for raising a protest? ... and how is the church going to see the perpetrators of abuse clearly if it can't see its own conceptualization of God as abuser?*

However, this doesn't explain the hysterical clerical reaction to the media who report on priestly abuse.

And as we have seen, when the child abuse scandal blew up, clerics came out fighting. They claimed that the whole thing had been blown out of proportion by hostile media figures who were determined to persecute them for their stand on abortion. They denounced any person or journalist who exposed the abuse as 'an enemy of the Church', aided by greedy lawyers scrambling to get their hands on the Church's billions through the 'priest litigation business'. Pope John Paul II seemed to agree that repeated sexual abuse of minors was nothing compared with the crime of publicising it. He complained that the public exposures violated the priest's right to keep the secrets of the confessional (especially his sexual antics). He further argued that priests should be above the law, especially as paedophilia was only a petty personal sin, and he protected Cardinal Hans Herman Groer, who had molested 2,000 boys over twenty years.

Other clerics blamed the Second Vatican Council (1962–65) for having created, so they said, a climate that encouraged priests to abuse children, especially as the priesthood clearly attracted those with a predisposition to paedophilia. Some even suggested that not all of the victims were as innocent as they seemed, and blamed the children themselves for having given their grown-up tormentors the 'come on'. In England, Cardinal Murphy-O'Connor (who had repeatedly protected and reassigned arch-paedophile Father Hill) claimed that journalists were conducting a witch-hunt against him. He accused them of relentlessly attacking Roman Catholicism itself, as he tried to turn the tables on those who had exposed him. Cardinal Ratzinger (later Pope Benedict) went further and blamed secular society – 'It has to do with our highly sexualised society ...' – attempting to portray the abusers as, in fact, the real victims. Of course, he also blamed the 'widespread false morality' of birth control and abortion for his priests' paedophilia. He felt that praying would ease the suffering of the children.

There is evidence that Ratzinger himself has been directly involved in covering up multiple child rapes: firstly by Father

Peter Hullerman, under Cardinal Ratzinger's authority in Austria in the late 1970s; and then in the case of Father Lawrence Murphy, who abused 200 deaf boys for decades in Wisconsin, USA. This case had been referred to Ratzinger as Head of the Congregation for the Doctrine of the Faith (i.e. the Inquisition). Ratzinger covered up both scandals and, despite the publication of names and dates (e.g. in *Der Spiegel*) and he dismissed both stories. Guilty or not, as Pope he now claims immunity from prosecution in any international human rights court, by virtue of being a Head of State (even though the Vatican is not a State in any recognised sense of the word). As Lord Acton observed in 1887:

Power tends to corrupt, and absolute power corrupts absolutely ... There is no worse heresy than that the office sanctifies the holder of it.

By his refusal to confront the issue of his paedophile priests, Pope Benedict XVI has surely forfeited the right to claim authority on any matter of faith or morality, but in Easter 2010, he stooped even lower when he dismissed the whole sickening worldwide outrage as mere 'petty gossip'. Meanwhile, a Vatican spokesman further nettled gays everywhere by claiming that paedophilia was caused by homosexuality.

When confronted with the Secret System (as it had been formally laid down by the Holy Office in 1962), the bishops responsible claimed that they did not understand paedophilia. They had no idea that paedophiles would re-offend as often as opportunities arose, and therefore they were guilty of nothing more than ignorance. This is another blatant lie. The bishops were well aware of their Church's 1,800-year heritage of serial paedophile behaviour in priests. They had masses of clinical evidence available at their fingertips from the Church's own care centres for problematic priests, such as those run by the Servants of the Paraclete. This organisation was founded in the 1950s in the USA to deal with problem priests. Its founder, Father Gerald Fitzgerald, was convinced that child abusers were totally incapable of changing their ways, and he recommended that all such offenders should be immediately laicised and kicked out of the church, without wasting time trying to reform them.

Yet the Secret System remains unchanged. Clerics are still unmoved by the estimated 750,000 living victims whose lives they have destroyed; nor have they made any commitment to tackle paedophilia within their ranks in the future. Instead they have blamed society, abortion and even the victims, but never the perpetrators.

Perversely, we may thank those grasping US lawyers who saw the Church as a golden goose – they were the ones who encouraged victims to come forward to expose the whole scandal, even though their motivation was often not justice, but money. And to some extent we may blame the continuation of the Secret System on those insurance companies and financial consultants to the Church who have advised concealment of as much of the outrage as possible.

In 2011, the clerics' lawyers tried a new ploy. They stated that the relationship between a priest and his bishop was not that of employee and employer, and that the bishop therefore had no vicarious responsibility, nor had the Church any financial responsibility, for damage done by a priest in the course of his duties. This is even though they concede that priests act on a bishop's behalf, in accordance with the bishop's directions, and that bishops have the authority to hire and fire priests.

The Catholic Church is probably the wealthiest institution in the world. It chooses to spend its millions on expensive lawyers, hiring them to exploit legal loopholes and technicalities to 'prove' that it has no assets and that it has no responsibility for its employees – the priests and bishops. To be on the safe side, the various dioceses have kept busy, squirreling the bulk of their vast property assets into inaccessible, anonymous 'trusts', leaving their books almost bare, certainly not worth pursuing for compensation. Victims have nowhere to turn, for whenever the question of the Church contributing financially to the consequences of its behaviour has been raised, 'Lies, obfuscation and institutional secrecy have been the hallmarks of a church establishment that ostensibly embodies virtue' (Justine McCarthy, *Sunday Times*, 10 July 2011). Clearly, money is of far greater concern to clerics than the broken lives of their wide-eyed victims, and the high moral code of the Vatican can surely be summarised as: 'Never give a sucker an even break!' As usual, money is at the root of the clerics' disgrace.

Long before priestly paedophilia was exposed as a worldwide problem, and certainly since it has been, it was surely up to the clerics in Rome to deal decisively with it. And they did nothing, beyond redefining 'allegations of abuse'. The same clerics who have pontificated so obsessively, and who continue to complain about low standards of sexual morality in secular society, have presided over the systematic rape and mental torture of innocent children. They have been positively abetted in this by a hierarchy which has knowingly protected the grossest offenders, keeping them provided at all times with pastures green, and done nothing to help the victims.

> *Any other organisation, and any state, that turned a blind eye to the molestation of so many children, and that not only refused to punish the perpetrators but set them up to re-offend, would be condemned at the UN and at international conferences, and would be made the subject of vitriolic reports by Amnesty International and by Human Rights Watch, and there would be calls to refer the case to the International Criminal Court.*
>
> Geoffrey Robinson QC, *The Case of the Pope: Vatican Accountability for Human Rights Abuse*, Penguin (2010)

It is because the Vatican can skip between being an unworldly religion one minute, and a hard-nosed quasi-state the next, that it is so hard to pin down.

And now the clerics complain that they are unfairly ignored. Cardinal Cormac Murphy O'Connor whined in May 2008, 'I am unhappy about various attempts to eliminate the Christian voice from the public forum,' as he sanctimoniously drew attention to the reluctance of some governments to accept clerical interference in matters of secular morality. It ill befits such an insensitive and manipulative organisation to be crying 'Foul' at a time like this. For to abuse a child is to violate an innocent, which is to sink lower than most people could imagine. It is beneath contempt. For a priest to sodomise a trusting child in his care is the ultimate treachery. It is at once a physical, mental and spiritual attack, which inflicts pain, anguish and emotional desolation, leaving the child seriously damaged for the rest of its life, to the extent of suicide in many cases.

> *But whoso shall offend one of these little ones which believe in me, it were better for him that a millstone were hanged about his neck, and that he were drowned in the depth of the sea.*
> Matthew 18:6; Mark 9:42; Luke 17:2

We can see clearly now how the Church has exploited ScapeGod: 'He would tell me that this was what God wanted, God would be pleased with me.' Whenever a Cleric mentions God, it's ScapeGod he is talking about. The true God, if he exists, is innocent!

Part II has shown how certain clerics have exploited ScapeGod to impose every kind of evil on the world. In order to preserve their wealth and their anachronistic power structure, they have individually and collectively opposed democracy, disinterested scientific inquiry and social, technical and medical progress. They have promoted division, repression, censorship and theocratic control, while blaming God for the collateral damage – without ScapeGod, they would have been powerless. Clerics claim to be the true arbiters of morality and the purveyors of God's great love, yet many of them have shown themselves to be unfeeling, sadistic, immoral and in some cases even psychopathic. Behind the crosiers and the mitres and the purple and gold palliums, behind the façade of saintly expressions and unworldly morality, we seem to have unearthed some pretty savvy 'operators'.

PART III

COULD IT ALL BE A CON TRICK?

By coincidence, the saintly expressions and façades of unworldly morality utilised by clerics are also the confidence trickster's favoured tools. This prompts the question: Could it really be that theistic religions have been cynically hijacked by certain senior clerics as means of securing power and privilege for themselves? Maybe they really believe that they are actually relaying God's instructions. Or could it be that that certain religions were created and designed expressly for the purpose of making money for their clerics? Is it all a conspiracy? It is hard to accept, but we will consider these possibilities in Part III.

After reading Part II, most moderate people will surely concede that Christianity has so far been something of a blight on humankind. This has largely been due to the naivety, or else the cynicism, of certain senior clerics, the self-same class of people who specified the dogma and ceremony in the first place. The circumstantial evidence overwhelmingly suggests that the monotheist religions have been exploited by clerical deviants wishing to impose their troubled minds on the rest of humanity, and that they pose a threat to the very survival of the human race. Most unbiased lay people, however, still generally feel that religion does more good than harm, and that the harm is the price we unfortunately have to pay to receive God's blessing and everlasting happiness in the next world. Christians may have been exploited in the past, and even in the present, but they think their turn will surely come in the next life …

This assumes, of course, that there will *be* a next life. It seems unlikely that God Himself is as clerics have described him, because the actual existence of this intangible, unresponsive, dependably silent God of Abraham has never been demonstrated. It is questioned by many, and not just by antitheists, atheists and agnostics, but also by believers in other gods like Vishnu and Ahura Mazda and by non-theistic religionists such as Buddhists and Confucians, as well as by a great many nominal Christians, who outwardly profess to believe in 'Him', but are not so sure deep down.

Fortunately for clerics, there is absolutely no way of verifying whether or not the God of Abraham really exists. If he does then he's a wayward God, for, despite his supposed ability to do anything at all – literally anything – there are three things that this omnipotent being chooses never to do: firstly, he refuses to communicate directly with ordinary people, except through the agency of senior clerics – and what's the point of that? Secondly, he refuses to feed or clothe these, his indispensable spokesmen, preferring to leave them dependent on charity – if he's employing them, he should pay them! (see 1 Timothy 5:17) Finally, although this omnipotent God could use his terrifying powers to demonstrate his existence to the whole world with absolute authority any time he chooses ... he chooses not to. In fact, he pretends not to exist at all. He has even cunningly arranged that all arguments in favour of his existence are unsound, and this despite his son's advice that you should 'let your light shine before men' (Matthew 5:16). Clearly, if God exists, then he wants to be left alone. However, clerics constantly pester all humankind to badger him with worship and requests for special favours.

If God wants us to do something for him, then surely he will make his wishes clear to us – he will at least make himself known to us, instead of playing silly beggars. As George Washington complained,

> *I am approached ... by religious men who are certain they represent the Divine Will ... If God would reveal his will to others on a point so connected to my duty, it might be supposed he would reveal it directly to me.*

Christianity is a 'revealed' religion, but it has been revealed only to senior clerics. They tell us that God's purpose in pretending not to exist is to incline us to disbelieve in him so that he can test our willingness to believe without evidence – and what is the point of that? They tell us that this is why God has arranged that we can never know what his purposes are – which seems to contradict their own simultaneous claims to know God's

128

purposes. There is, of course, another possibility, which is that this God doesn't exist, and clerics are deceived by wishful thinking. Or maybe, as I have suggested, some of them know that the Christian God doesn't exist, and have chosen to exploit human gullibility for their own benefit. The French commentator CF Volney (1757–1820) was certain of it:

> *They everywhere attributed to themselves prerogatives and immunities, by means of which they lived exempt from the burdens of other classes ... They everywhere avoided the toils of labour, the dangers of the soldier, the disappointments of the merchant ... Under the cloak of poverty, they found everywhere the secret of procuring wealth ... They styled themselves the interpreters and mediators [of God] always aiming at the great object to govern for their own advantage ...*

Sadly, this cynical-sounding scenario fits frighteningly well with the observable facts. Jefferson, in his draft Bill for Religious Freedom, felt:

> *That ... fallible and uninspired men have assumed dominion over the faith of others ... Hath established and maintained false religions over the greatest part of the world and through all time ... that to compel a man to furnish contributions of money for the propagation of opinions of which he disbelieves and abhors is sinful and tyrannical ...*

Humankind has long realised that clerics,
> *... knew nothing of benefit to man; they were utterly ignorant of geology – of astronomy – of geography; – that they knew nothing of history; – that they were poor doctors and worse surgeons; – that they knew nothing of law and less of justice; that they were without brains and utterly destitute of hearts; that they knew nothing of the rights of men; that they were despisers of women, the haters of progress, the enemies of science, and the destroyers of liberty.*
> *The Works of Robert Ingersoll (1833–99), Volume 1*

More recently, so-called New Atheists such as Christopher Hitchens have accused many of those promoting the various religions of using forged foundational documents and of sustaining their positions through lies and fear. As we have seen in Section II, Church leaders have persistently opposed free enquiry, freedom of speech and individual liberty, while promoting ignorance, guilt, sexual repression, torture, murder, violence and hatred. They have been, and continue to be, ready accomplices of racism, sexism and genocide.

Scapegoating is recognised by psychologists as a natural human tendency. Machiavelli (in *The Prince*) advises, however, that you must pick your scapegoat cautiously, taking care that it can be held responsible without fear of contradiction or retaliation. A disastrous set of trade figures can be attributed to 'world conditions', with the certainty that world conditions cannot retaliate. Perhaps the real fault lies with 'procedures' – such intangible scapegoats can be safely blamed for all sorts of things. God similarly makes an excellent scapegoat: 'It is God's will that millions are starving' safely absolves those responsible. They can be quite confident that God won't contradict them, because God pretends not to exist, and he never talks to ordinary people. God's guaranteed silence is the foundation stone that has enabled clerics to exploit and capitalise on his name with impunity, and upon which they have built their multibillion worldwide God industry. They know that God will never deny their claims. Nor will he ever expose their duplicity. Nor will they ever have to pay for having used his name so shamefully.

ScapeGod has been exploited since feudal times to do the dirty work of the wealthy and powerful. Even Napoleon asked:

> *How can you have order in a state without religion? For when one man is dying of hunger near another who is ill of surfeit, he cannot resign himself to this difference unless there is an authority which declares, 'God wills it thus.'*

More recently, in June 2003, President Bush II justified his aggression against Iraq with: 'God told me to strike at Al Qaeda and I struck them, and then he instructed me to strike at Saddam which I did.' God never contradicted him.

Ever since Constantine, it has suited the ruling classes to have the masses believe that each person's station in life has been divinely ordained: 'The rich man in his castle, the poor man at his gate, God made them high and lowly, and ordered their estate.' As Karl Marx famously observed, religion is a sedative that helps to prevent the masses from rising up against the injustice and unfairness that rulers impose on them. This is why kings and governments have always patronised clerics, and clerics have always spread the notion that the ruler's position has been divinely ordained. The relationship between church and ruler continues, each supporting the other in various quiet ways. Christian clerics teach the people that their suffering is in accord with God's will and that they should meekly accept it; that being unfairly exploited and humiliated is somehow virtuous; that 'in a moral sense, poverty means wealth' (Pope John Paul II); and that justice will come in the next life after we are dead. They point out that Jesus made no attempt to rebel against the occupying Roman overlords, but taught that we should give to Caesar that which is Caesar's. Christian clerics to the present day generally enjoy the protection of those in power.

In Part III, I intend to show that Christianity is falsely founded on a number of grounds, and that the particular God that Christian clerics invoke is a paradoxical absurdity that cannot possibly exist, a very obvious ScapeGod (though, for all I know, other gods may well exist – a lot depends on what you mean by 'God'). I have no wish to offend believers gratuitously, but by making this point I hope to encourage them to question the motives of those men who pronounce that it is God who is telling them to inflict their horrors on our race when it is so very obviously ScapeGod.

I am conscious that I am one of a small minority of disbelievers living in a community of professing Christians. The onus is therefore on me to explain why I think I'm right and they're all wrong, and why the majority of clear-thinking, intelligent people believe and even cling tenaciously to their professed faiths. I attempt to do this in chapters 9 and 10 with reference to some elementary psychology, and conclude Part III by reporting how traditional Christian belief is slowly declining, even as Islamism and dumbed-down versions of Protestantism are thriving.

CHAPTER 8

THE SHAKY FOUNDATIONS OF
CHRISTIANITY

Religion is founded on the fear of the many and the cleverness of the few.

Stendhal (1783–1842)

Christianity provides the answer to all our dreams – a caring God of infinite justice, truth and love watching over us, followed by everlasting life where we will be reunited with our loved ones, and where we will enjoy perfect happiness for ever. What more could anybody yearn for? It sounds perfect, too good to be true. Unfortunately, a dream is not made true just because we wish it were so, and the most convincing lies are the ones we tell ourselves.

True believers should have no need to keep reaffirming to each other how much they believe. If you really believe, for example, that the sun will rise tomorrow morning, you simply plan your life accordingly. There is no need to regularly attend meetings to affirm to others how much you believe it. Yet weekly religious liturgies consist of little more than clerically-led public professions of abject guilt for imagined sins, followed by public professions of belief in the dogma – it is almost as if churchgoers are trying to convince themselves.

Christians are obliged to believe in the literal truth of each of the articles of faith specified in their Creed. If they don't believe, then strictly speaking, they're not Christians and they won't qualify for the Heavenly goodies. Christianity and Islam both claim to be sources of ultimate truth about the whys and wherefores of our existence. Both make definite claims that are supposed to be *literally true.* So when, for example, Christians proclaim: '... I believe in ... the resurrection of the body, and life everlasting,' they are publicly asserting that they believe that after they die, their bodies will be physically raised up and will

133

continue to exist in some other place. They mean this not allegorically or metaphorically or poetically, but absolutely literally. Now, when scientists and logicians analyse the evidence upon which such fundamental tenets of Christianity as these are founded, they discover them to be paradoxical, and not literally true … literally false, in fact. As you would expect, clerics splutter that 'God cannot be tested!' But they don't explain why not. Maybe it is because they are fearful that they will be exposed as opportunists. Christianity is a somewhat top-heavy edifice, built upon questionable grounds and facing a rising tide of scientific knowledge. In Luke 6:49, even Jesus himself warned against building a structure without proper foundations, because, 'The moment the torrent strikes, it will collapse and its destruction will be complete.' So let us examine some of these foundational beliefs upon which the edifice of Christianity stands.

Shaky Foundational Belief No. 1: Immortality and Heaven

If the bible is so mistaken in telling us where we came from, how can we trust it to tell us where we're going?

Justin Brown

The possibility of an afterlife is a fundamental component of religious doctrine, perhaps because clerics' threats and promises would have little persuasive power without such a prize. Christians are required to believe that after they die physically, their 'spirit' somehow continues to live. Depending on whether or not they have been baptised and have led obedient, virtuous lives, they are arbitrarily assigned by God/Jesus either to everlasting happiness in Heaven, or to perpetual perdition in Hell.

There is no mention of any afterlife in the Old Testament (though the New Testament makes up for the omission), but from the beginning Christian clerics and their wealthy patrons exploited the promise of a blissful life after death to compensate for the suffering and injustices they themselves imposed on the masses during their lifetimes. They found the concept useful in preventing the powerless from rising up in rebellion against those injustices – Karl Marx famously noted in his 1843 *Critique of Hegel's Philosophy of Right* that the notion that it is harder for a rich man to enter Heaven than for a camel to pass through the eye of a needle was as effective as opium in placating the exploited masses and preventing them from rebelling. The notion of an afterlife is useful when preparing soldiers for battle; and useful also when recruiting to the faith ordinary mortals with a natural fear of death. The prospect of a happy afterlife has also provided a powerful incentive for the masses of ordinary people to grovel and beg their clerics' to forgive their imagined sins. The threat or promise of an afterlife has always been exceptionally good for clerical business.

Conversely, the atheist or agnostic sees no reason for believing that humankind will receive fair treatment – nature is not fair, as should be obvious to any impartial observer of the injustices of life on Earth. Bertrand Russell pointed out that if you bought ten dozen eggs and the first dozen turned out to be rotten (as is life on Earth for many millions of people), only a cleric would reason that the remaining nine dozen must be of surpassing excellence.

Primitive man probably saw death as the loss of some animating spirit from the body, instead of the mere cessation of bodily functions. He might have reasoned that this spirit, this 'soul', had not necessarily died but had simply gone somewhere else, maybe to some 'Heaven'. Such dualistic reasoning satisfies humankind's yearnings for immortality, and Jesus took great pains to promise the physical resurrection of the body. But let us reject ghoulish notions of corpses rising out of their graves, and suggest for a moment that the faithful believe instead that a person's essence is located in the brain. The genetic inheritance, the memories, the beliefs, the mannerisms and habits that we call personality are all duplicated in an immaterial 'soul' which exists in a different state, a sort of ethereal backup disk. Whereas the cells and synapses of the brain dissolve at death, this soul somehow continues to 'exist', and it is in this form that we might hope to live on forever, ecstatically in Heaven or agonisingly in Hell.

Unfortunately, scientists tend to spoil this wishful dream by asking, perversely, what such a soul or disk might be made of – energy? Or matter? Or … what? What forces hold it together and, leadingly, how might it interact with ordinary matter? Scientists believe that they already know all the things that influence normal electron behaviour at normal energy levels (the Dirac equation), and the list definitely doesn't include spirit energy or even spiritual particles. Christians already believe that non-human animals do not have souls, so it seems improbable that something as basic as the amino acids, proteins or other complex molecules that all animals – including humans – are assembled from have them either.

The subjective evidence of near-death experiences is discredited by recent research. This suggests that the sensations felt at the point of death have a biological explanation – there is a final burst of brainwave hyperactivity as blood flow to the brain ceases. Spiritualists also seem unable to produce any objective evidence of an afterlife. Sceptical societies thrive on such challenges – back in 1964, the American sceptic James Randi publicly promised $1 million to anyone who could provide experimentally verifiable evidence of the occult, and fifty years later the money is still intact. We would surely have heard of any scientific evidence for the supernatural; there would have been no shortage of research funding available to anyone who might find even the slightest hint of it (as for example with the Turin shroud). However, all the evidence so far supports the conclusion that humankind is just another species of animal – and, as already noted, not even Christians believe that animals have souls.

Bishop Barnes of Birmingham argued that man,

… can build Westminster Abbey. He can make an aeroplane. He can calculate the distance from the sun … Shall, then, man at death perish utterly? … The universe has been shaped and is governed by an intelligent purpose.

Surely it would be foolish to waste such genius? Well, death may indeed seem wasteful to us, but there is no evidence that the universe has any 'intelligent' purpose, and it certainly *doesn't* share our ideas of wastefulness. Dawkins' notion of the selfish gene probably gives a better idea of nature's purpose, or rather, its lack of purpose, and this unfortunately doesn't involve immortality for individual humans.

Pascal's Wager (as expressed by Blaise Pascal, French mathematician and philosopher, 1623–62) appears to offer a logical reason for professing belief in the Christian concept of immortality – if you're wrong, there's nothing to lose and if you're right, you win eternal life, whereas those who proclaim disbelief are in a lose/lose situation. Unfortunately, this is a false dichotomy – there are thousands of possible theisms and hence, thousands of possible ways of being wrong (www.godchecker.com describes 2,850 different deities). So even if there is an afterlife, devout Anglicans could just as easily end up in Shi'ite Hell. Here is a better wager: lead an ethically virtuous life; appreciate and enjoy it to the full and ignore every one of the religious doctrines available, only one of which, at best, can be right. If it turns out that there is indeed a judgemental God, depend on It/Them/Him/Her to reward you for a life constructively used. This life, now, is the only one you can be sure of; if you give it up to self-sacrifice and cringing in church in the hope of winning everlasting life elsewhere, and then it turns out that there is no 'elsewhere' or it is the wrong 'elsewhere', then you've blown everything.

As for our spiritual destination, Hell is supposedly more horrible than your worst nightmare. It is where the souls of all sinners and unbaptised people end up. Purgatory is where souls go to be punished by torment before they enter Heaven, where they hope to devote themselves to an eternity of praise and adoration, total self-sacrifice and grovelling sycophancy (what Christopher Hitchens called 'a celestial North Korea'). Catholics know about Purgatory because their infallible Church has always taught it. In fact, the same Church used to sell indulgences to short-circuit the Purgatory process, a practice which prompted the observation:

> *There is not a word spoken of it* [purgatory] *in all Holy Scripture, and also if the pope with his pardons may for money deliver one soul hence, he may deliver him as well without money; and if he deliver one, he may deliver a thousand; if he deliver a thousand he may deliver them all; and so destroy purgatory; and then he is a cruel tyrant, without all charity, if he keep them there in prison and in pain, till men will give him money.*
>
> Simon Fish, *A Supplicacyon for the Beggars*, 1529

It looks suspiciously as if Purgatory is indeed a clerical scam designed to satisfy papal greed.

Clerics tell us that all humankind is destined to fry in Hell because of Eve's disobedience in the Garden of Eden, with Christian baptism the only way to rid our souls of this inherited Original Sin. As we saw in Chapter IV, they also teach that a soul enters a human egg at the very moment of conception, meaning that the soul of an aborted foetus is guilty of original sin, and it goes straight to Hell. Since approximately one third of all fertilised ova abort naturally, the God who loves us all sends hundreds of millions of souls annually straight into an eternity of unmitigated torture. Hence the notion of Limbo, a sort of nothing-place which, for the past 700 years has been home to the souls of all unbaptised babies until December, 2005, when Pope Benedict abolished it on the unlikely grounds that it's unlikely – though he never told us what he did with all the souls.

Anglicans now similarly disown the notions of Hell and Hellfire as too difficult to sustain in the twenty-first century. They now describe Hell as 'a state of separation from God'. But if we've lost Purgatory, Limbo and Hell ... where does that leave Heaven?

Irish historian WEH Lecky explains:

... as is customary with a certain school of theologians, when they enunciate a proposition that is palpably self-contradictory, they call it a mystery and an occasion of faith.

History of European Morals, London, 1911

This is not a terribly solid foundation to build a Church on.

Shaky Foundational Belief No. 2: The Bible is the Word of God

The church says the earth is flat: but I have seen its shadow on the moon, and I have more confidence in a shadow even than the church.

Quote by Robert Ingersoll in 1873, which he attributed to Ferdinand Magellan

Scriptures: the sacred books of our holy religion, as distinguished from the false and profane writings on which all other faiths are based.

Ambrose Bierce, *Devil's Dictionary*

The notion that any ancient book could be an infallible guide to living in the present gets my vote for being the most dangerously stupid idea on earth.

Sam Harris in *New Statesman,* 25 July 2011

The Bible is 800,000 words long, and more than a hundred million copies of it are sold or given away each year. It is available, at least partially, in over 2,400 languages. Not that anyone actually reads it: a Gallup survey in the most Christian country of all, the USA, found that less than half of Americans could name the first book (Genesis), only a third knew who delivered the Sermon on the Mount (not Billy Graham), sixty percent couldn't name even half of the ten Commandments and twelve percent were under the impression that Noah married Joan of Arc! Yet for hundreds of Protestant denominations, the Bible is the basis of their faith, and Christians are required to believe that it is the very Word of God, even though it is in fact a compilation of 66 different books (73 for Catholics), written by at least forty different authors and selected by ancient clerics from a much greater choice of texts variously produced between the eighth century BCE and 120CE.

The first five books (the Pentateuch) appear to consist of Jewish myths and folk stories, especially as there is no archaeological evidence to support the historicity of any of the events or the people they report. So it seems probable that Isaac, Joseph, Moses, Noah and Aaron never existed, and that God's supposed gift to Abraham of all the land from the Nile to the Euphrates was, in fact, just so much wishful thinking. The presumed purpose of the Pentateuch and the notion of one almighty God who 'chose' the Israelites, was presumably put about by their leaders to provide cohesion and hope for a rag-tag band of homeless people. The notion that their God is a sadistic, bloodthirsty killer who will help them to defeat their enemies has united and sustained the Jews through many travails.

The manuscripts of the New Testament began to be written as soon as would-be clerics realised that Jesus' prediction of the imminent end of the world had been mistaken. They needed a more solid foundation for the new religion, if it was going to be around for a while. Leaders were appointed, and these clerics naturally rejected the option of having every believer equally gifted with God's grace. They began to direct the masses, make rules, specify rituals, and appoint lesser officials. The early Christians had many different understandings of the new faith, and the various leaders found it necessary to denounce the heresies of those who disagreed with them. We see this in some of Paul's letters, in which he preaches against 'false teachers' – who were, of course, themselves producing tracts denouncing Paul's understanding of the faith.

Even in the ranks of the purists among early Christians, enthusiastic scribes made frequent changes in the scriptures, usually in order to stress their understanding or to diminish an alternative understanding of the text. Eventually, in 382, the more powerful leaders arbitrarily agreed to omit several relevant documents from the New Testament. These include the Gnostic gospels, especially Thomas' gospel which contradicts the 'approved' version of Jesus' life and death; another by Peter; one by Jesus' supposed brother; and another by Philip, suggesting that Jesus had a relationship with Mary Magdalene.

Constantine instructed his 'spin doctor', Bishop Eusebius of Ceasarea, to produce fifty copies of the approved version of what was to become the New Testament. Eusebius skilfully managed to give the impression that this severely chopped version represented the only true Christian view, though the discovery of the Nag Hammadi manuscripts in 1945 and the Dead Sea scrolls near Qumran in 1947 have cast new and even more controversial light on Jesus' life and teaching. As Robin Lane Fox confirms (in *The Unauthorised Version*, Viking, 1991), the entire New Testament is merely 'a list of some books which some Christian bishops approved and asserted more than three hundred years after Jesus's death', which describe 'a tiny proportion of Jesus's life (three years out of perhaps forty or more: the narrative time of the incidents in the fourth Gospel covers barely two-and-a-half months)'.

Paul and the Gospellers never met Jesus, but deluded or not, they clearly believed what they wrote about Jesus and his teaching. However, scholars have identified whole sections of the Gospels which have been inserted or changed by later scribes. For example, the entire story in John (7:53 to 8:12) of the woman taken in adultery who was about to be stoned to death, when Jesus said, 'Let him who is without sin be the first to cast a stone,' was not part of the original. Nor was, 'Consider the lilies of the field ...' Nor were the last twelve verses of Mark (16:9–20), which introduce the notions of speaking in tongues and immunity from poison – now foundational to Pentecostalism with its 300 million adherents. They were added by a later hand. Nor, probably, did the words, 'This is my body which has been given for you; do this in remembrance of me,' (Luke 22:19) ever appear in Luke's original gospel – they, too, seem to have been added later. Mark's text describing Jesus' conviction on a charge of blasphemy appears to have been changed to emphasise the responsibility of the Jews for Jesus' death, probably in order to promote anti-Jewish sentiment among the early Christians.

Over the centuries before the invention of printing, the texts – mistakes and all – were copied and recopied by scribes. Roman philosopher Celsus observed that with each fresh translation, they would '... reform it so that they may be able to refute the objections raised against it'. It was added to and subtracted from since then, especially by Pope Gregory VII, so that what we find in the Scriptures today, including the four canonised gospels, no longer have much value as God's Word. The Bible is now simply what some ancient clerics wanted us to believe – from the beginning Eusebius openly boasted (in *Ecclesiastical History*) that he had magnified whatever glorified the church and omitted whatever might discredit it. Then there was the forged 'Donation of Constantine' and the notorious Isidorian forgeries (the 'False Decretals'). Even Cardinal Ratzinger confessed that, 'the Gospels are a product of the early Church', an effective admission that the legitimacy of the papacy itself hangs on folklore and forgery.

> *The Bible is none other than the voice of Him that Sitteth upon the Throne! Every Book of it, every Chapter of it, every Verse of it, every word of it, every syllable of it ... Every letter of it is the direct utterance of the Most High!*
> John William Burgon, biblical scholar (1813–88)

Alas! The notion that the present confused Biblical mess is the inerrant Holy Word of God seems ridiculous. Even if the original manuscripts were indeed inspired by God, we simply don't have the originals. All we have are highly edited, error-ridden, distorted translations of copies of copies of copies of copies of the originals, which are nothing like the original supposedly inspired words. According to Bart Ehrman (in *Whose Word Is It?*, Continuum, London, 2006), there are more differences between the manuscripts than there are words in the Bible, and how can we know what the words mean if we don't even know what they are? Yet there are hundreds of Protestant denominations, from Apocalyptists to Methodists, from all the Fundamentalists of every stripe to Anglicans, whose dogma and beliefs are all founded on these error-ridden biblical 'teachings'.

The King James Bible of 1611 was translated from a Greek text, which was in turn based on a manuscript by Erasmus published around 1520, which is now known to contain many important inaccuracies, including those mentioned above. Yet the King James version was used as the standard until well into the twentieth century – some fundamentalists now claim that it is the King James Bible that is the inerrant word of God, and not the original writings! Other theologians claim that parts of the Bible should be treated metaphorically or symbolically, though they tend to disagree on the questions of which parts are metaphor, which are symbol and which are supposedly literal, and by whose authority we are to be guided.

In *The Age of Reason*, Thomas Paine looked at the Bible as one of many books:

> *The Persian shows the Zend Avesta of Zoroaster, the law-giver of Persia, and calls it the divine law; the Brahmin shows the Shaster, revealed, he says, by God to Brahma, and given to him out of a cloud; the Jew shows what he calls the law of Moses, given, he says, by God, on the Mount Sinai; the Christian shows a collection of books and epistles, written by nobody knows who, and called the New Testament; the Muhammadan shows the Koran, given, he says, by God to Muhammad: each of these calls itself a revealed religion, the only true Word of God, and this the followers profess to believe from the habit of education, and each believes that the others are imposed upon.*

Surely, only one at best of the hundreds of conflicting 'sacred' texts can be the true word of God? And the Bible, which supposedly contains '19,000 provably false statements, along with fourteen unambiguous affirmations that the earth is flat, along with sixty additional passages that historians have identified as assuming a flat earth' (William Harwood in 'Sig

Heil, Pope Ratzinazi', *Humani*, Nov/Dec 2006) is self-evidently not the one. John E Remsberg found 610 self-contradictions in its pages (e.g. 'I have seen God face to face' (Gen 32:30) and, 'No man hath seen God at any time' (John 1:18) – you'll find most of them at www.infidels.org).

If God really did inspire the Bible, then it says very little for his scientific knowledge, his clarity of thought or his editorial skills that after two thousand years, Christians disagree more than ever over what he was trying to tell us. His ambivalent book has spawned more than 1,200 Protestant denominations in the USA alone (according to a speaker at the Millennium World Peace Summit of Religious and Spiritual Leaders, 28 August 2000), each claiming to be the only true Christians. Some of them, such as Martin Luther King's Baptists, use Biblical quotations to promote human rights, while others on the Religious Right use different Biblical quotations to justify the very opposite. It seems that in real life, those who purport to follow Jesus' teachings actually follow just the bits that suit them. Christianity can now be whatever you want it to be, and it need not bear any relationship with any of Christ's teachings, though all denominations agree with 1 Timothy 5:17–19, which advocates that those who direct the affairs of the Church should be well paid, in turn quoting Jesus, 'a workman is worthy of his hire' in Luke 10:7.

Much to the satisfaction of Roman Catholic clerics, who maintain that the scriptures provide insufficient authority for the faith, and that the traditional authority of the pope is supreme, the Bible has turned out to be a very wobbly foundation stone upon which to build so politically powerful and wealthy a group of institutions as Protestant Christianity.

Shaky Foundational Belief No. 3: Jesus Was the Son Of God

Christians are required to believe that Jesus was a manifestation of God himself and simultaneously the Son of God, as officially declared at Nicea in 325. Christianity is ostensibly founded upon Jesus' life and teachings, but as we have just seen, most of what we know about him is found in the four Gospels which were written on parchment centuries after his death, long after Christianity had become established as a serious political force, so presumably what was written was intended to serve some political purpose. The parchments were loosely based on selected earlier references to Jesus, which had been written on papyrus decades after his death by men who had never met him – Mark probably wrote the first version of Jesus' adventures around the year 70CE, hoping to impress his readers by throwing in a few Mithran fables to emphasise Jesus' Godlike nature. These documents are all that remain after other records were destroyed and libraries burned. This was also done to serve somebody's political purpose. As we have seen, biblical scholars have found changes to the earliest texts which cast doubt on everything we think we know about Jesus.

In trying to get to know him, John Hick complained that we have to view him 'through thick layers of first- second- and third- generation Christian faith' (*Jesus in History and Myth*, 1986). This has inevitably obscured and distorted our picture; and the inconsistent reports of different stories from his life confuse the issue further. Even the Catholic Church (in the 1943 encyclical *Divinio Affante Spiritu*) admitted that the literal sense of the scriptures was 'not always obvious' – except to Catholic clerics of course.

Some sources tell us that Jesus was born around 0CE of a virgin (though if he developed from an unfertilised ovum then 'he' would have had to be female). Others tell us that the Holy Ghost impregnated his mother, and yet others suggest that it was an off-duty Roman soldier. Jesus himself was a poor Palestinian – he would have looked and dressed like any other dark-skinned Palestinian of typical short stature, around 1.6m tall. He was born and died a Jew, he worshipped the Jewish God, kept Jewish customs, and interpreted Jewish law, but he was neither educated nor a rabbi. Rather he was a charismatic itinerant preacher who hated arrogant, autocratic clerics and reacted against what he saw as their hypocritical customs and conventions. He knew that he was assured of their condemnation and a probable death penalty after his outburst in the temple when he overturned the money-changers' tables. He was executed around 33CE.

As for the finer details, the New Testament is such a contradictory mess that it is very difficult to differentiate between fact, tradition, opinion, political influence and subsequent amendments, so it is impossible to say with any confidence who Jesus was. Some scholars (e.g. RJ Hoffmann and GA Larue, *Jesus in History and Myth*, Prometheus Books, 1986) have proposed that the biblical material is mostly legend, while others (e.g. GA Well in *The Historicity of Jesus*) have even suggested that it is unlikely Jesus ever existed. After all, archaeologists can find no evidence of his existence, and there is no contemporary reference to him during his lifetime. Others argue that whether or not he was real flesh and blood is not important.

Some say that Jesus was a figment of Paul's imagination. None of Paul's letters (written around 50–57 CE) contains any hint that Paul thought Jesus was a real person – he seems more of a mystical being, like Mithras or Hercules. Paul never mentioned Jesus' birth, his miracles or his teachings, though he dwelt on the crucifixion. When the gospels were eventually written to tell the story of Jesus the man, significant parts of them look suspiciously like propaganda designed to fit with Old Testament prophesies of the promised Messiah who would be the saviour of the Jews, together with bits of Mithraist lore in order to make Jesus sound extra special and win more converts. By presenting Jesus as a Heaven-sent revolutionary figure who had probably been the promised Messiah, but who had been martyred, the gospel writers knew that they had a figurehead who could not be 'got at' by the Roman authorities or their enforcers.

Assuming that he existed, and accepting that he is usually viewed through a rosy haze – as a man of peace who preached the Sermon on the Mount and healed sick people on the Sabbath – the gospels nevertheless show less attractive aspects of the man. For example he comes over as a Jewish racist views who, when sending out the disciples to heal the sick, instructed, 'Do not go among the Gentiles [non-Jews] or enter any town of the Samaritans [the people of Samaria].' (Matthew 10:5) He himself refused to help a Canaanite woman (i.e. from western Palestine), saying, 'I was sent only to help the lost sheep of Israel ... it is not right to take the children's bread and cast it to the dogs.' (Matthew 15:26) John Hartung (in *Sceptic* 3:4, 1995) reckoned that 'Jesus would have turned over in his grave if he had known that Paul would be taking his plan to the pigs' (i.e. to the non-Jews around the Mediterranean).

In contrast to modern Christian obsessions with the sanctity of the family, Jesus was openly anti-family: Matthew 19:29 reports his claim that, 'everyone who has left houses or brothers or sisters or father or mother or children or fields for my sake will receive a hundred times as much and will inherit eternal life'. Matthew 10:34–36 declares, 'For I have come to turn a man against his father, a daughter against her mother, a daughter-in-law against her mother-in-law – a man's enemies will be the members of his own household.' Luke confirms (14:26), 'If anyone comes to me and does not hate his father and mother, his wife and children, his brothers and sisters – yes, even his own life – he cannot be my disciple.'

Though Jesus also taught that we should love our enemies, he clearly hated not only his family but also the scribes and Pharisees, as exemplified in the Seven Curses (Luke 11:42–52). As for his enemies, Jesus wanted them destroyed: '... bring them here and kill them in front of me' (Luke 19:27), and he threatened that anyone who ignored his teaching would be tortured sadistically forever in Hell. Jesus the anti-clerical revolutionary repeatedly attacked the arrogant and sanctimonious scribes and Pharisees, abused whole cities, and challenged even those who weren't involved when he declared, 'He who is not with me is against me.' (Luke 11:23) As for his prophetic powers, 'I did not come to bring peace, but a sword,' (Matthew 10:34) was practically his only truly prophetic remark.

As to whether or not Jesus was the son of God, Dr Jeaneane Fowler concludes that, 'The Jesus that is portrayed by the gospels does not really come across to us, on balance, as divine; he might have been an exceptional human being, but he seems human nevertheless.' (Jeanane Fowler in *Humanism: Beliefs and Practices*, 1999) He certainly reacted badly to criticism, hurling abuse at the Pharisees (orthodox Jews) when they merely asked for some evidence to support his incredible claims:

> *You hypocrites! You are like whitewashed tombs which look beautiful on the outside but on the inside are full of dead men's bones and everything unclean ... You snakes! You brood of vipers! How will you escape being condemned to hell?*
> Matthew 23:29–33

This is hardly the cool, reasoned response you would expect from the Son of God. He sounds only too human – and therefore another loose foundation stone.

Shaky Foundational Belief No. 4: Christianity Is Founded On Jesus' Teachings

> *Jesus proclaimed the coming of the Kingdom ... what came was the Church.*
> Alfred Loisy

Christians were persecuted for three centuries after Jesus' death. Then Constantine converted and gave their senior clerics political power, giving them the opportunity to become hugely wealthy. This required some rapid changes in Christian teaching, such as moving from loving your enemies to killing them; from opposing torture to torturing; and from despising wealth to coveting it. Saint Augustine had an aptitude for justifying these reversals – he rationalised that Jesus' teaching applied only to life in heaven, while here on Earth we must allow ourselves to be guided by the Church; and that fighting and killing are perfectly acceptable if they are done in the Church's name and the cause is 'just'. Thomas Aquinas subsequently relaxed the requirements for a 'just' war to one merely whose 'intentions' are good – hence the notion that the road to Hell is paved with good intentions.

Whereas Jesus was a social egalitarian who sought neither wealth nor political power, Christianity as we now know it is obsessed by wealth and power. The Jesus who so hated the pretentious Pharisees would surely have disapproved of today's Church of Rome with its authoritarian clerics, its ostentatious wealth and ultra-right-wing politics, its perverted notions of morality and its arrogant claim to infallibility, not to mention its 1700-year history of torture, murder, hypocrisy and political intrigue. Other Christian Churches have similarly become a 'binding burden on men's backs', because from being a religion that once celebrated Jesus' teaching, Christianity is now fixated on his death ... and sex and money, of course.

Jesus expressed socialist views, insofar as he wanted an egalitarian society whose members would accept no authority except God's:

> *I believe Christ was a great revolutionary ... His entire doctrine was devoted to the humble, the poor ... I'd say there's a lot in common between the spirit and essence of his teachings and socialism ... I believe that Karl Marx could have subscribed to the Sermon on the Mount ... There are ten thousand times more coincidences between Christian gospels and Communism than between Christian gospels and Capitalism.*
>
> Fidel and Religion by Brazilian Catholic friar Frei Betto, Havana, 1987

These are the words of Marxist Fidel Castro, who was consistently targeted by a Church whose bishops claimed to model their lives on Jesus' example, but who lived in palaces, and whose predecessors had built the most magnificent cathedrals and amassed treasures and the finest works of art, paid for with money taken from the poor.

Nietzsche in particular was enraged by what he saw as the cynicism and hypocrisy of clerics, and his writings contain

149

passionate records of his disgust. Yet clerics assure us that Christ's presence is still to be found in the modern Church because, 'Jesus mediates God's power and channels it with God's instructions down to the ordained clergy here on earth.' This obvious godswallop is their only justification for their existence.

There's nothing new in any of this. Almost every religion, from Buddhism to Presbyterianism, has been founded upon the teachings of a charismatic philosopher, whose message subsequently became so distorted that the founder would now disown it if he could recognise it. Reactionary religious leaders in the Vatican, in the Religious Right in the USA and in certain Muslim communities have become so obsessed with political power that they have lost sight of their prophets' messages. They now preach twisted dogma that is authoritarian, sexist, reactionary, anti-liberal, pro-greed, anti-democratic and anti-egalitarian. Consider, for example, Jesus' admonition 'judge not lest ye be judged' (Matthew 7:1), in the context of the Inquisition. Or consider clerical warnings that it is a sin not to attend church, in the light of Jesus' advice: 'When you pray, do not be like the hypocrites, for they love to pray standing in the synagogues ... When you pray, go into your room, close the door and pray.' (Matthew 6:5–6)

The central theme of Jesus' mission was clearly based on his expectation that the end of the world would arrive with a bang at any moment: 'Some who are standing here will not taste death before they see the kingdom of God come.' (Mark 9:1) Much of his teaching was clearly intended as last-minute advice to a handful of doubting Jews: 'Go, sell everything you have and give to the poor' (Mark 10:21). As we know, he was so completely wrong that even the famed medical missionary and theologian Albert Schweizer described him (in *The Quest for the Historical Jesus*, 1906) as a 'deluded apocalyptist' who went to his crucifixion believing that it would initiate the end of time.

Clearly, Jesus never once envisaged that his teaching would be claimed as the basis for an enduring worldwide religion of more than two billion people. He spoke in riddles, advocated few rules and, unlike Mohammed, wrote no books and left no formal teaching. Christianity owes far more to Paul than to Jesus, but modern Christianity owes very little to either of them. Its clerics have consciously distanced Christian dogma from Jesus', and to a lesser extent from Paul's, teachings over the years. Modern Christianity may capitalise more heavily than ever on Jesus' rose-tinted PR image, but it clearly has little in common with Jesus' ideals – and that's another foundation stone gone.

Shaky Foundational Belief No. 5: The Christian God Is the One True God

The Large Hadron Collider has been built in the hope of proving the existence of the Higgs boson and of finding dark matter. Paddy Power, an online Irish bookmaker, is offering the impossibly short odds of 100 to 1 that the machine will also discover God.

There are religions, such as Buddhism and Confucianism, that have no need for gods, but for Christianity the notion of one God who takes an active interest in every one of us is foundational. Four or five thousand years ago, the early Israelites were motivated by a clever subterfuge put about by their leaders. They were told that there was just one all-powerful God, who had 'chosen' their particular society. In exchange for their devotion and obedience this God had undertaken to promote their interests above all others, even to the extent of promising them a homeland. This notion successfully united and encouraged them in their travails; the belief in themselves as God's Chosen People has sustained them practically to the present day.

Christians inherited the same omnipotent, male God of Abraham. As children we were taught about 'Our Father who art in Heaven', and we cosily envisaged him as some sort of Father-Christmassy 'Daddy in the sky', which was nice. But in school we learned that he wasn't nice at all: Exodos 20:4 reports his command, 'Thou shall have no other gods before me, nor shall you bow down to any graven images, for I am a jealous God, punishing the children for the sins of their fathers to the third and fourth generation.' God now sounds like an insecure, vindictive bully: 'Bow down to me or I'll get your kids ... and their kids ... and *their* kids ... and maybe even THEIR kids!'

Leviticus (26:14–39) goes on to describe God threatening to,

> ... *bring upon you sudden terror, wasting diseases and fever that will destroy your sight and drain away your life ... I will multiply your afflictions seven times over ... I will send wild animals against you and they will rob you of your children, destroy your cattle ... you will eat the flesh of your sons and the flesh of your daughters. Your land will be laid waste and your cities will lie in ruins.*

This is the God who banished from his altar anybody 'who is hunchbacked or dwarfed, or who has any eye defect ... or who has damaged testicles' (Leviticus 21:20), as if they didn't already have enough problems. It is the God who approved of slavery and child-beating, who wanted human sacrifices, who killed first-born babies, and who demanded nothing less than death for heretics, blasphemers, adulterers, witches and anyone who worked on the Sabbath; the God who Himself exterminated tens of millions of innocents using flood, starvation and disease ... So much for Daddy in the sky. If this vindictive sadist is the 'loving' father who is waiting to greet them in Heaven, then maybe Christians need to rethink why they want to go there.

There are those, like Bishop Richard Harries of Oxford, who complain (e.g. in the *Observer*, 16 April 2006) that the critics of religion tend to focus, as I have just done, on the worst excesses of professed religious belief. He admits that the God of the Old Testament is a highly improbable concept, a Straw Man that atheists can knock down with ease. Harries objects that the Straw Man ploy is a trick of rhetoric, even though this particular Straw God came straight from his own Bible, and is quoted in context. Nevertheless, this Christian bishop calls it a verbal trick.

In fact, this Christian bishop wants us to ignore the Old Testament completely, more than three-quarters of his whole Bible, because he admits that it is obvious nonsense that discredits his case! Well, why not the New Testament as well?

There will always be those like Bishop Harries who demand the right to discard evidence and redefine God every time they find themselves backed into a corner. But okay, we'll play by Harries' rules and concentrate on the infinitely just God of the New Testament, whose punishments now last for all eternity instead of a mere lifetime. This is the loving God who ignored his only son when he cried out, 'My God, my God, Why have you forsaken me?'

A lot depends on exactly what you mean by 'God', and the only way to avoid Harries' constant-redefinition ploy is to insist that God's proponent first defines his particular concept of 'God'. One explicit definition is written by respected Christian theologians in the *National Catholic Almanac*. This informs us that, 'God is the creator of everything except himself, he is male, he is eternal, omnipresent, all-merciful, unchanging, perfect, and he is actively concerned with the thoughts and behaviour of every individual human.' He is also 'immortal, immutable, incomprehensible, ineffable, infinite, invisible and just ...' and a whole lot more besides (*1968 National Catholic Almanac*, edited by Felician A Foy, OFM Paterson: St Anthony's Guild, 1968, p.360).

I will resist the temptation to ask how they know so much about this incomprehensible being. And I would surely be accused of attacking another Straw Man if I challenge this version of God because, in their efforts to impress us, the authors have clearly overburdened their God with such a heavy assortment of far-fetched and contradictory qualities that not even they can conceive of Him. They now call these issues 'mysteries'. I will not waste the readers' time by refuting this obviously man-made concoction.

So let us redefine God again, but this time confine him merely to being the eternal 'supreme being' which chose to create the universe and which Christians believe to be omnipotent and infinitely kind, merciful and just. This definition runs straight into the problem of evil. These qualities are incompatible with a creator who gave us earthquakes, cancer and the Holocaust, because if God doesn't want to prevent these things, then he's not infinitely kind, just and loving, and if he's not able to prevent them then he's not omnipotent. We would happily have settled just for all things bright and beautiful, but God deliberately created evil, and so he is not the all-powerful nice guy that Christians worship. Any father who could watch unmoved while his children suffered in the Gulags, in Auschwitz and in the Rwandan killing fields is clearly unworthy of worship.

Paschal reasoned, 'We must be born guilty, or God would be unjust.' Since God is supposedly infinitely just, such mass sufferings of innocent people must be God's punishment for sin, despite Jesus' self-sacrifice to save us all. The very notion that natural disasters are God's punishments for our sins, and that innocent children need to suffer for the sins of adults, is inconsistent with the concepts of mercy and justice. If the Holocaust failed to cause the Jews to wonder about their loving, all-powerful God, who had promised to protect his Chosen People above all others, then it says much for the power of their faith, but very little for the power of their reasoning.

There is a breed of charismatic Christians who claim that God is not like that; that neither the scriptures nor the intellect can lead us to knowledge of God. It can only be derived from personal experience, and those who claim to have experienced God's presence are immune from doubt – they *know in their hearts* that God is there; they have *felt* his touch, and they have spoken with Jesus personally! Subjective sensations such as these and spiritual 'oceanic' experiences (with or without the help of magic mushrooms, psilocybin, fasting, monotonous drumbeats, extreme fatigue or similar aids) genuinely affect people who are searching for 'the Truth'. Unfortunately they no more prove the existence of the Christian God than they prove the existence of Krishna or Shangri-la, which can be similarly 'experienced' by those who long to do so. These are merely subjective psychological/neurological sensations in brains that are predisposed to belief. Christians are easily able to dismiss Krishna as 'obviously' false without any hard evidence of his absence, yet they are unable to accept that others can similarly reject *their* God, because there is no evidence for his existence either.

The root of the problem seems to be that an abstract intellectual concept, 'God', has been made easier to grasp for lay people by ascribing human attributes to it. The clerics responsible for this subterfuge must be aware that the anthropomorphised description is false and misleading – a trick of rhetoric, in fact. According to Douglas Fox (*New Scientist*, 27 November 2010), the tendency to anthropomorphise inanimate objects is ingrained in human nature, especially in lonely and insecure people. Xenophanes was opposing anthropomorphic notions of the gods as long ago as 600BCE.

The God we have been discussing so far has a gender, intelligence and emotions. He has the ability to punish and to love and to heal illness. But 'God' is really no more than an abstract concept, an ethereal notion. As Comte-Sponville pointed out (in *Atheist Spirituality*, Bantam Press, 2009):

> *Where the absolute is concerned, all forms of anthropomorphism are naïve and ridiculous ... if God is inconceivable, then nothing justifies our conceiving of him [sic] as a Subject, a Person, a Creator, a Protector, a Benefactor or the embodiment of Justice and Love ... Ineffability is not an argument.*

Yet clerics persist in telling us that 'He' is the Father; that 'He' is compassionate, loving and merciful. One now suspects more than ever that 'He' is simply ScapeGod.

At this stage all that God's apologists can do is redefine 'God' yet again, using ClericSpeak and obscurantism, rhetorical ploys, tricks of authority and implication. Hans Kung now tells us that God:

... is in fact the infinite in the finite, transcendence in immanence, the absolute in the relative ... God is therefore the absolute who includes and creates relativity, who, precisely as free, makes possible and actualises relationship: God is the absolute-relative, here-hereafter, transcendent-immanent, all-embracing and all permeating most real reality in the heart of things ...

I won't argue, because I have no idea what he is talking about. However, this doesn't sound like the sort of three-in-one god who talks exclusively to clerics and has strong views about sex. Anyway Kung goes on to contradict himself: 'God is always beyond our concepts and definitions ...'

Paul Tillich, in *The Shaking of the Foundations*, defined God as 'the infinite and inexhaustible depth and ground of all being ... Being itself ...', the existence of which need not be demonstrated, '... since a God that has to be demonstrated would not be a God at all'. Nobody can deny any of this, since it is mostly meaningless ClericSpeak, but at the bottom of it is a profound truth: 'If we could fully comprehend God, then God would not be God' (Victor Griffin, Dean of St Patrick's Cathedral, Dublin, 1969–96). This is to say that the Christian God must be unknowable *by definition*, and Its existence cannot, *by definition*, be refuted. This is a pathetic attempt to prevent God from ever being backed into a corner.

However, respected science philosopher Karl Popper, in the process of arguing that there can be no such thing as absolute truth or objective knowledge, points out that all scientific discovery involves a process of conjecture and refutation, trial and error. Concepts are developed, tested and, if found to be false, rejected. He notes that ideas and theories can only ever be tested for falseness, never for correctness, and so any concept that cannot somehow be tested for falseness is meaningless. In other words, any extraordinary claim is empty and valueless unless it can conceivably be refuted. Here we have a claim for a supernatural being that cannot be refuted *by definition*, and so for Popper, as for most thinking people, such a proposition is pointless and unworthy of further consideration. All we are left with is a meaningless God, a nothing. A nothing to worship; a nothing to fall down at the feet of; a nothing to give our lives over to – and worshipping nothing is pointless.

Quite independently of Popper, Wittgenstein had already decided, 'A nothing will serve just as well as a something about which nothing could be said.' Simon Blackburn explains (in *Think*, OUP, 1999):

Many people think that the difference between being a theist, believing, and being an atheist, unbelieving, is incredibly important, but if nothing does as well as something about which nothing can be said, it vanishes.

In fact, we can equate God with non-existence:

God is not matter; neither is nonexistence. God does not have limitations; neither does nonexistence. God is not visible; God cannot be described, neither can nonexistence.

George H Smith

Christopher Hitchens took a short cut: '[W]hat can be asserted without evidence can be dismissed without evidence.'

Unabashed, clerics now claim that secular philosophers simply don't understand theology. They imply that atheists are too blind or stupid to see what clerics can see clearly, claiming that the god that I have just disproved is not the God of Christianity. Of course, they now know better than to say what they think it *is* (I think it is ScapeGod). It's true that atheists don't understand theology; but this is only because they don't believe in God – and most of them will have read more about theology than most Christians. For surely, when someone proposes the existence of something for which there is absolutely no evidence – like pixies at the bottom of the garden, or flying spaghetti monsters – the burden of proof should rest with the proponent. There should be no need for the rest of us to have to disprove the existence of these fantasies.

Theists sometimes complain that scientists are inconsistent – they profess belief in the existence of quarks and black holes and dark matter, without any idea what they are, whilst refusing to accept the possibility of a Christian God. The scientists can easily reply that we can infer the attributes of quarks, black holes and dark matter by observing their effects on the universe, whereas the Christian God seems to have no effect whatsoever. Kai Nielson (in *God Talk*, 1864) concluded, 'given the very peculiarity and obscurity of the concept of God we are not justified in believing in God if no good evidence can be given.'

What we know is what the Christian God is not: it is not natural; it is not a 'he'; it is not detectable; it is not determinate. It is the negation of every real quality that we can conceive. In fact, its most glaringly obvious negative quality is that it is not there; it does not exist. Sceptics are surely justified in their belief that the God of Christianity is a paradox, a ScapeGod, a self-contradictory, man-made fiction put about by those with a vested interest. Devout Christians will tell you that this is the ultimate proof of God's omnipotence – 'He' doesn't even need to exist to work 'His' miracles! 'Away with your reason, my religion dreads nothing but being understood' (Robert Ingersoll on Thomas Paine). Clerics claim they can explain the things that we can't understand, such as spirituality or the purpose of the universe, by positing a God which we can understand even less. Abstruse and inexplicable by definition, He is nevertheless gratefully accepted by those who have difficulty with the notion that humankind is a purposeless accident of nature. But the Christian God doesn't exist, and without its God the key-stone is gone and the whole Christian structure must surely collapse.

Shaky Foundational Belief No. 6: Religious Certainty

The whole notion of a supernatural being lurking up in the sky seems irrational, and my experience of the world has never once given me the slightest reason to suspect that such a being exists. However, I am conscious that my experience of the world is purely subjective and constrained by my limited senses.

Evolution has arranged that different species of animal have developed the senses they need to survive in their particular environments, and humankind is just one more species. There are lots of things in the world that my senses fail to report – radio waves, polarised light and magnetic fields, for example – so I must be wary of dogmatically asserting anything about 'reality' based merely on my limited experience of it, and I am therefore hesitant to claim that something that could be regarded as a god could never have existed

The sad fact is that we can never gain objective knowledge about anything at all. Even something as 'obvious' as, say, a solid silver coin, seen obliquely, appears to be elliptical and coloured according to whatever light is shining on it, even though our brains tell us that it is 'really' circular and coloured silver. But is it really solid? Science has shown us that all matter is assembled from zillions of sub-microscopic atoms, each consisting of an incredibly tiny nucleus surrounded by even tinier electrons all whizzing around relatively vast volumes of free space. Our 'solid' coin is, in fact, 99.9999999999999% empty space! How objective is it, then, to talk of the solidity, shape or colour of something so ethereally composed? Obviousness is further confounded when we enter the micro-world of quantum theory, and the mega-world of space-time relativity, where mathematics is the only language that can be used to describe the otherwise unimaginable. We must conclude that for us humans, there can be no such thing as objective reality – all we can be sure of is that nothing, nothing at all, is what it seems to be.

Locke warned against 'entertaining any proposition with greater assurance than the proofs it is built upon will warrant', and proofs based on reason, common sense and sensory experience are clearly insufficient to maintain any assertion that a supernatural 'being' or 'force' may or may not exist. 'Nothing exists except atoms and empty space; everything else is opinion,' said Democritus back in 370BCE. Protagoras agreed: 'Of the gods, I can say nothing – neither that they are nor that they are not, nor what they are.' All we can reasonably claim is open-minded agnosticism, especially as the agnostic is in the happy position of having nothing to justify or prove or explain. He or she isn't necessarily anti- anything, and the agnostic offends no-one except the cleric.

'I am a scientist and think in terms of probabilities not certainties, and so I am an agnostic,' said James Lovelock (in *The Revenge of Gaia*, Allen Lane, 2006). US journalist Natalie Aungier put it differently:

I don't believe in God, gods, godlets or any sort of higher power than the universe itself, which seems quite high and powerful enough for me. I don't believe in life after death … reincarnation, telekinesis or any miracles but the miracle of life and consciousness, which again strike me as miracles in nearly obscene abundance.

Christianity is founded upon concepts that Christians proclaim to be literally true: the gospels, the notion of everlasting life, Jesus as the son of God and his teachings, and especially God himself. They are certain of the truth of these things – they are the very foundations upon which the whole edifice of Christianity is based. Without any one of them it must collapse – and we have just seen that not a single one of them stands up even to cursory examination.

Clerics have striven to promote Christian dogma using reason and mysticism. Reason, however, has turned out to be a tool better suited to denying the religion, and mysticism is discredited by Nietzsche's simple observation: 'Mystical explanations are considered deep. The truth is that they are not even superficial.' Arguments for and against the existence of the Christian God have occupied philosophers for 2,000 years, yet they have got us absolutely nowhere and no imminent breakthrough is expected. Clerics are still scratching fruitlessly for inconclusive scraps of circumstantial evidence to support the mere possibility of their God's very existence.

But if, as I suggest, the Christian enterprise is specious, with a handful of clerics supposedly taking man's needs and desires to God and returning with God's commands and authority, knowing all the time that there is no such thing as God; if the venture is indeed such an obvious scam, how can I explain away the three-and-a-half billion clear-minded, intelligent people who appear to accept clerics' claims to God's (or Allah's) authority without question? This is the subject of Chapter 9.

HOW CAN SO MANY INTELLIGENT
PEOPLE BE SO WRONG?

We are all tattooed in our cradles with the beliefs of our tribe.
Oliver Wendell Holmes Snr, medical writer
and lecturer (1809–94)

Advertisements for commercial products invariably show the
users wearing happy smiles and affirming the effectiveness of
the product. Christianity, on the other hand, offers weeping
women, misery and death. Its body copy is packed with sadistic
promises of eternal damnation, together with calls for self-
sacrifice and suffering. Its logo is a corpse nailed to a scaffold. Its
offices are gloomy, cold churches surrounded by graveyards.
And bundled with this package comes the catalogue of horror
and depravity that we saw in Section 2. Its unique selling
proposition is a tedious eternity chanting psalms. Surely no one
but a gullible sado-masochist would choose such a product,
especially one with such dubious credentials and such a terrible
track record. Yet Christianity claims over two billion satisfied
users, and Islam more than a billion more. How can this possibly
be?

In fact, there are several good reasons why people profess
belief in Christianity. Significantly, though, not one of them
requires that Christianity is necessarily well founded, true or
even virtuous.

Culture – Belonging and Believing

If you come from India, then you probably have Hindu roots.
This is not because Hinduism is the one true religion (it isn't),
nor because you have figured it out and it makes sense (it
doesn't). It is simply that Hinduism is a part of your culture, the
traditional way of life you were born into. Human babies are

born with an ability to learn amazingly quickly, an ability which stays with them through their formative years up till the age of seven or so. Indian babies soon pick up the language, dialect, customs, ideals, aesthetic tastes and rituals of those around them, enabling them to gain acceptance into their society.

During their formative years, children have a strong predisposition to copy the behaviour and accept the wisdom of those around them, thus saving them from having to rediscover everything that their ancestors have already found out along the way.

Your culture gives you a sense of identity, security and comfort. A common culture is what binds a society together, providing its members with a psychologically indispensable sense of belonging. So if you have been born in the West, you are probably a Christian, not because Christianity has anything much to commend it (it doesn't), but simply because it is part of Western culture, a large component of who we are. Differences between cultures reflect the outcomes of past wars of conquest, or the religious conversions of kings and mass conversions of ancient societies. For Muslims in particular, religion is a large component of their daily culture.

Traditions must be learned, but they soon become taken-for-granted norms that the members of a given culture simply don't see as distinctive features, just as a fish is unaware of the water it swims in. Like a pair of spectacles that distorts the way we see, our cultures are invisible to us, and yet we interpret the world through these cultural lenses – they provide the framework through which we judge and evaluate what we see. Our culture seems to us to be natural, timeless, obvious common sense, a true reflection of reality. But by turning cultural myths into perceived reality, it provides a means for concealing manipulative ideological and religious forces so that they 'go without saying' – membership of a given culture means unquestioningly taking for granted its dominant myths and beliefs and attitudes. Nevertheless, different cultures see the world in quite different ways – again like spectacles, other people's cultures are obvious to us, though we are unaware of our own.

Most major religions date back thousands of years, having been founded out of ignorance and superstition. This is especially true in places where living was particularly difficult, where people needed something to believe in, no matter how improbable. Ancient religious lore and fable were subsequently passed down from generation to generation as a component of the cultural identity of a community, and these various religious traditions still invisibly influence a society's values and attitudes to the present day. Thus it is that people's professed religious beliefs are more dependent on the prevailing culture in the place where they spent their formative years than on the credibility of those beliefs. So we find predominantly Buddhists in Sri Lanka, Hindus in India, Muslims in Saudi Arabia and Christians in America.

We in the West no longer depend on God in our daily lives. God has been replaced by technology, medicine and entertainment, but we are still reluctant to express a culturally 'alien' opinion, because we all have a strong psychological need to be accepted by those around us. We want to belong, and to be seen to belong, to society, and so we tend to pay lip service to our culture. What I'm positing is that very few of those who profess Christianity, and step back to think about it, actually believe in the literal truth of the Christian creeds. They profess Christianity mainly to express their cultural identity, in order to 'belong'. 'Few really believe. They mostly only believe that they believe or make believe [that they believe].' (John Lancaster Spalding, US Roman Catholic bishop, 1840–1916) In most Christian denominations, this is all that is asked of them. Clerics are happy so long as the laity behave like believers. The doubting members of the congregation, surrounded by respected peers all apparently professing faith and devotion, will influence each other. Clerics only want large numbers of compliant churchgoers, and the churchgoers only want to be recognised as members of the group by those around them. It is quite conceivable that inside the church, everybody is fooling everybody else.

In Ireland, for example, many people refer to themselves as Catholics because Catholicism is part of Irish culture. Professing Catholicism is for them as much an expression of Irish patriotism as of religious belief, especially during the recent 'Troubles'. It could be that a similar patriotic need to belong is the main motivator for those professing Christianity in America, especially in light of Vice President George Bush Snr's statement (in Chicago in 1987): 'I don't know that atheists should be considered as citizens [of the USA], nor should they be considered patriots. This is one nation under God.' Maybe this is why only three percent of Americans admit to atheism.

Childhood Conditioning

By education most men have been misled;
So they believe, because they so were bred.
The priest continues what the nurse began,
And thus the child imposes on the man.

John Dryden in 1687

Men are born ignorant, not stupid. They are made stupid by education.

Bertrand Russell

Article 26.3 of the Universal Declaration of Human Rights (UDHR) states that 'parents have a prior right to choose the kind of education that shall be given to their children', and a large number of parents choose education that includes religious indoctrination of their children into their own religious beliefs and practices. Beliefs that have been culturally inherited tend to become compulsive when reinforced by deliberate indoctrination, because what children learn during their formative years seriously influences their view of the world long after they have left childhood behind. This is especially so if the dogma has been asserted repeatedly by authority figures, with great reverence and commitment, and with no consideration of the possibility of doubt.

If, in early childhood, certain fundamental views and doctrines are paraded with unusual solemnity, and an air of the greatest earnestness never before visible in anything else; if, at the same time, the possibility of a doubt about them is completely passed over, or touched upon only to indicate that doubt is the first step to eternal perdition, the resulting impression will be so deep that, as a rule ... doubt about them will be almost as impossible as doubt about one's own existence.

Arthur Schopenhauer in 'Religion: A Dialogue', 1851

This process of Confident Repeated Affirmative Presentation (CRAP) of a message is known by modern psychologists as 'conditioning', but they knew about it even in Old Testament times: 'Train up a child in the way he should go, and when he is old he will not turn from it' (Proverbs 22:6). Or, as the Jesuits coldly put it, 'Give me a child until he is seven, and I will have him for life.' The incredible capacity of children to learn during their formative years has been highlighted by language guru Noam Chomsky. He observed that children learn their native language much too quickly, too accurately and with too few mistakes for this to be the result of any ordinary trial-and-error learning process. Evolution has arranged that infants are uniquely equipped to take on board whatever their environment presents to them, because the sooner they can understand the workings of the world, the better their chances of survival. In 2010, the Catholic Church alone ran 67,848 kindergartens and 93,315 primary schools worldwide (Data from *Agencia Fides*), with probably as many Protestant, Muslim and other schools of religious indoctrination all touting for business, usually at the taxpayers' expense.

Young children tend to assume that there is design and intention behind all natural events, so anthropomorphism comes naturally to them. Some psychologists surmise that even without prompting, they would invent God anyway. But clerical conditioning is so additionally effective that many of those who today claim to have lost their faith still feel guilty about imagined 'sins', and still feel the cultural pressure to subject their own children to the same process; thus 'the child imposes on the man'. In Hans Andersen's story of the emperor's new suit of clothes, all the adults who had been conditioned by their education pronounced that it was a fine suit, they even admired the style and the colours. It took a simple child, unfettered by indoctrination, to point out that there was no suit and the emperor was naked! Similarly, it takes a child who has never been blinded by the fog of religious conditioning to see clearly when a cleric is talking bullshit. Believers, meanwhile, are taught that it is blasphemous, dangerous even, to question their clerics, who are inspired by God himself.

In a religious society, a child soon finds that life is easy so long as it conforms to cultural norms, whereas failure to do so brings disapproval. Primary school children are exposed to peer pressure as the cultural indoctrination becomes formalised, and as also does the punishment for transgressing the rules. Children quickly learn that the easiest way to get on in the world is to accept what they are told without question. Peer pressure provides a good reason for conforming, because children are unsure of themselves. They find comfort in numbers, by joining groups and adopting mutual opinions. It is easy to believe that religious dogma is absolutely true when there is no alternative and everyone else already seems to believe it. There is a Chinese proverb – Three Men Make a Tiger (a.k.a *argumentum ad populum*) – to the effect that, if an unfounded premise is repeated by many diverse individuals, it will soon become accepted as truth. At this stage, peer pressure has become an overarching influence, and the conditioning of children is complete by the time they leave primary school. They are blinded by religious myths, mistrustful of those of other cultures, submissive to those in authority, and helplessly dependent on God's mercy.

Many people feel that parents should not have the right to foist their religious beliefs on to their young children. Article 18 of the UDHR proclaims: 'Everyone has the right to freedom of thought, conscience and religion,' and Article 19 adds: 'Everyone has the right to freedom of opinion and expression.' You may ask just how 'free' is the thought, religion or opinion of a child whose education has included deliberate indoctrination into a particular belief system?

Most clerics require religious parents to produce large families, and then to impose their religion on their children, in order to out-breed rival religions. Until recently, this probably accounted for much of the natural spread of religion, with Catholics and Muslims in particular being explicitly urged by their respective clerics to outbreed each other in a race of 'strategic demography'. Tertullian's notion that, 'Each one of us is free to adore whom he wants [since] the religion of an individual neither harms nor profits anyone else,' is clearly quite wrong – a person's religion affects the fortunes of the clerics who seek power over him. 'Greater numbers mean greater power and influence in a worldly, though not necessarily in a spiritual sense.' (*Enough Religion To Make Us Hate* by Victor Griffin, The Columba Press, Dublin, 2002)

Authority

A soldier is conditioned, like one of Pavlov's dogs, to obey a command from an officer as an involuntary conditioned reflex, without thought or hesitation. To some extent we all instinctively tend to respond to commands from those who appear to be 'in authority'. This was famously demonstrated by Stanley Milgram of Yale in 1963, when he got passers-by to take part in an experiment ostensibly to do with punishment and learning: a volunteer was given a (fake) device which, he was told, would deliver an electric shock to a Learner (who was really an actor) sitting in an 'electric chair'. The volunteer was told to administer painful shocks to the Learner if he answered questions wrongly. Milgram, wearing a doctor's white coat and an air of confident authority, instructed the volunteer that he was to increase the voltage each time the Learner got a wrong answer, assuring him that the Learner would suffer no 'permanent damage'. Subjects dutifully obeyed, and even though the Learner cried out and begged to be released, they kept upping the voltage. They continued even with the Learner banging the wall and shrieking to get out – 62% of them took it all the way to what they thought was 450 volts! The volunteers believed that they were inflicting severe pain on the Learners, and happily continued merely in response to the perceived authority of a total stranger wearing a white coat!

Clearly, self-proclaimed authority is a powerful manipulative tool, all the more so when everybody else seems to acknowledge that authority. The Vatican claims over a billion followers, a hotline to almighty God, and papal infallibility. It possesses overwhelming cathedrals and tasteless displays of immense wealth. It uses theatrical devices to speak with a solemn authority that leaves little opportunity for doubt and none for questions – whereas Milgram's only authority prop was a white coat. No wonder that children in primary school are so easily influenced by men persuasively calling themselves 'Father' (despite Jesus' injunction in Matthew 23:9: 'Do not call anyone on Earth "father".')

Predisposition to Belief

It may seem that when children reach adulthood, they are free to reconsider what they have been taught. Generally speaking, though, they choose not to. Perhaps this is because they have also been conditioned to fear such freedom: one big lesson we all learn is that the least painful way through life is to shut up and follow the crowd. Loners who express contrary opinions are seen by most as troublemakers.

Personality is a good indicator of susceptibility to religion, and about ninety percent of people in the western world are belongers, those who run with the crowd. They are conservative, and have little interest in theorising, preferring to be guided by tradition because they feel secure with the things they know. These people defend the *status quo*, patriotism, the law and the prevailing religion. Believers tend to be extraverted optimists who willingly submit to the mood of an emotive crowd. This explains why charismatics get to meet God so frequently, as they find themselves in large, fanatical gatherings of swaying, sweating, swooning devotees.

> *There is no opinion, however absurd, which men will not readily embrace as soon as they can be brought to the conviction that it is generally adopted ... They would sooner die than think ...*
>
> Arthur Schopenhauer (1788–1860)

These conservatives are the 'doers', while the remaining ten percent are the 'thinkers', liberals who prefer 'to debate all aspects of a topic before failing to reach a conclusion'. These liberals supply the ranks of the agnostics and atheists.

Religiosity is also related to perceived social security. Inequitable, insecure societies tend to be more religious than those societies whose inhabitants feel secure and fairly treated. Countries like Denmark, Norway and Sweden are the most atheistic, whilst those countries like the USA – where 'socialism' is a dirty word – and others too poor to provide a secure existence or a good education for their inhabitants, tend to strong religious conviction.

Researchers are beginning to find that certain characteristics of the brain (an overactive dopamine D4 receptor for example) predispose people to religious credulity. Some brain chemicals, which are controlled by certain genes (such as VMAT2), seem to be associated with meditative states such as prayer and with 'spiritual' feelings. These genes are thought to control a person's predisposition to spirituality, which commonly takes the form of religious belief – though for others it can manifest itself through, for example, music appreciation or artistic expression.

A capacity for religious belief confers an evolutionary advantage on those who have it, by uniting people in communities where they enjoy the benefits of mutual altruism, and it is postulated that humankind therefore has an inherited predisposition to spiritual belief. (Dean H Hamer, a geneticist at the US National Cancer Institute, in *The God Gene: How Faith is Hardwired into our Genes*, 2004) Anthropologists surmise that social cooperation and mutual empathy gave primitive man a reproductive advantage over go-it-alone, non-social individuals. Recent studies into social groups also indicate that the stability of religious communities is greater than that of secular communities, so the stronger the religious convictions of a group, the greater will be its durability. This increases the likelihood that predisposition-to-religious-belief genes will be passed on to subsequent generations. It is also possible that potential mates expect that religious believers will be more dependable than freethinking loners, giving those with a religion gene a further edge in the genetic stakes.

Voluntary Adult Conversion

There are millions of wretched people in the world who have nothing now, and have nothing to look forward to. It is surely no coincidence that all of the great religions originated, perversely, in the most God-forsaken places – burning deserts where nature was absent, where fatigue, discomfort and thirst could make a cleric's promises of rivers of milk and honey seem irresistible. Desert sand has always been the most fertile soil for religion, where life is hard and communities need something, anything at all, to cling to. But such is the state of the world that many ordinary people in developed countries now feel unable to cope with the ever-increasing pace of technological developments. Traditional cultures have been swamped by globalisation and ongoing threats of international conflict. People feel that their lives are out of control and their self-esteem is threatened. They feel they need a father-figure to hang on to. There are also millions of frustrated people who need answers to unanswerable questions. And then there are the people, most of us in fact, who are insecure and who yearn to belong to a community. All of these are potential candidates for a belief system that promises to ease their discomfort. Feuerbach saw the Christian churches as 'some kind of insurance company'.

There is no doubt that atheism, taken seriously, can be hard to live with. There are many who brashly proclaimed atheism with the impetuousness of youth, but who in later years felt isolated and frightened. Attracted by the reassurance of belonging to a group of believers, many such people have consciously faced the choice between false but comforting hope and pitiless but bracing truth, and have freely chosen the former, suppressing or rationalising away the dissonance. We believe what we want to believe, and many adults still want to believe in the father-figure-in-the-sky who is patently missing from the cold, monetarist-minded, secular society we live in.

The placebo effect can be amazingly effective. A belief that white pills will take away pain can indeed cure you, even though the pills contain only sugar – it is the belief, not the pill, which does the trick. Religious people will tell you that if you are truly seeking God, then God will make it/him/herself known to you, and psychologists confirm that if you are emotionally yearning for some experience of divine presence, then you will tend to interpret experiences in such a way that they will seem to fulfil your wishes. As already noted, the most persuasive lies are the ones we tell ourselves. Blaise Pascal felt that it was only necessary for those who want to believe to,

Follow the way by which they began: by acting as if they believe, taking holy water, having masses said, etc. Even this will naturally make you believe and deaden your acuteness.

Sigmund Freud posited that religious beliefs are 'fulfilments of the oldest, strongest and most urgent wishes of mankind', and that veneration of a father figure originates in childhood. Freud suggested that belief in God is no more than wish-fulfilment arising from a repressed infantile yearning for protection and security. The subject rationalises that,

The statements of religion cannot be confuted by reason, [so] why should I not believe in them since they have so much on their side – tradition, the concurrence of mankind, and all the consolation they yield?

Freud immediately qualified this with the observation that, 'Ignorance is ignorance: no right to believe anything is derived from it.'

Expedient Conversions

Many adults proclaim religious belief for reasons of expediency, quite insincerely and purely as a means to an end. Historically, Christian clerics of various stripes have threatened those of other faiths and none with the choice of conversion to Christianity or exile and death. Not surprisingly, many chose to convert, though clearly, no thinking person can simply 'decide' to believe in a particular God. True religious conviction is a personal thing that cannot be forced into or out of a person's mind by legislation or logic, or even at the point of a sword. However, many have tried and many more, whole nations in fact, have paid lip-service to obligatory religious beliefs.

Throughout the world, people profess a religion or change religions in order to divorce or remarry, or to make themselves eligible for something otherwise barred to them. In many countries a career in the public service or in the judiciary is available only to those of certain faiths (or, at least, to those prepared to swear religious oaths). Doctors' and nurses' jobs in 'faith' hospitals, and teachers' jobs in 'faith' schools, are legally barred to those of the 'wrong' faiths. In America, any aspiring politician, or any scientist seeking funding, will have little hope of success unless he or she professes Christianity, and access to certain schools and universities is also available only to those of the 'right' religion. In some Islamic countries, there is a strong financial incentive for conversion to Islam, as non-Muslims are discriminated against through extra taxes and legal barriers to owning property or running a business. In India, Hindu Dalits (or 'untouchables') have an obvious incentive to convert to a rival religion.

Involuntary Adult Conversion – Missionary Activity

Whenever a natural disaster strikes an undeveloped nation, provoking fear of starvation and disease among the population, there you will find proselytising missionaries. Frightened people tend to heightened suggestibility. They will clutch at straws, and missionaries use their fear manipulatively to persuade them to accept religious beliefs. In China, for example, US sociologist William Liu noted that, as the country's leaders became increasingly interested in capitalism and the old communist social services started to crumble, hundreds of millions of superstitious peasants in remote areas became so fearful that they eagerly converted to Christianity and Islam, prompted by the thousands of western missionaries who quickly exploited the situation. Joseph Kahn claimed (*New York Times*, 25 November 2004) that there were now more churchgoing Protestants in China than in the whole of Europe. Finnish evangelist Reverend Johan Candelin announced: 'The revival of the Christian church in China is by far the biggest and most significant in the history of Christianity.'

Missionaries thus capitalise on suffering in undeveloped nations. The 'Hellelujah wallahs', as they are known in India, move among starving, uneducated people, Confidently, Repeatedly and Authoritatively Proclaiming (remember CRAP?) their unique knowledge of the 'Truth'. With elaborate rituals, mysterious words, strange music and inflexible rules, they have managed to 'dazzle men by their solemnity and confuse them by their complexity', in the words of John Robertson.

Christian missionaries have left a trail of broken societies and trouble wherever they have gone in the world, to the extent that they often needed military protection to cover their proselytising activities. Military garrisons have been followed by colonial powers and ultimately by the forced suppression of whole continents. In Africa, there are many who now equate Christianity with exploitation:

> *When the missionaries arrived, the Africans had the Land and the Missionaries had the Bible. They taught us how to pray with our eyes closed. When we opened them, they had the land and we had the Bible.*
>
> Jomo Kenyatta, first president of independent Kenya

The Big Lie

> *It is easier to fool people than to convince them that they have been fooled.*
>
> Mark Twain

In light of what has been said, it is hard to accept that such an incredible supernatural belief system as Christianity has been accepted at face value on such an enormous scale – involving billions of adherents over thousands of years. Yet it could be that its very incredibility is what makes Christianity believable.

The Big Lie is any lie so outrageous that it is almost impossible to believe that anyone 'could have the impudence to distort the truth so infamously' (Adolf Hitler, *Mein Kampf*, 1925). The Big Lie becomes credible by virtue of its very incredibility – no one would dare say such an outrageous thing if it weren't true. In 1941, Hitler's propaganda minister Joseph Goebbels wrote (in *Churchill's Lie Factory*): 'The English follow the principle that when one lies, one should lie big, and stick to it. They keep up their lies even at the risk of looking ridiculous,' and it is a fact that people will believe a big lie before a little one. If the lie is repeated frequently enough, and is seasoned with a little manufactured supporting 'evidence', and providing that any contradictory information is suppressed or denigrated, then people will accept the uttermost nonsense. The success of the Big Lie technique as a wartime propaganda tool shows how easy it is to persuade even whole nations to accept incredible claims; the more outrageously incredible, the better.

175

In any case, the masses of ordinary people are said to be readily deceived, especially in matters that don't particularly interest them. The majority of people are lazy thinkers, who find it easier to accept that the world was created from nothing by an omnipotent God than to struggle with scientific explanations. Machiavelli observed that the masses 'are always impressed by appearances' more than by substance. Cecil King, as head of the Mirror newspaper group, claimed:

Only the people who conduct newspapers and similar organisations ... have any idea quite how indifferent, quite how stupid, quite how uninterested in education of any kind the great bulk of the British public are.

Adolf Hitler felt much the same about the Germans: 'The receptive powers of the masses are very restricted, their understanding is feeble and they quickly forget.' HL Menken put it in a nutshell: 'No-one ever lost money under-estimating the intelligence of the general public.' Not clerics, anyway, who succeed largely because, 'their stronghold is the ignorance and thoughtlessness of the majority'. (John Mackinnon Robertson in 'Godism', a tract included in *Papers for the People*, published in 1896 by Truth Seeker Company of Bradford)

In this chapter we have reviewed some of the reasons why people profess Christianity – and you may have noticed that not a single one of them required that Christian beliefs or values themselves be true or good, or even sensible. But Nietzsche's rhetoric is too glib:

To accept faith just because it is customary, means to be dishonest, to be cowardly, to be lazy. And do dishonesty, cowardice and laziness then appear as a presupposition of morality?

No, we have seen that people, including clerics themselves, initially accept the faith of the culture they are born into because they are psychologically conditioned to do so, not because they have made a considered decision to copy everyone else. Once conditioned, there is little question of conscious choice, because there are now deep psychological forces at work resisting change, as we will see in the next chapter.

CHAPTER 10

CLINGING TO BELIEF

Religious belief ... involves a significant emotional and financial investment over the years. The older you are, the more of your life you've invested as a believer, and if you decide to give it all up a long way into your life, it probably makes you feel a bit daft.

Sid Rodrigues, scientist

Self-Image and Rationalisation

Seventeenth-century Dutch philosopher Baruch Spinoza claimed that comprehension is the same as belief: once you learn something and understand it, then you will believe it, and it will require a subsequent act of deliberate repudiation if you are subsequently to disbelieve it. This fits in with the Law of Primacy – the psychological principle that whatever you learn first takes root and becomes entangled in the interlocking and interdependent mosaic of your understanding of the world and its workings. Even if there is convincing contradictory evidence available later, it will take a very reluctant and conscious effort to untangle and displace this primary learning.

The Law of Primacy explains much of the power of childhood conditioning. Beliefs are like the unconscious actions we live our lives by. In much the same way as we can walk down the road without ever thinking of the mechanics of what we are doing, beliefs are pathways that similar impulses regularly take through the synapses of the brain. Just as a river cuts an ever-deeper path to the sea, so beliefs become ever more entrenched the longer and more fervently they are held. We are creatures of habit, and just as it is difficult to persuade an old river to take a different course, so it is difficult to persuade ingrained neurological impulses to take a different path through the brain.

Recent research by neuroscientist Professor Antonio Damasio has demonstrated that even the most rational person is also very much influenced by emotion. In fact, emotion comes before reason, and it can unconsciously direct our line of thought in one direction rather than another, so that a lot of what we believe to be cold reason is actually rationalisation. It is indeed noticeable that when a person's religious (or political) beliefs are challenged, the believer will tend to become emotional, and argue as if their personal honour and pride are at stake. Psychologists now suspect that self-esteem also has a lot to do with it.

All people are similar in many ways – we all look and behave roughly the same; we are all motivated by similar stimuli; and, though experience sometimes suggests the opposite, most of us believe that honesty, honour and attention to duty are good and virtuous. Self-esteem is the degree to which we approve of our self-images, and psychologists tell us that normal people have a deep intrinsic need for a unified and favourable self-image. It should be noted that Christian clerics equate self-esteem with sinful 'pride', and advocate (though they don't practice) self-loathing, which psychiatrists consider particularly harmful.

When considering normal human behaviour, we generally reckon that we have free will and are therefore responsible for our own behaviour. It seems self-evident that we identify objectives, and then behave in logical ways to achieve those objectives: 'I'm hungry, so I'll get some food.' However, psychologists have noticed that we often behave apparently irrationally, and that the behaviour frequently precedes the stated objective: 'I just ate some food ... I guess I must have been hungry.' In this case, my behaviour was actually motivated by some deeper psychological drive or need (e.g. insecurity) of which I was not consciously aware. Now I am at a loss to understand why I just ate when I wasn't hungry. In order to maintain my self-image as a sane and sensible person, if questioned about it, I must devise a plausible-sounding reason. This sequence of behaving apparently irrationally, and subsequently inventing a seemingly sensible reason for it, is known as 'rationalisation'.

Let us say that, on an unconscious sexual or status-related impulse, I foolishly bought an overpriced sports car that I can hardly fit into. The only way I can maintain my self-image is by subsequently inventing some logical-sounding reasons for having bought it – 'it holds its second-hand value' – in order to explain away my behaviour. We frequently behave seemingly irrationally in response to subconscious drives and urges, and our self-image is challenged whenever we find ourselves doing crazy things such as smoking, being angry or wearing impractical clothes. This leads to uncomfortable mental stress known as 'cognitive dissonance' – 'I'm sane but I'm behaving foolishly' – that we normally deal with by rationalisation.

But it isn't always easy to rationalise. Sometimes we can't think of a good reason for our behaviour, and when this happens the cognitive dissonance becomes particularly stressful. A man who sees himself as a Christian and who successfully resists a frontal argument attacking his faith will rationalise the experience to reinforce his self-image as a believer. This is known as the inoculation effect, as the psyche defends itself from an invasion of new concepts. If he had been unable to defend his beliefs and could no longer rationalise, it may seem that this man must abandon his Christian self-image and reinvent himself as an atheist. Not so! The devastating impact on a man's (and especially a cleric's) self-esteem of discovering that a belief system which has sustained him since childhood now turns out to have been false would be gut-wrenching; it would be overwhelming, and so there are other, more likely, outcomes from such a scenario.

If he can't rationalise, our subject will try to discredit the contradictory evidence, or the messenger who brought it. He will suspect a trick, or he will put the information out of his mind. If the evidence is thrust into his face, he is likely to become scornful, cynical, angry and irrational, and maybe go out and get drunk. There is an overwhelming need for him to believe that he is right. This is much more important than actually being right. He must rationalise rather than be rational; explain away rather than explain. Thus, a full frontal attack on a person's religious beliefs usually serves only to reinforce those beliefs – this is known as the 'backfire effect'.

The tendency to hear, see and believe only those things that don't cause dissonance or anxiety is called 'denial'. It deflects prejudiced people (that's every one of us, including you and me) from seeing objective truths. It is involuntary, taking place in the subconscious, so we are not aware of it. It can also take a number of forms, such as:

- Selective attention – failure to see contradictory pieces of evidence.
- Belittling or distorting the significance of evidence.
- Obsessing about how things ought to be, whilst ignoring things as they really are.
- Selective amnesia – suppressing disturbing thoughts and memories from conscious awareness: we forget, and then forget that we have forgotten (this is fertile ground for psychiatrists).

Many people who now doubt the truth of their religion were conditioned during childhood to feel guilt about their questioning behaviour. This makes the denial of obvious facts and the acceptance of obvious fallacies less painful; even virtuous. As with the Big Lie, the more ludicrous the belief they are defending, the more virtuous a person feels in defending it. Thus it is most unlikely that a person, least of all a priest or a cleric, would abandon a conditioned religious belief by force of argument alone.

Most people are today probably living in some degree of religious denial. They are vaguely supported by memories of Pascal's Wager (What if God does exist ...?) and subconsciously protecting their self-images by avoiding stressful situations where they might be exposed to dissonant evidence. They will read only those newspapers that support their political prejudices, socialise only with people who hold consonant opinions, and avoid books such as this one, that might challenge their beliefs. We tend to believe what we want to believe, so that, when faced with a credible challenge to their religious beliefs, devout people tend to retire into their traditional ways of thinking. They close their minds and become doggedly inflexible, and the last thing they will do is to open up and give the challenge fair consideration. This is unfortunate, because such obdurate and dogmatic behaviour promotes ignorance, and sometimes even violence.

One further point: all of our experiences are subjective – if two people share the same adventure together but hold different attitudes to it, then subjectively they experience different adventures. Consider a scary ride at a fairground for example: Alan is relaxed and enjoying the fun, and his glands are releasing 'happy hormones', giving him a sense of wellbeing; Ellen, sitting next to him, is terrified, her brain demanding adrenalin without delay to prepare her for instant flight. The objective experience of the fairground ride is identical for them both, but subjectively they are each on a completely different trip, simply because they have different attitudes to the experience. In a similar way, a person's attitude to religion influences his or her experience of it. For a believer, for example, praying has measurable psychological and physiological benefits that the sceptic can never share, and faith healing works because the subject *believes* that God will make it work (placebo effect), whereas sceptics don't, and therefore it doesn't. The believer's belief is thus reinforced by his subjective experiences, just as the atheist's disbelief is similarly reinforced by his lack of subjective experiences.

Esteem Value

If we must make a big sacrifice or suffer great pain to achieve something, we rationalise that it must have been worth it – otherwise, as sensible, rational beings, we wouldn't have put ourselves to so much trouble. Consequently we tend to esteem those things that cost us most, whether in money, time, effort or discomfort, and to place little value on things we achieve easily. We will esteem an exclusive club that costs thousands to join, has a waiting period of years, and imposes demeaning initiation rites on new members more highly than the local social club which is open to everyone, even if it offers better facilities.

Similarly, a high-maintenance religion will be more highly esteemed than one that demands little in the way of personal sacrifice. The Muslim, whose faith demands that he must pray five times every day, observe Ramadan, Hajj to Mecca, give 2.5% of his annual income to charity, refrain from drinking alcohol, and accept without question its irrational beliefs and extensive behaviour prescriptions, will hold his belief in higher esteem than the Anglican, whose faith imposes relatively few demands.

Thus the most successful churches are the ones that make the greatest demands on their followers, and the most loyal congregations belong to those churches that treat them the worst. The faithful will tend to rationalise that since they, as sensible individuals, voluntarily belong to such demanding organisations, then the organisations must be worthy of ever greater humiliation and suffering. This is probably why Catholic and Muslim women, who are slighted and belittled by their respective religions, tend nevertheless to be more devout than men.

Random Reward Effect

Similarly, the man who works in good conditions for a good employer who pays generously and reliably will be less appreciative and less hardworking than the man working in dirty and dangerous conditions for a demanding employer who pays poor wages, especially if there is no guarantee that he will pay at all! The first man will be complacent and hard to please; the second will be hardworking and loyal. The notion of random reward – maybe you'll get paid, but maybe not – is recognised by psychologists as one of the most potent forms of behavioural (operant) conditioning, with the greatest resistance to extinction of learned behaviour. The effect has been intensively studied by psychologists, because it accounts for gambling addiction and is therefore the foundation of the multi-billion-dollar gambling industry. But it also explains the power of prayer, where the supplicant begs God to make his wishes come true – because occasionally wishes do come true. People who are prayed for do recover from serious illnesses; some prayerful students do pass difficult exams; some fortunate people survive earthquakes that kill thousands of others; and sometimes it doesn't rain on the parade. These occasional 'successes' motivate believers to believe in the power of prayer, while the failures are ascribed to 'God's will'. The random nature of the reward makes the supplicant all the more devoted to prayer, and all the more resistant to those who argue against the effectiveness of prayer.

Escalation

We have seen that a person who holds an irrational belief must occasionally defend the belief against reasoned criticism, and that the more ridicule and discomfort that he or she suffers in protecting the rationalised belief, the more he or she must rationalise that it is right. Furthermore, the more that people are required to invest in their religion, the more they will be motivated to protect their investment. Thus belief begets greater belief. This phenomenon, the tendency of opinions to push from the moderate towards the extreme, is known as 'escalation'. Hatred begets greater hatred; love begets greater love; and religious fervour begets greater religious fervour.

Some bizarre cases of mass manipulation are attributable to the escalation phenomenon, wherein sequences of small steps have led sane people into quite incredible situations. The American anti-communist hysteria and the arms race during the Cold War were frightening examples. Or consider the case of the Reverend Jim Jones, who, in 1950s Indiana, founded a religious sect called the People's Temple. Initially he asked for small contributions to help spread a message of interracial brotherhood. Then he asked those who made this voluntary sacrifice, and had therefore rationalised that Jones' set-up must be a worthwhile cause, to make incrementally bigger contributions. The more they gave, the more they had to rationalise their behaviour deeper into Jones' control. Eventually he got them to sell their houses and give him the proceeds. Then he persuaded them to join a commune in the Guyanan jungle in South America, cut off from any possible counter-influence and surrounded only by like-minded believers. Here they had to make further sacrifices, in the forms of hard work and sexual favours, and further rationalise that 'the cause' made it all worthwhile. Finally, in 1978 when he thought the game was up, he told them, 'The time has come to meet in another place.' He distributed a cyanide and lemonade drink, and ordered his followers to poison their children and then themselves. All 913 of them, mothers and fathers and children, voluntarily killed themselves – just because Jim Jones asked them to!

Group Psychology

It is easier to manipulate large groups of people than it is to persuade one individual to hold a different attitude from everyone else. This is because, as we saw in Chapter V, a person who joins a random group – of, say, blue-eyed people – will be predisposed to be loyal to the group, tending defensively to adopt the attitudes of other group members in order to reinforce the sense of one-ness. He/she will exaggerate the differences between this group and other similar groups, enjoying the boost to self-esteem and confidence that comes from belonging to the group, even though in objective terms that person may have nothing significant in common with the other group members. People who share similar emotions also tend to identify with each other, whether they are united in love (of God, say) or hatred (of a scapegoat).

Young and insecure people in particular have a greater need to belong than to believe. Social psychologist Solomon Asch dramatically demonstrated this in his conformity experiments in the 1950s, in which peer pressure led participants to give obviously wrong answers to questions. Most ordinary people can be led quite readily to deny the evidence of their own eyes by their desire to conform. Individuals will often deny their own strongly held beliefs and preferences rather than stand apart from the crowd, especially if they feel inferior to the crowd members in any way. Astute propagandists use this phenomenon to create a sense of unity where there really is none, manipulating group members' professed beliefs by preying on their sense of loyalty to imagined group ideals, such as evangelical dogma.

Undeniably, there is something emotionally satisfying about being a member of a crowd – you feel good, confident, anonymous, powerful and unbeatable, free to yield to the 'personality' of the crowd, and these shared emotions tend progressively to bind everyone tighter. Football fans experience the gratification of crowd euphoria every weekend. Nietzsche summarised: 'Madness is the exception in individuals, but the rule in groups.'

So while attendances at mainstream churches are in decline, the charismatic Pentecostal churches exploit crowd psychology by giving congregations a real psychological kick from their highly emotive sing-along 'worship experiences'. The crowd's raised suggestibility makes them easier to manipulate, especially when they are given something to get emotionally roused about, such as an object of adoration (say, Jesus) or a scapegoat (like communism). Evangelist Billy Graham used to stage-manage his rallies to rouse his thousands of followers into fervours of religious ecstasy twice nightly, and three times on Sundays. Some all-male American dominance theology meetings, with their fascist salutes, are too evocative of Nuremberg for everyone's tastes, however.

These psychological phenomena cast doubt on the cynical notion that all clerics are only in it for the power and the money. Most of them started their careers in the Church as teenagers, straight from school and still under the influence of childhood indoctrination and peer pressure. Subsequently, throughout their whole lives in the Church, they will have been surrounded only by like-minded colleagues, never exposed to the real, secular world and never having any reason to question their faith.

Undoubtedly there are some who really believe that God guides and advises them. Others may have occasional doubts, but, having come so far and invested so much of their lives in the system, they will be under enormous self-imposed psychological pressure to rationalise away doubts and commit themselves ever more fervently. There are yet others, the most senior in the hierarchy, who must deal with the more practical side of the Church's affairs, and must wheel and deal and resort to dirty tricks to protect the Church and its assets. These are men who have little time for spiritual matters, and who must be cynical about the whole business, but they are in such exclusive positions that they can enjoy the power and the good life.

However, despite the psychological imperative to reinforce one's belief whenever it is actively attacked, there are millions of people who are gradually losing their faith under the passive, dripping-tap influence of living in a secular world that no longer depends day-to-day on God. In this world, traditional clerics are beginning to sound slightly ridiculous when they speak, and we continue to progress educationally, socially and technically despite the efforts of clerics. In the next chapter, we consider this gradual secularising effect.

CHAPTER 11

SLOWLY LOSING FAITH

When the committed football fan will stand in the cold and rain for two hours every Saturday to watch his team, we have to suspect that those who explain their lack of church involvement by considerations other than lack of belief are fooling themselves or fooling the researchers.

Steve Bruce, *Religion in Modern Britain*, Oxford: OUP (1995).

Men occasionally stumble over the truth, but most of them pick themselves up and hurry off as if nothing ever happened.

Winston Churchill

There has been no sudden collapse of religious belief in Europe, because there never was any great depth of belief in the first place. We were misled by the large numbers of regular churchgoers who paid lip-service to religion, but who turned out to be belongers rather than true believers. One wonders how extensive this phenomenon might be elsewhere – social pressure to conform is powerful, and maybe all believers, deep-down, are really belongers, simply following the crowd. However, there have been some important changes, and the old, traditional religions are slowly declining.

Secular Influences

In Britain or France, you can live your life without ever thinking much about the religion you were born into, because it doesn't intrude into your daily activities. Scientific ways of thinking have exposed religious myths for what they are. We know now that Galileo and Darwin were more or less right, and that the popes were absolutely wrong. Science enables us to live longer, healthier lives with no recourse to God. Even Christians admit that antiseptic is more effective than exorcising demons when tackling disease, just as fertiliser is more effective than sacrificing a goat in making crops grow. Very few would now attribute a fatal train derailment to God's wrath – rather, they would look for the buckled rail and the lapsed maintenance schedule. Believers and atheists alike feel confident that the sun will rise on time tomorrow, whether or not God commands it. God has become redundant, no longer needed in people's daily lives. In Indonesia and Egypt, just as in Afghanistan and Saudi Arabia, religion plays a large and important role in daily life, and religion is passively absorbed as part of the environment, but in Western Europe that environment has now become secular, and secularism is what is passively absorbed.

Religious believers in Europe have been increasingly exposed to temporal experiences. Books, films and the news media have become openly critical of religion, especially of Islam and US Christian fundamentalism, and they gleefully report misdemeanours or indiscretions by the more pompous clerics. Other factors influencing the gradual loss of clerical power include secular education, consumerism, the disintegration of the traditional family, foreign holidays, and the drabness of religious rituals that depend on parrot-like repetition and discourage all mental activity. Old habits die hard, but the world has changed radically – its population has doubled in the past forty years; electronic communications have been with us for less than thirty years, yet they have introduced radically new lifestyles; unregulated global 'free' trade is now rife. So much has changed that tradition has become irrelevant, and cultural norms no longer offer cosy refuge.

A steady stream of scientific discoveries is rapidly filling the gaps in our understanding of nature, wherein God used to be found, and social attitudes have changed too: In the UK, Margaret Thatcher's October 1978 claim that 'there is no such thing as society' and that self-interest is virtuous, and her scornful description of ethically principled members of her Cabinet as 'wets' hardened subsequent generations. Social morality was devalued, and the growth of popular capitalist sentiment and unregulated mega-businesses has led to an obsession with money and the self. There is a dwindling interest in community affairs, which often used to be focussed around the local church.

In rural communities, attendance at church on Sunday is an opportunity for members of the community to bond openly together. Neighbours are missed if they fail to show up, and there will be gossip if they are wearing anything but their Sunday best. The psychological pressure to conform can be overpowering. But rural communities are threatened – young people are increasingly moving to the cities, where they are anonymous and where the echoing churches offer little sense of community. The flight from rural society has thus further eroded religious observance.

After Vatican II (1962–65), when Catholics were expecting some slackening of the impractical rules relating to sex, the pope chose instead to tighten them. Popular hostility to *Humanae Vitae* – which in 1968 reaffirmed Catholic opposition to artificial birth control – and the general refusal by women to accept it, together with the further papal humiliations of women, gays and others, have been further factors in the alienation of clerics from their so-called 'flocks'.

Clerics' efforts to restore their authority has only made them look ridiculous. In Ireland, for example, Catholic clerics taught that a married woman facing 'condomistic intercourse' with her husband must forcefully resist, like a virgin threatened by rape: 'She may not remain passive. This means forceful active resistance ...' (Malachi O'Doherty, *Empty Pulpits*, Gill and Macmillan, Dublin, 2008) The same source mentions that Reverend J McCarthy warned that tampons 'could easily be a grave source of temptation, especially to those with strong physical desires'.

Such outrageous interference into private affairs was naturally resented. The subsequent introduction of the contraceptive 'pill' turned out to be a hugely empowering development for women, who were now able to control their own (and their daughters') lives, no longer dependent on sham Victorian notions of respectability. The recent revelations about clerical connivance with paedophile priests were the last straw for many who have consciously turned their backs on Rome.

We now know that our galaxy, the Milky Way, is 100,000 light-years in diameter and 1,000 light-years thick; that there are around 170 billion similar galaxies in the universe; and that there are perhaps ten thousand billion billion planets, of which Earth is but one. This knowledge together with the recent discoveries of astro- and nano-physicists tend to make the assertions of the primitive authors of the Bible seem risible.

It was a television programme about astronomy that caused my wife, ultimately, to leave the Church. She wasn't expecting to have her religious beliefs put to the test when she switched on, and she found the programme so interesting that she forgot to go into denial. It might equally have been a news item about a tsunami killing thousands of children, or maybe a priest's fatuous sermon at a friend's funeral, or a radio discussion about other people's religious beliefs – innocent seeds like these take root in people's minds. Other people lapse from their faith because they consider that the religious people around them are hypocritical and judgemental, or that the dogma is too rigid and unsympathetic, or, in my case, that clerics are too obsessed by power and money.

Fewer than ten percent of the population of the UK now regularly attend religious services. Religious baptisms, weddings and funerals are in decline, and the change from routine unthinking behaviour has, in itself, further obliged people to start thinking. For example, whereas there was never previously a choice between going to church or not (you simply went), churchgoers now have to make a conscious decision to go. Those belonging-type individuals, who used to attend church simply because most of the people around them attended, no longer go, because hardly anyone else does.

Multi-culturalism

Religion comes to us as part of our culture, and it acts like a lens to show us a distorted version of the world. But in our modern, multi-cultural world, where long-distance travel is relatively easy and people of different cultures increasingly interact, we soon discover that there are other cultures and other religions that other people hold equally passionately. At first they seem deviant, immoral, rude and primitive. Gradually, though, their presence makes us aware of our own cultural lenses, and it eventually dawns on us that our self-evident truths are not self-evident to everyone. In this way, the improbable religious beliefs of others bring home to us that our own religious beliefs are hardly any more probable.

As Catholics, for example, we smirk when we first learn that Hindus pray before statues of their god Shiva's penis; or that Buddhists believe in reincarnation as an animal; or that Muslim 'martyrs' expect seventy-two virgins when they arrive in heaven; or that Jehovah's Witnesses are quite certain that 144,000 of them will shortly be physically lifted into Heaven. Such knowledge, however, may eventually prompt us to wonder about our own certainty – for example, that our priests can turn wine into blood, or that the pope is infallible. It may even lead us to wonder about our all-seeing, all-powerful God, the one who pretends not to exist and who wants us to play celestial hide-and-seek with him. By contact with other cultures we slowly become aware of our own religious prejudices. Some of us become sceptics and, as cultures continue to intermingle, purse-lipped Christians increasingly have to acknowledge that there's nothing special about their particular brand of virtue.

Weakness of true belief

I certainly had no idea how little faith Christians have in their own faith till I saw how ill their courage and temper can stand any attack on it.

Harriet Martineau, English suffragette (1802–76)

Religion is primarily a social thing, culturally inherited, a bit like patriotism. It seems probable that many of those who loudly profess religious belief are really more interested in belonging than in believing, and what they chant so devoutly is a poor guide to what they believe deep down. Unwittingly, they go through the motions in order to be seen by their peers to be members of religious society, but they betray the shallowness of their beliefs when, whilst chanting that the world is God's plaything, they actually behave as if they expect the laws of nature to hold. Most evidently, the televangelists, who preach vociferously about the terrors of everlasting Hell, seem to show little urgency in their own personal attempts to avoid it.

Philosopher Daniel Dennett noted (in *Breaking the Spell*, Penguin, 2006) that those who practice primitive folk religions don't think of themselves as practising a religion at all, since their religious observances are an integral part of their day-to-day lives as hunters or farmers. They don't keep telling each other how much they believe in God, any more than we go around asserting our beliefs in bacteria or electrons, because where there is no doubt, there is no need to speak of faith. But organised Christianity speaks of little else, which would seem to imply that there is a great deal of underlying doubt, especially among those who most loudly and repetitiously profess their faith. One may wonder if Christians really believe in the literal truth of any of what they profess when they recite the Apostle's Creed:

> *I believe in God the Father almighty, creator of Heaven and Earth, and in Jesus Christ His only son, our Lord who was conceived by the Holy Spirit, born of the virgin Mary ... He shall come again to judge the living and the dead. I believe in the Holy Ghost, the holy catholic Church, the communion of saints, the forgiveness of sins, the resurrection of the body, and life everlasting ...*

What do they think a Holy Spirit is? And does anybody *really* believe that Jesus will come back to judge every person who has lived over the past 2,000 years? And who or what do they think they are talking to? Because if they don't really believe all this stuff, they shouldn't really call themselves Christians.

It seems that clerics are more concerned with uniformity of *professed* belief than with uniformity of inner belief. The document *'Dominus Iesus*: On the Unicity and Salvific Universality of Jesus Christ and the Church', written by the then Cardinal Ratzinger and ratified by Pope John Paul II in June 2000, differentiated between what Catholics must 'firmly believe' and what they are merely 'required to profess'. So the Vatican at least seems to acknowledge that you can profess something even though you don't believe it.

Semi-Catholicism

> *There are two ways you can observe a religion. You can either assume that everything in it, as the commandment from an omnipotent, omniscient, omnipresent being, must be followed to the letter, or you can – you know – pick and choose the bits that are convenient.*
>
> > Matt Kirshen in 'How to Have the Perfect Jewish Christmas'

Semi-Catholics pick and choose the bits of the dogma that are, you know, convenient, and they reject the rest. Clerical dogma is important to clerics, but not to the Semis. They are perfectly happy to let the pope make his infallible pronouncements about faith and morality in Rome, while they decide for themselves what to believe and what is ethical. These Semi-Catholics don't necessarily think much about it, but they don't believe that the pope is infallible or that using condoms will condemn them to everlasting perdition. They generally prefer to depend on their own consciences rather than on the pope's anachronistic dogma. It is harder for a Catholic to change his professed Church than for a Protestant, who has hundreds of denominations to choose from, and so the Semis continue to wear their Catholic badges, though, strictly speaking, they too are now Protestants.

In Latin America in the 1960s, many devout Catholic priests working among oppressed people reacted against the stream of anti-socialist propaganda flowing from Rome. They initiated what became known as the Liberation Theology movement, which sought social equality and justice for the downtrodden masses, and enjoyed support from the poor peasants who had grown to mistrust fascistic Catholic dogma. These priests were welcomed wherever they worked, especially in Guatemala, Peru, and El Salvador, but definitely not in Rome. The pope denounced them as revolutionary Marxists, and set Opus Dei on them. Today, the people of Latin America recognise two Catholic churches: there is the People's Church, which supports social justice for all, even women, and is made up of millions of people guided by Jesus' supposed ideals; and there is the pope's Church, consisting of a few misogynistic old clerics in Rome, where 'The Vatican is primarily a political and financial power institution functioning behind the pope's façade of spirituality,' (John M Swomley, *The Humanist*, Nov/Dec 1997) and where Jesus' socialistic teaching sticks in their throats. The pope is impotent in the face of such mass disobedience, but rather than excommunicate the lot of them, he prefers to tell the world that he still speaks with authority on behalf of 1.1 billion Catholics, since this is the source of his power.

The Semis are open to accusations of insincerity and hypocrisy, and outsiders dismiss them as impossible to reason with, yet there are an awful lot of them: the Liberation Theologists; all the alienated Catholic women; and the tens of millions of ordinary men (and priests) who feel that the pope has lost the plot. The Semis cannot see why outsiders consider that they are hypocritical to call themselves Catholics, because all their co-religionists feel exactly the same, and anyway, hypocrisy within the Church is commonplace. Yet Archbishop Diarmuid Martin is unyielding:

One cannot pick and choose different elements of God that appeal to them ... you end up defining your own God ... you can't be an individualistic Christian. A Christian belongs to a faith community and must share the faith.

> 'Moving On? Catholic Ministry in Ireland', *The Irish Catholic*, 9 November 2006

Pius XI similarly warned:

... let the faithful also be on their guard against overrated independence of private judgement ... for it is quite foreign to everyone bearing the name Christian to trust his own mental powers ... a characteristic of all true followers of Christ, lettered and unlettered, is to suffer themselves to be led in all things that touch upon faith or morals.

St Ignatius Loyola explained:

We should always be disposed to believe that that which appears to us to be white is really black, if the hierarchy of the Church so decides.

No matter how much you model your life on Jesus' teachings, you can never be a 'true follower of Christ' until you submit completely not to Christ, but to Rome. So the Semis call themselves Catholics and the Church happily counts them as members, whilst telling them that they're not.

New Age

The popular interest in New Ageism attests to the fact that at least some of the people who stop believing in religion don't believe nothing. 'The truth is much worse, they believe anything.' (Malcolm Muggeridge, British journalist, 1903–90) New Agers claim to seek 'universal knowledge' through the 'oneness of humanity'. They employ Indian gurus, Eastern mysticism, spiritualism, holism, astrology, esoterism, dreamwork, Feng Shui, Ayurveda, Qi Gong and similar strange practices, according to personal taste, to get it. New Ageism is characterised by rejection of the mainstream dogmatic religions in favour of individualism. Its popularity attests that there will always be those who want more, and that no matter how comfortable they are in this life, they will always want another.

The rise of superstition and the fall of Orthodox Christianity

In his article 'Fading Faith' (*Free Inquiry*, February 2010), the agnostic and sceptic James Haught makes the point that, 'Increasingly, supernatural faith belongs to the third world.' Here, primitive belief in invisible gods, witches, angels, miracles, prophecies and exorcisms still survive, and anti-intellectual religions such as Revivalism, Pentecostalism and Islam are all thriving.

America: To Haught's third world, we should add the USA, whose hostility to socialism leaves its people feeling insecure and exposed, and where more than three-quarters (78%) of the population claim to be Christians. Damon Linker (in *The Theocons: Secular America Under Siege,* Doubleday, 2007) reckons that the US is effectively a theocracy, where religion is seen as an essential component of patriotism, essential also for upward social mobility. But the situation is fluid – a 2008 survey by the Pew Forum on Religion and the Public Life showed that 44% of Americans belong to religious traditions other than those in which they were raised. This volatility of professed faith is largely explained by the fact that the Clerics who operate the various churches in America tend to compete for new members the way that washing powder brands compete for new customers in Europe. There is a huge variety of 'religious' products on offer, each of them bidding to be more attractive than the others. Americans are nowadays generally more interested in self-fulfilment than in devoting their lives to some unresponsive God, and individual clerics must address this simple fact, or lose out to those who do.

The tail now wags the dog, insofar as US congregations now define the sort of Christianity they want, rather than simply accepting what some embittered old clerics tell them they must accept. Go-ahead, business-minded clerics (known as pastorpreneurs) now use high-powered marketing techniques to determine the exact needs of their targets, and then set up their churches to offer just that. After spending a fortune on market research, they have established that what Americans most want from their church is a sense of community – just like everyone else, in fact.

Accordingly, the pastorpreneurs have built mega-churches standing in perfectly manicured grounds with enormous car parks, comfortable seats and modern décor. Their jazzed-up services feature videos, modern music and drama. As added hooks, they run special-interest groups for anyone from weight-watchers to motorcycle enthusiasts, and sporting and entertainment facilities, crèches, children's day-care centres and citizens' advice centres. There are special churches for cowboys, gays, down-and-outs and even for liberals, with the emphasis at all times on excellence of service. It is no more spiritual than a shopping mall, but it does provide that sense of community that the customers want. Though it may seem more like a privatised social service offering self-help and feel-good, it is what Americans call Christianity – and the money is pouring in for the pastorpreneurs, who enjoy fancy homes and private jet planes.

In 2006, there were over 120 mega-churches (each with a capacity of at least 2,000) in the USA, with Lakewood in Houston, Texas, boasting a 500-strong choir and 30,000 weekly attendees. With over a thousand different denominations to choose from, there are enough varieties of 'Christianity' in America to suit most tastes – though they all hold the same views in matters relating to patriotism, sex, abortion, divorce, the family and gun-toting. They all support the same theo-con Republican politicians, they all preach similar mega-distortions of Jesus' teachings, and they all promise salvation in exchange for lots of money. As traditional 'intellectual' Protestantism slowly dies, lowbrow evangelical Protestantism is thriving, which is to say that while well-educated Americans are increasingly turning away from supernaturalism, the less educated masses are moving toward revivalism – the born-again fundamentalists, evangelicals and Mormons are all thriving.

Pentecostalism is a good example. It was founded in 1906 in a run-down area of Los Angeles by William Seymour, a charismatic African-American who based his teaching around Mark 16:17–18: '... And these signs will accompany those who believe. In my name, they will drive out demons, they will speak in new tongues, they will pick up snakes with their hands and when they drink deadly poison it will not hurt them at all ...' The speaking-in-tongues, or glossolalia, bit really caught on, and in no time his small group were all eagerly talking gibberish. Despite serious doubt about the validity of these verses tacked on to the end of Mark's gospel, the group grew. Within three years the movement had blossomed, as Seymour's word spread across America and around the world. Pentecostalism is now a worldwide faith system, with over 300 million followers, many of whom believe that the Holy Spirit can give them supernatural powers to speak in tongues, as well as float in mid-air and cure sickness. It is the fastest-growing religion in the world, a political and economic force to be reckoned with.

There are hundreds of less successful, but equally improbable, evangelical denominations in America. They all preach the same stuff about being born again, about the Bible being the literal Truth, about Creation, the Commandments, the impending apocalypse, exorcism, miracles ... and money of course. These happy-clappy evangelical churches probably represent a popular reaction to the strictures of Calvinism and traditional Christianity. Their leaders are not great scholars, or even deep thinkers – in fact they are probably the most active dumbing-down force in America – but they are charismatic, emotive orators, and their meetings are powerful and exciting, emphasising fervent religious experiences over traditional 'book' theology.

Despite appearances, these worship events don't just happen. They are carefully scripted, choreographed and stage-managed by skilful manipulators of human emotions, people who know how to wind up a congregation and give them a great religious 'experience'. Like other big American corporations, they are going global – in Latin America, Africa and the Far East, US-style Pentecostalism is already well established. In Brazil there are 24 million Pentecostal Christians. In Guatemala, Pentecostals worship in the biggest building in all Central America, a 12,000-seater church with a heliport and parking space for 2,500 cars. The main Pentecostal church in Santiago, Chile, dwarfs this, with seats for 18,000. On the other side of the world, five of the ten largest mega-churches on Earth are to be found in South Korea – one such church in Seoul claims to cater for 850,000 worshippers. But the whole over-the-top, go-get-'em business model, with its promises of upward mobility and worldly success, clearly has 100% American roots.

In their book *God is Back* (Penguin Books, London, 2010), John Micklethwait and Adrian Wooldridge attribute the spread of American-style Christianity to four things: 1) the high-powered approach to marketing and promotion; 2) the philanthropical nature of middle-class America, where there is no welfare state to help those in need; 3) the US-based Christian radio and TV networks, such as Trinity Broadcasting Network and Christian Broadcasting Network, which reach into practically every backwater of the world; and 4) the armies of Evangelical Missionaries. In 2005, there were 115,700 full-time American missionaries working abroad. These are well-dressed, well-prepared, well-financed, and well-trained people, supported by one-and-a-half million short-term missionaries, who together contribute a further 30,000 man-years – a formidable influence in poor and backward countries.

Britain: The situation in Britain is confused by the fact that although almost three-quarters (72%) of the adult population claimed to be 'Christians' in the National Census (2001), this number was flatly contradicted by statistics produced by the

Christians themselves: the English Church Census (carried out every seven to nine years) reported that in England in 2004, only 7% of Christians actually attended church during any given week. This figure is corroborated by Christian Research's *Religious Trends 2002/2003* (table 2.14.1), which showed church attendances at 7.4%, while 90% of the population manifested no religion at all. And most of those attending in urban areas were immigrants. So the Christian churches, which might have been expected to exaggerate their numbers, were contradicted by the findings of the wholly secular National Census, which actually did exaggerate those numbers by a factor of ten!

The difference may be partly explained by noting that the word 'Christian' means different things to different people. For the devout few, it is confined to those who conscientiously observe the teachings and rituals of a Christian Church; while for the heterodox many, it seems to cover 'anyone who occasionally refrains from committing adultery or dishonouring his/her father and mother'. Further distortion will have arisen from the traditional British reluctance to admit to atheism. And the Catholic policy is to count as members all those who have been baptised into the faith and have not yet been buried, so this would include a lot of semi- and lapsed Catholics. Whatever the reasons for the discrepancy, it is important, because Census returns influence government policy on matters such as faith schools, censorship, social cohesion, women's rights, children's rights, foreign aid and charitable status. Government policy in all these areas is badly misinformed by Census returns suggesting that there are ten times as many Christians in the country as there really are.

British people are still nostalgic about traditional Christianity and regret its passing, and though they don't believe the traditional teachings, they have never rejected them either. In their efforts to hang on to the few that remain, Christian clerics have swept the sadism and fascism under the carpet. They have cooled the fires and diluted the brimstone, and have put their demands for poverty and chastity to one side. They have reinvented Christianity, turning from bible-thumping rants in

201

freezing chapels towards soft-focus strummed guitars and saccharine smiles, whilst all the time assuring us that nothing has changed.

Developed countries: Christian observance is declining markedly in Scandinavia, France, Germany, Japan, Australia and New Zealand, where education and social services have reduced people's dependence on God. In Western Europe, the experience of centuries of bitter and twisted Christianity, followed by two world wars, has made people mistrustful of utopian promises. As the number of visible secularists has increased in each location, so the rate of decline in religious observance has increased, further suggesting that most people are guided by those around them.

Eastern Europe: The demise of communism in the late 1980s brought with it a renewal of interest in Christianity. In those previously atheistic Iron Curtain countries religion was like forbidden fruit, and had always seemed desirable. The Vatican showed a great and sudden enthusiasm to negotiate special concordats and diplomatic relations with the ex-communist states, and the Church even spuriously claimed to have been instrumental in bringing about the collapse of Communism. At around the same time, the upsurge of Islamic militancy provoked many previously passive Christians to react by nailing their colours to the mast of militant Christianity, many of them supporting the state of Israel against the 'Axis of Evil', by which they meant Islam.

The Beginning of the End?

The biologist PZ Myers, writing in the *New Statesman* (25 July 2011), said:

> *I don't just reject religion, but actively oppose it in all its forms – because it is fundamentally a poison for the mind that undermines our critical faculties.*

Meanwhile well-known philosopher AC Grayling (who describes himself as an 'antitheist' – holding that all religions are untrue and the influence of churches is positively harmful) sees these events as the death throes of once-powerful groups of clerics over-reacting to their loss of power and influence. He argues that some in the Muslim world have reacted so noisily and violently to the forces of globalisation that other religious groups have felt obliged to voice their respective demands. Politically-correct politicians have over-responded, and the media have over-hyped, effectively amplifying a small minority interest into a seemingly overwhelming movement. But Grayling feels that this is no more than their last desperate bid for attention. Let us hope that he is right, because the upsurge in Muslim militancy and the rightist Christian reaction to it is hardly comforting.

Nor should we forget that the traditional churches still have unimaginable wealth and enormous political influence. They haven't gone away, and there will always be those who need to believe – God will continue to exist for as long as the reasons that brought him about in the first place continue to exist. Nevertheless, in Western Europe we can clearly see that traditional authoritarian religion is declining in popularity and *de facto* secularism is flourishing. When we compare the differences in the beliefs of ordinary people in Western society today, there already seem to be more practising secular Humanists than Christians, as a straight comparison demonstrates:

Credo	Humanists	Christians
Self-esteem is…	essential	a sin (pride)
Put your trust in…	knowledge	blind faith
Pleasure is…	to be enjoyed	to be shunned
Emotions are…	normal and natural	to be suppressed
Women are…	Equal	inferior
Alien beliefs are to be…	debated	rejected, belief and believer
Life is to be lived…	to the full	on your knees
Doubt and uncertainty…	are natural	are sinful
Children's education should…	encourage critical thinking	Indoctrinate with religion
Morality comes from…	evolution and reason	God and his clerics

Part III has explained how, despite standing on obviously false foundations, Christianity nevertheless claims over two billion adherents. These include many clerics who have successfully rationalised the counter-arguments and who now sincerely believe that they are party to God's wishes, whatever they conceive God to be. But there are a lot of other clerics who display very few Christian virtues. If we can judge them by their actions, then, as we will see in Part IV, they are less interested in God's wishes than in temporal wealth and political influence.

Part IV

Follow the Money

Part IV contains further circumstantial evidence to support the notion that modern Christianity owes little to God or the Bible or Jesus, or even Paul, and that it owes considerably more to powerful interests and elite clerics.

CHAPTER 12

THE GOD BUSINESS

*I am surrounded by priests who repeat incessantly that their
kingdom is not of this world, yet they lay their hands on
everything they can get.*

Napoleon Bonaparte

*The church is a bank that is constantly receiving deposits but
never pays a dividend.*

Lemuel Washburn, US writer

Christianity is supposedly founded on the teachings of a poor
itinerant preacher, who despised wealth and who warned that
the wealthy were doomed. Yet modern Christian clerics have so
twisted Jesus' teaching that greed is now seen as virtuous,
enabling Mammonists such as Lord Brian Griffiths, Goldman
Sachs adviser on executive bonuses, to claim: 'The injunction of
Jesus to love others as ourselves is an endorsement of self-
interest.' (Bloomberg News, 21 October 2009) He was claiming
that Jesus would applaud the banker, already in receipt of a
hundred times the average industrial wage, who then awards
himself a generous 'executive bonus'. Lord Griffiths has not
been contradicted by any prominent clerics, so we may assume
that mega-money is now seen as God's reward for being a good
Christian. After all, as televangelist Jim Bakker asked, 'Where in
the Bible does it say a church has to be non-profit?' Bakker raked
in $150 million a year from his Praise The Lord (PTL) business.

The clerics of the Mormon Church do not release details of
their finances, but in July 1997, *Time* magazine reported that
they had ten million members worldwide, and an annual
income of $5.2 billion with assets of around $30 billion. In 2007,
they claimed 13,194,000 members, so we may assume that their
income was well over $10 billion. This is not bad for a big

corporation, let alone a religious sect, but it is not enough – clerics want more.

Quoting Malachi 3:8–9, Dr Dale A Robbins complains:

The Lord Almighty said, 'Will a man rob God? Yet you rob me.' But you ask 'How do we rob you?'. 'In tithes and offerings. You are under a curse – the whole nation of you – because you are robbing me. Bring the whole tithe into the storehouse ...'

He explains:

Robbery is the act of taking something that doesn't belong to you ... It is extremely fair of God only to require a tenth to be returned to him, since he owns 100% of the planet. Robbery is a serious offence, and a person guilty of robbing God will be 'cursed with a curse'. Some claim that they can't afford to pay their tithes. But 'Can you afford to be cursed ... can you afford to be considered a thief or robber of God's property? The part that God claims ... is the first and best 10%.'

But even this isn't enough. Dr Robbins also wants offerings: 'An offering is that which we give voluntarily out of our own property after the tithe has been subtracted.' He then instructs that on the first day of the week you are to bring your tithes and offerings and give them, not to God, but, of course, to Dr Robbins.

There are said to be 1,500 different Christian denominations in the USA, twenty-four of which claim over a million members. Altogether, 'The United States has 350,000 churches whose members donate nearly $100 billion per year.' (James Haught in 'Fading Faith', *Free Inquiry*, February 2010) Most are small, but some are mega-churches run as businesses, with hundreds of full-time employees and heavy investments in communications technology, including radio and television stations, each of which can regularly bring in over $1 million per week.

The televangelists openly and unashamedly exploit ScapeGod to tout for money. Paul Crouch puts it this way:

If you have been healed or saved or blessed through Trinity Broadcasting Network and have not contributed to [the] station, you are robbing God and will lose your reward in heaven.

He goes on, 'God, we proclaim death to anything or anyone who will lift a hand against this network ...' He urges viewers to send him $1,000 cheques even if they can't afford it: 'Write the cheque anyway as a step of faith, and the Lord will repay you many times over ...' (though not until after you're safely dead, of course). These preachers of the Gospel of Prosperity, such as Crouch, Ken Copeland and Creflo Dollar, are after serious money, measured in millions.

The Catholic Church is the oldest multinational business corporation in the world. By the middle of the twelfth century, despite all Jesus' teachings about the virtues of poverty, Church officers were amassing so much wealth that Arnold of Brescia felt obliged to remind them publicly that 'bishops who hold fiefs, and monks who possess property cannot be saved'. This was not what they wanted to hear, so Pope Adrian IV (the English pope) arranged for Arnold to be captured, hanged and burned. His ashes were thrown into the Tiber, thus proving that Jesus was wrong about camels passing through eyes of needles. It was a convincing argument.

With the pope as its CEO, the Vatican operates a worldwide franchise system based on the weekly offerings and bequests of its supposed 1.166 billion members. There are 412,886 parishes in 2,864 dioceses worldwide, with each diocese operating as an independent cost centre. It has been accumulating wealth for many hundreds of years, and is almost certainly the richest enterprise in the world. Its assets include some of the world's most valuable land sites, including the sovereign state of Vatican City, and over a million other large buildings. These include around half a million churches and chapels and as many presbyteries; over 200,000 schools with playgrounds; over 5,000 hospitals and around 16,000 homes for the elderly; 10,000 orphanages, 30,000 rehabilitation centres and 10,000 other institutions; plus cathedrals, bishops' palaces, seminaries, monasteries and convents. Most of these stand on several hectares, and usually in prime urban locations (data from *Agenzia Fides*, 2010). Kevin Cahill reported in the *New Statesman* (14 March 2011) that,

> *The Pope is understood to own all the land of the Catholic Church's institutions, religious orders and dioceses ... The estimated total of the land held by the Pope is around 177 million acres.*

That is 72 million hectares, across the globe, and guesstimates as to its total value produce figures of tens, or even hundreds, of trillions of dollars for the land and buildings alone. In Ireland in 2007, the Sisters of our Lady of Charity sold a green site for €20 million per hectare ... work it out for yourself. (The Holy See values St Peter's Basilica and other historic buildings at €1 each, so it tends to understate its true assets somewhat, lest anyone thinks it is obscenely wealthy.) The Catholic Church's assets also include innumerable priceless and irreplaceable works of art, including paintings by the likes of Giotto, Caravaggio and Raphael, and sculptures by Michelangelo, as well as vast treasure in gold bullion and equity investments worth billions. The secretive Vatican Bank (*Istituto per le Opere di Religione*) is not subject to audit and releases no reports, but it accepts only gold and cash as deposits, so we may assume that it is solvent.

The pope, as successor to the poor itinerant Nazarene, is the nominal owner of all of this wealth, which equates with enormous political influence for the Catholic Church. Whenever the pope makes a visit abroad – usually at the host country's expense – the Vatican's PR machine squeezes the occasion for maximum publicity. Celebrities and powerful politicians publicly pay obeisance to the pontiff, who presents himself to the world as a saintly, unworldly man of love and peace, naïve in matters relating to money or politics. This same man presides over a uniquely wealthy and powerful political body with embassies and diplomatic relationships with all the main governments of the world, a seat in the United Nations and special concordats with many countries. He can afford to be humble.

Needless to say, such enormous wealth also attracts undesirables. In 1982, after the probable murder of Pope John Paul I, the Vatican Bank became embroiled in a financial scandal involving the Mafia and the looting of billions of dollars from its coffers (see David Yallop's books: *In God's Name*, Corgi Books London, 1984; and *The Power and the Glory*, Constable & Robinson, 2007). Michael Ryan (see www.churchsecurity.info) estimates that, every year, around $90 million goes missing from Sunday collection plates, embezzled by priests and clerics. Terence McKiernan (www.bishopaccountability.org) reckons that these reported losses are a fraction of the total – after all, it's an unaudited, cash-based system, and God can be relied on not to give the game away.

God Grot and Jesus Junk

Believers have always sought to visit the holy places mentioned in the Bible. They are encouraged by clerics, who know that 'being there' helps to confirm the beliefs that pilgrims bring with them. Local guides flourish as they bring travellers to see the various supposed sites and sell them supposed relics. The pilgrimage industry is a good money-spinner: today, if you visit any of the Catholic shrines and cathedrals around Europe, you will discover shops selling pictures of the Pope, candles, holy medals, rosary beads, tasteless statues and crucifixes, authentic Mass cards (in Ireland, there's a fine of €300,000, or ten years in prison, for selling 'bogus' Mass cards) and lots of books about Catholicism.

Visit an American religious outlet (usually attached to one of the 330,000 churches) and you will find lots more religious books, from all sorts of Bibles and biblical reference books to

Tim LaHaye's *Left Behind* Armageddon-fiction series (which has netted $650 million so far). There are religious mystery stories and even dieting books, like *What Would Jesus Eat?* Every angle is covered. All of the big publishing houses now have religious imprints, and together they sell $2 billion worth of religious books every year in the USA alone. You can also get Christian greeting cards and Christian jewellery, such as cross-nails pendants and gold crucifix lapel badges. Just before Christmas, you can buy a birthday cake for Jesus. There are CDs of religious pop music, such as Hank Williams' 'Jesus Died for Me', Johnny Cash telling us 'I Talk to Jesus Every Day', Carrie Underwood imploring 'Jesus Take the Wheel', or Bobby Bare pleading 'Drop Kick Me Jesus Through the Goalposts of Life'. While you're there, you can get yourself a genuine 'Praise the Lord' backpack. The market for such 'religious' products in the USA alone is worth over $6 billion per year.

Even in the secular world, we are constantly urged to 'put Christ back into Christmas' by buying and sending religious cards, buying and hanging angels from our Christmas trees, and buying and displaying toy cribs in our windows. Among the ranks of the non-religious there are plenty of people who are fascinated by 'the psychic' – in any general bookshop in Europe, you will find that the 'Religion', 'New Age' and 'Mind, Body, Spirit' sections are extensive. Superstition sells, whatever form it may take and however it may be presented.

In 2004, film producer Mel Gibson privately funded his somewhat anti-Semitic film 'The Passion of the Christ'. It grossed $365 million, alerting Hollywood to the potential of religious themes, and film companies are becoming actively involved with God. Indeed the world of God grot and Jesus junk is only just waking up to the true selling power of Jesus' name.

Charitable Status

The monumental corruption of the Catholic Church, as evidenced by the many sexual abuse scandals, is particularly

galling when one contemplates the vast (and covert) wealth of
that particular enterprise ... It's a racket.

Barbara Katz on church tax exemptions

I did not see why the schoolmaster should be taxed to support
the priest, and not the priest the schoolmaster.

Henry Thoreau (1817–62)

When a religion is good, I conceive it will support itself; and
when it does not support itself, and God does not care to
support it so that its professors are obliged to call for the help of
the civil powers, 'tis a sign, I apprehend, of its being a bad one.

Benjamin Franklin

A 'charity' is an organisation set up to give help and money to
those in need. This should not be confused with a business or
organisation which enjoys 'charitable status', which, in most
western countries, means eligibility for exemption from paying
income tax, corporation tax, capital gains tax, capital
acquisitions tax, stamp duty and dividend withholding tax, by
virtue of the beneficial nature of a body's activities. There are
four types of activities which most national tax authorities
normally accept as qualifying an organisation for charitable
status: 1) the relief of poverty; 2) the advancement of education;
3) purposes generally deemed to be beneficial to the community;
and 4) the advancement of religion. Now, most would agree that
the first three purposes are indeed beneficial and deserving of
financial encouragement from any given state. However, having
seen in Part II the enormous harm done in the name of religion,
and in Part III the probable bogus nature of it all, it is very hard
to understand how anyone can consider activities aimed at the
advancement of religion to be anything but seriously harmful.
Yet even secular states generously subsidise the advancement of
religion in this way, at the expense of those regular taxpayers
who do not enjoy charitable status.

The very notion of 'charitable status' evokes a misleading
image of a 'charity', of the kind that helps the needy. Most

religious organisations exist to maximise clerical influence and wealth, without a thought for those in need.

> *Religion supports nobody. It has to be supported ... It is a perpetual mendicant. It lives off the labours of others and then has the arrogance to pretend that it supports the giver.*
>
> Robert G Ingersoll

Clerics promote charity, all right, but what they're looking for is bequests, contributions and charitable gifts to themselves, usually from people who can ill afford them. Christopher Hitchens (author of *The Missionary Position: Mother Teresa in Theory and Practice*) noted that the money that Mother Teresa's Calcutta-based Missionaries of Charity raised to help the poor was in fact spent largely on religious proselytising, and one of her ex-staff remarked that most of the mission's tens of millions in charitable contributions sat earning interest in its bank accounts.

> *I think it is very beautiful for the poor to accept their lot, to share it with the passion of Christ. I think the world is being much helped by the suffering of these poor people.*
>
> Mother Teresa

And so her 'charity' helped the world further by increasing their suffering – one example among many of a religious 'charity' that takes from the poor and gives to the rich.

The charitable veneer and the benevolent public image are all-important. Five hundred years ago, Machiavelli noted that the masses were impressed more by appearances than by reality, and to those in the public eye he counselled:

> *... everyone can see what you appear to be but only a very few experience you as you really are ...*

So,

> *You should always* appear *to be sympathetic, trustworthy, kind, straightforward and devout, and indeed you should try to*

be so whenever possible, but if necessary you should be
prepared to act differently. Be careful, though, never to say
anything which does not seem to be inspired by one of the five
qualities listed above ... You need not necessarily have the
good qualities mentioned above, but you should certainly
appear to have them.

Niccolo Machiavelli, The Prince, 1513

Somehow, despite the reality of their disastrous record, their
arrogance and wealth, Christian clerics have managed to
appropriate for themselves appearances of all five of these
qualities: sympathy, trust, benevolence, simplicity and piety!

There are many individuals, both religious and secular, who
volunteer for truly charitable work for their own personal
reasons, and many charitable organisations, both religious and
secular, collect charitable donations and use them to good effect
by helping those in need. But in 2009 Pope Benedict, concerned
that Catholic charities were behaving too much like real
charities, issued his encyclical *Caritas in Veritate*. In this
document, he reminded them that their prime purpose was to
facilitate proselytisers (the pope preferred to call them
'evangelists') to gain access to potential converts and so to
advance the religion, whilst incidentally giving the Church a
valuable veneer of sympathy, trust, benevolence, simplicity and
piety. As Benedict said, 'The most tragic hunger and the most
terrible anguish is not lack of food. It's more about the absence
of God ...'

Clearly, the credit for truly charitable gifts and works should
go to the donors and the workers, and not to clerics. These
clerics, with Machiavellian artfulness, gain a benevolent public
image by occasionally berating Western governments for not
doing enough to help the victims of specific situations in the
undeveloped world which, often enough, they themselves
created by blocking attempts by secular organisations to feed the
starving, or to control overpopulation, or to fight the spread of
sexually transmitted diseases with condoms.

In the context of Dr Robbins' claim that 'robbery is the act of taking something that doesn't belong to you', it is pertinent to note that these incredibly wealthy institutions routinely 'steal' billions of dollars from taxpayers by virtue of their charitable status. The multi-million incomes of all proselytising religious sects are not only free of tax – many of them also attract government grants, gifts of land and property, subsidies and a multitude of other privileges. In Austria, Denmark, Sweden and Switzerland, the governments fund religion through the imposition of church taxes. In Germany until 2005, 8% of all personal incomes (including those of atheists) was taken by the State and given to the churches (in 1979, for example, the Catholic Church in Germany received the equivalent of two billion US dollars from this source alone), and without any obligation to show what they did with the money. There was no requirement to keep accounts, no audits and no conditions on how the money should be spent.

In France, and also in America, where Church and State are supposed to be separate, clerics nevertheless enjoy charitable status tax-wise, which helps to explain how obscure sects such as the Mormons and Opus Dei could have become so wealthy so quickly. Back in 1953, the author Ron Hubbard managed to get Scientology defined as a 'religion' so that he could claim tax-free charitable status for the considerable royalties from his 'Dianetics' books. A top Chicago banker avoided $80,000 property tax by calling himself a 'priest', and designating his $3 million mansion as a 'church'. In Thailand thousands of cults enjoy unaccountable and often fraudulent tax-free status, and in 1998 there were reports of some of the top Buddhist monks raking in $40,000 per day tax free for 'helping' the credulous to win the Lottery. In Russia in the 1990s, the Orthodox Church became a major importer of goods, exploiting its exemption from customs and excise taxes. And in Japan, where, according to the *Nikkei Weekly* in 1992, religious organisations registered with the Agency for Cultural Affairs didn't have to report the income they derived from their religious activities, the situation resulted in 180,000 new religions and cults collectively enjoying hundreds of billions of yen per year tax free, all at the expense of honest taxpayers. So far, nothing has changed. Without outside access to their accounts, it seems safe to assume that many, perhaps most, of these organised religions are little more than moneymaking rackets. There is no need to go to the Cayman Islands when the advancement of religion is the biggest tax haven of them all.

Social Services

Where a state's constitution permits, clerics are keen to set up their own private schools. Here they are free to indoctrinate each new generation of young children into their particular beliefs, isolated from distractions and contradictions from those of other, and no, faiths. Some religions also provide hospitals, perhaps in the hope of proselytising to the sick, receiving generous legacies from the dying, and to ensure that 'unapproved' medical practices are not undertaken. But whatever the superficial reasoning, they do it because they choose to and they don't do it for nothing. Religiously operated schools and hospitals take away some of the onus for providing these services from the State, and clerics therefore demand that the State funds their operations in full, including paying rent for the institution's buildings, which the State often originally built and now maintains.

As we have seen, segregated schools are socially divisive, and by supporting them a state creates resentment among those citizens, especially the taxpayers, who are ineligible, by virtue of their beliefs or lack of beliefs, to avail of the religiously run facilities they are paying for. Northern Ireland provides an object lesson: the segregated Catholic and Protestant schools, housing, hospitals, employment and even sports facilities can end up creating State-subsidised ghettoes that cost considerably more than the basic financial cost of providing and running them. Subsidised segregation of the citizens within a state is immoral because it creates victims – all citizens should be treated equally, in facilities that are accessible to everyone. The simplest way to achieve this is to make all state-funded services totally secular, leaving any group that wants to indoctrinate their children with religion to do so in their own time and at their own expense.

Clerics in the USA have exploited their charitable image by taking over the running of some of the government's social welfare activities, including managing the funding that was previously administered by civil servants. Thus, under the guise of promoting religious freedom, George Bush's Faith-Based Initiatives greatly expanded government subsidies to proselytising religious institutions. The State now gives millions of dollars of aid money directly to clerics, to spend as they see fit on welfare schemes for down-and-outs and drug addicts, without any controls to prevent them from favouring those of their own faith, or blocking assistance to those of no faith, homosexuals, unmarried mothers, or anyone who refuses to espouse their right-wing theology.

As far as life's inevitabilities are concerned, clerics may *claim* that they can avoid death, but they know for sure that they can avoid taxes. It seems that most US-based pastorpreneurial and televangelist operations are primarily intended to earn a tax-free profit for their respective organisations, as are many of the newer religious cults such as Scientology and those that have sprung up recently in the Far East. With regard to the older, more traditional religions, quite apart from their financial assets and investments, they have built their churches, mosques and schools on valuable land sites which today represent enormous wealth. This must be operated pragmatically by senior clerics skilled in managing money, artful in dealing with 'the markets', avaricious in taking advantage of tax breaks, ruthless in putting pressure on governments to contribute to their expenses, and devious in hiding their assets from the public gaze. This is their job, as employees of the Church. It seems quite obvious that many of the senior members, the clerics of most organised religions, are more interested in the money-and-influence aspect of the business than in God.

CHAPTER 13

POLITICAL POWER

Everywhere that religion has ever held temporal power, the result has approximated Taliban-style rule.
> AC Grayling, *The Form of Things*, Phoenix, London (2006)

Jesus instructed his followers to fulfil their obligations to the State, rendering 'to Caesar that which is Caesar's and to God that which is God's'. He was clearly advocating a secular state, quite separate from clerical religious authority, with neither having a right to interfere with the other. But all of that ended before it had even started, when the Roman emperor Constantine gave political authority to the clerics of the early Christian Church. Power went straight to their heads, and God's spokesmen incited vicious persecution – 'out of love', according to Augustine – of any individual, heathen, unbeliever or heterodox Christian who failed to toe their particular line. Jesus' brand of Christianity was a big loser in 325 in Nicea. Peaceful, secular society was another, with its freedoms surrendered, its morality debased, its knowledge discarded and its tranquillity thrown into turmoil. While they presented a holy, pious face to the world, with clasped hands and eyes raised to heaven, those early Christian clerics wielded an intolerant and vicious political power that was to last for centuries throughout Europe. Though they have now lost much of that power, the Christian churches are still thoroughly Machiavellian political institutions, interfering in temporal State affairs to push their own agendas. There is no good reason why they should not be scrutinised and treated the same as all other political institutions, open to investigation, criticism and ridicule where appropriate. Instead, even unbelievers are expected to treat these self-seeking opportunists with deference and reverence.

Clerics and State

It cannot be overemphasised that the Church (whichever denomination is under discussion) is essentially whatever its clerics say it is, and what is good for the Church is good for its clerics. So when we talk of the respective interests of Church and State, we are really considering the interests of a few senior clerics versus those of a democratically-elected government mandated to protect the rights and welfare of its citizens.

Article 18 of the Universal Declaration of Human Rights (UDHR) states:

> *Everyone has a right to freedom of thought, conscience and religion: this right includes the freedom to change his religion or belief, and the freedom, either alone or in community with others and in public or private, to manifest his belief in teaching, practice, worship and observance.*

It is important to emphasise that it is individual people that have human rights, *not* their beliefs or organisations. People are also free to worship whatever they wish – Allah, the sun or their ancestors – provided that they practise their religion with consideration for those who don't share their beliefs. But clerics demand special privileges: they claim the right, for example, to exempt themselves from taxes and to demand generous grants and subsidies; and to have blasphemy laws to protect them from fair criticism, along with many other special concessions, as we will see.

In an Ipsos MORI poll dated 24 November 2006, 42% of respondents complained that the government pays too much attention to clerics. But governments must listen when clerics speak, if only because the media will give them extensive coverage – clerical utterances can be depended on to cause controversy, which is what sells newspapers. There are, however, sound political reasons why governments must listen when clerics talk, and we will consider four of them: 1. religion as a power prop; 2. the potential of clerics to cause trouble; 3. overt clerical influence; and 4. covert clerical influence.

Religion as a Power Prop

The Roman statesman Seneca observed: 'To the ordinary citizen all religions are equally true. To the philosopher, they are all equally false. And to the rulers, they are all equally useful.' The general perception that religion is 'virtuous', 'benign' and even 'peaceful' is constantly stoked by those in power, who hope that by association with the religious, they will also be perceived as virtuous and benign.

What is more, religious congregations are easier to control than hordes of free-thinkers, especially if they believe that their political leaders are appointed by God, that their stations in life are divinely ordained, and that their duty in life is therefore to obey without question and to accept their inferior status without complaint, as used to be the case until quite recently. But even today, religious people tend to be passively conservative and patriotic. They support the forces of law and order and the status quo and, as such, they are a political leader's dream.

The Potential of Clerics To Cause Trouble

By rights, their divisive, intolerant, anti-feminist, homophobic, immoral attitudes should debar clerics from any position of influence in any society. Yet their potential to make political trouble gives them special access to the corridors of power because, despite misgivings on the part of policymakers and legislators to the effect that much religious dogma is alien to the very notion of human rights, Art 18 of the UDHR obliges governments to facilitate their citizens in exercising their right to 'manifest' their beliefs, however perverse. In multicultural societies this can give rise to a clatter of bizarre demands for exclusions, exceptions, privileges and, of course, subsidies, in matters such as morality, free speech, diet and health, often compromising those governments of goodwill that try to accommodate them. For example:

- Morality as enforced by State laws often conflicts with ideas of morality held by clerics, leading to disputes on matters of censorship, heresy, blasphemy and family affairs, including polygamy, mixed marriages, arranged and under-age marriages; and also in matters relating to abortion, family planning, divorce, genital mutilation and self-mutilation. Clerics and church spokesmen complain that their 'rights' to manifest their beliefs are being violated.
- Some believers manifest their beliefs in antisocial ways; some are subversive or rebellious; some refuse to pay taxes or serve in the armed forces; some clerics try to give effect to the notion that apostasy is punishable by death; some practice honour killing; others would deny the basic rights and freedoms of women, homosexuals and atheists.
- Some public manifestations of belief involve large groups of emotionally aroused people who disturb the peace and threaten security. Religious rallies and marches are often offensive and even deliberately provocative, as for example in Northern Ireland.
- Arbitrary religious dietary taboos can cause problems in hospitals, schools, prisons and in the armed services, especially as different religions have different feast days and days of rest. It is clearly impractical for authorities to provide specially prepared foods of every variety, or to allow members of every faith to observe different working days if society is to function, but this gives clerics cause to complain that their right to manifest their belief is being denied.
- Organisations such as the British Farm Animal Welfare Council, the RSPCA, and the British Veterinary Association claim that the Jewish and Muslim requirements for Kosher and Hal-Al slaughter are cruel, and they lobby the British government to ban these primitive practices on welfare grounds. In the UK, however, religious groups have been given exemption from animal welfare legislation because,

cruel or not, such a ban would contravene their pointless religious taboos.

- According to the Muslim Council of Britain, Muslim schoolchildren must be excused from dancing lessons; they need segregated music lessons; they must be provided with individual changing cubicles for sports activities; and they should be provided with special prayer rooms with washing facilities – 'in order to foster greater integration' with the other kids! They also demand (and get) sexually-segregated swimming pools – Leicester offers sessions for women to swim fully clothed. In Bristol, special Muslim apartments are built in which the toilets face away from Mecca. (Micklethwait and Wooldridge, *God is Back*, Allen Lane, 2009)
- Proselytising is obligatory in the manifestation of some faiths, yet the evangelists' messages and their means for disseminating them, as well as church bells and amplified religious chanting and music, are often unacceptable to the rest of society.
- Missionary work and proselytising is sometimes used to cover subversive political activity (e.g. US 'missionaries' in China).
- Some clerics claim to be offended by routine public health measures, such as water fluoridation and vaccination, even when there is a danger of an epidemic affecting the whole community. Others encourage parents to refuse to allow medical treatment for their children, or allow them access only to faith healers or prayer alone. When the State intervenes for humanitarian reasons, it stands accused of interfering in their right to manifest their beliefs.
- Clerics demand special State-funded schools and hospitals for members of their respective faiths – the schools to facilitate conditioning children into the faith; the hospitals to provide only those treatments and chaplains approved of by clerics. Governments that cannot accommodate the demands of each different faith, and those of no faith, stand accused of discrimination.

- Some people are offended by religious symbols, e.g. crucifixes, in public places, or by priestly garb, burkhas, or jewellery announcing the wearer's faith.
- Clerics, and others, can object to ceremonies involving singing the national anthem, swearing religious oaths and swearing allegiance to the flag.
- Clerics demand loyalty to their religion above loyalty to the State, claiming that their God takes precedence over mere citizenship. They are emphatic in their claim that Canon Law or Sharia Law supersedes the State's laws and systems of justice. They can often be hostile to the very State that defends their right to make trouble, rousing their followers to defy those State laws that conflict with their teaching.

In many such individual issues as those listed above, a few clerics can carry disproportionate weight. They have an incentive to lobby intensively, whereas the overwhelming majority of lay people, the ones who will be required ultimately to pay for a proposal, don't even bother to inform themselves about it. The legislator who opposes the proposal will attract hysterical opposition from the few who would benefit from it, with only weak support from those on his side – his easiest course is to support it.

In July 1964, Roman Catholic Archbishop Hurley observed:

> The State has no religious obligations whatsoever under the New Testament. The consequence of this is that the Church cannot demand of the State, even of a State representing a completely Catholic society, that it use political powers in favour of the Church. To make such a demand is to ask the State to act ultra vires [i.e. beyond its authority].

Nevertheless, the Vatican makes no secret of its hostility to certain secular laws enacted by democratically elected governments. In 1992, Cardinal Alfonso Trujillo claimed: '... legislators, politicians, physicians and scientists have a duty of conscience to be the defenders of life in this war against the culture of death.' One may have thought that he was talking about the Pentagon and its stockpiles of WMDs, but no, he's not concerned with *that* culture of death; abortion was, as usual, the obsession. Earlier in that same year, New York Cardinal John O'Connor had re-emphasised that '... attacks on the Catholic Church's stance on abortion, unless they are rebutted, effectively erode Church authority on all matters, indeed on the authority of God himself.' (ScapeGod, of course.)

Clerics in general, and the papacy in particular, regard political democracy as the road to perdition. Cardinal Ratzinger argued that '[t]ruth is not determined by a majority vote', and in 1995, John Paul II issued encyclical *Evangelium Vitae*, attacking the principles of liberal democracy and questioning the legitimacy of the democratically elected US government. His encyclical seditiously instructed Catholics to defy those civil laws that he deemed unacceptable.

> *It is precisely from obedience to God* [i.e. me] *that the strength and courage to resist human laws are born. It is the strength and courage of those prepared even to be imprisoned or put to the sword, the certainty that this is what makes for the endurance and faith of the saints ... cooperation* [i.e. with the State] *can never be justified either by invoking respect for the freedom of others or by appealing to the fact that civil law permits or requires it.*

John Paul II went on to advocate martyrdom in the fight for the pope's supremacy over laws passed by democratically elected governments: 'Life finds its centre, its meaning and its fulfilment when it is given up.' The pope was advocating sedition and treason to the death to enforce his authority! If the Vatican claims to be a State, the rules of international diplomacy are clear: it has no business interfering, even superficially, in the affairs of any other State. Whenever challenged on this, the Vatican suddenly forgets that it is a State, and becomes an intermediary, humbly conveying God's Word. Islamic clerics similarly teach that the need for obedience to the State is secondary to obedience to God's (i.e. their) law. They similarly encourage martyrdom when the State fails to toe their line.

Such anti-authoritarianism seems incongruous coming from such arch-authoritarian organisations, yet their arrogance in this is breathtaking: the Vatican, for example, wants all predominantly Catholic States to make its dysfunctional notions of morality enforceable on all citizens, including non-Catholics. Pope Pius XI, who described artificial birth control as 'criminal abuse', wrote:

> *Governments can assist the Church greatly in the execution of its important office, if, in laying down their ordinances, they take account of what is proscribed by divine and ecclesiastical law* [i.e. me], *and if penalties are fixed for offenders.*
> Encyclical *Casti Connubii*, p.45 of the English translation

Pope Paul VI (1963–78) made a similar plea:

> *To rulers, who are those principally responsible for the common good, and who can do so much to safeguard moral customs, we say: Do not allow the morality of your peoples to be degraded; do not permit by legal means practices contrary to natural and divine* [i.e. my] *law.*
> Encyclical *Humanae Vitae*, p.17, para 3

The pope demands that the whole world, atheists and all, obey his dictates above those of the State.

The Religious Right aspires to replace democracy with theocracy. It wants to return to the Dark Ages, to be ruled by clerics whose 'revealed teachings' would justify Taliban-like tyranny. They speak of God's love and justice, but this would inevitably introduce systems of control that are totalitarian and unethical. When the Taliban took control of Afghanistan, its Ministry for the Prevention of Vice and the Promotion of Virtue mandated public executions for apostasy, adultery and homosexuality; bans on TV, music and sport; and severe

227

discrimination against women and girls. New penalties were introduced, such as amputation and live burial.

In a similar theocratic society, in 1939 after the Spanish Civil War, Catholic clerics declared that every Spaniard was henceforth decreed to be a Catholic. Compulsory indoctrination classes were brought in, along with forced baptism and renaming of orphans. Attendance at Mass became obligatory, and a priestly denunciation was virtually a charge of treason. Priests took over education and changed the curriculum to emphasise their dogma. Divorce and civil marriage were abolished and the penalty for abortion was increased. Church representatives were placed on every civil committee. All dramatic works and films needed an ecclesiastical licence, and clerics were given responsibility for the censorship of books. The role of women reverted to domestic servitude, while women without families were obliged to join charitable organisations. Finally, every new employee was required to have a certificate of spiritual cleanliness from a priest. The pope praised the dictator Franco for having thus brought 'honour, order, prosperity and tranquillity to Spain'.

More recently in Poland, the post-communist government ratified a concordat with the Vatican in 1998, guaranteeing clerics special privileges. The constitutional separation of Church from State was repealed and aspects of Catholic dogma were enforced on all citizens through criminal law. Religious instruction became compulsory in all schools. A censorship law enforced respect for Catholic values. Abortion was outlawed. All draft legislation had to pass scrutiny by clerics – e.g. they rejected a proposal to remove religious grades, which discriminated against non-Catholics from school certificates. The State gave generous assistance to certain Catholic publishing houses, and of course it gave special tax allowances and exemptions for clerics themselves. (These details were contained in an open letter, dated 15 March 2001, from Polish Humanists Andrej Dominiczac and Barbara Stanosz, addressed to members of the European Union.) At the UN Commission on the Status of Women, forty-fifth session, the Polish Minister for Family Affairs formally opposed attempts to outlaw discriminatory practices against women. In the draft European Constitution, Poland held out for a mention of God and the Christian tradition. The *Economist* (24 March 2007) noted that the League of Polish Families (a minority coalition partner) wanted to ban abortion and the teaching of evolution throughout the whole of Europe: 'To secular liberals in the rest of Europe, all this makes Poland seem like a bastion of medieval barbarism.'

The Vatican has negotiated undemocratic concordats with several European states, giving it extraordinary influence and special, legally enforceable powers and concessions in those states. These can include the power to control the education of a state's children, and the exemption of Catholic clerics from certain obligations. Many of the concordats between the Church and the pre-WWII fascist regimes of Portugal, Spain, Italy and Germany are still in place, while new concordats are still being forged, as in Poland, Romania and Slovakia. There are twenty-five concordats currently in force (see www.concordatwatch.org for a state-by-state commentary). The Vatican has diplomatic relations with 177 of the 192 member states of the United Nations, which is significant when you recall Michael Shea's definition of diplomacy as 'saying and doing some very nasty things without ever seeming to'. No problem for these clerics.

Overt Clerical Influence

Until quite recently, preachers simply instructed their flocks from the pulpit in the way they should vote in national elections and referenda. Sheep-like, their flocks obeyed, and since the flocks totalled tens of millions, no aspiring politician could afford to ignore or offend them. Today in India, a supposedly secular nation, the political parties fall over each other in their eagerness to please the so-called 'vote banks', which provide votes en masse as dictated by their religious leaders.

In Europe, such direct clerical interference has waned, and religious spokesmen now only speak on behalf of a tiny percentage of the millions they claim to represent. For example, the pope speaks ostensibly on behalf of the Catholic Church in the metonymical sense of 'the one billion-odd claimed members of that Church worldwide', whereas in actuality he merely reflects the views of the Catholic Church in the synecdochic sense of 'a few dozens of ancient clerics in the Vatican'. He is an entirely unrepresentative spokesman, as are the Muslim clerics and *mujtahid* who similarly interpret the Koran, and the Protestant preachers in the USA who tell us what they think the Bible ought to mean. They have no right to pronounce to the world what Christians, Muslims, Jews or Atheists believe, or what they should believe, and they certainly have no right to interfere in secular government. But that doesn't stop them from doing so, quite brazenly and overtly.

Fortunately, when they speak, they often alienate more people than they win over. For example, when asked if the Vatican's demands for the EU to enforce Catholic dogma on non-Catholics might explain the growth of anti-Catholic prejudice, the spokesman replied:

> *One must keep in mind that, when the Church intervenes on great moral issues posed by the political context, it does not present proofs of faith, but gives arguments based on reason which she considers valid and, therefore, acceptable also for those who do not believe.*
>
> Archbishop Lajolo, Vatican Secretary of Relations with States, in an interview with Italian newspaper *La Stampa*, 29 October 2004

In this case, the 'arguments' turned out to be unacceptable to unbelievers and believers alike.

In the USA, despite laws forbidding charitable-status institutions from taking sides in election campaigns, clerics openly veto political candidates. In the 2004 presidential election campaign, Catholic bishops very publicly censured Catholic John Kerry for failing to promise to enforce Vatican policy if elected, even though such a promise would have been unconstitutional. He lost to George Bush, who would have had no such scruples.

Roman Catholic interests are also very well represented in the United Nations. For example, Vatican City is the world's smallest city-state (108.7 acres), created in 1929 when fascist leader Mussolini signed the Lateran Treaty with Pope Pius XI. It originally qualified for access to the UN by virtue of its ownership of a radio station and postal service (the International Telecommunications Union, founded in 1865, and the Universal Postal Union of 1874 are two of the oldest international organisations, and founder members of the United Nations Organisation in 1942), and certainly not by virtue of being a nation. Vaticanian is not a nationality. Nevertheless, Vatican representatives started attending sessions of the United Nations General Assembly in 1951. In 1964 they installed permanent observers in the UN HQs in New York, Geneva and Vienna, with direct involvement in the work of at least fifteen high-powered bodies. Nor was the General Assembly ever invited to ratify its presence. The Holy See was never invited to participate. Instead, according to Pope John Paul II, 'Pope Paul VI initiated the formal participation of the Holy See in the UN Organisation, offering cooperation of the church's spiritual and humanitarian expertise[!]'

In July 2004, the Holy See gained the right formally to participate in the debates of the General Assembly – the right of reply, the right to have its communications issued and circulated as official documents, and the right to co-sponsor relevant draft resolutions. In the UN, Vatican City (population 750) sits alongside China (population 1,300 million), and it enjoys the power effectively to veto the urgent wishes of the rest of the world. It has exploited this power to the full, with an impressive record of obfuscation and obstruction of all sorts of reforms. The Catholic Church is also a member of the African Union, the Organisation of American States, and similar inter-governmental bodies. It certainly punches far above its weight in the world of international diplomacy.

The UN is a diplomatic organisation where delegates wheel and deal and try to compromise on controversial issues, whereas the policies of the Holy See and Islamic states are determined by rigid dogma with no room for manoeuvre. This caused the former head of Amnesty International, Paul Sane, to complain of the:

> ... unholy alliance between the Holy See, Iran, Algeria, Nicaragua, Syria, Libya, Morocco and Pakistan [that] has attempted to hold for ransom women's human rights at UN conferences.

Beijing Plus Five conference, 2000

At the Cairo Conference on Population and Development, the Holy See joined forces with the OIC (Organisation of the Islamic Conference, a group of 56 Islamic nations) to block the availability of condoms and abortion to the world's poorest. In 2008, again collaborating with the OIC in the UN Human Rights Council, clerics of the Holy See were instrumental in limiting the right to freedom of speech in the Universal Declaration.

Jesus famously instructed Christians to avoid mixing political matters with religious affairs ('Give to Caesar ...'), but in 1903, Pius X contradicted Jesus, saying:

> ... whoever judges the question fairly must recognize that the Sovereign Pontiff, invested by God with the Supreme Magistracy, has not the right to separate political matters from the domain of faith and morals.

Since this time, the Vatican has consistently shown more interest in political power than in the souls of its rapidly evaporating flock.

UN Secretary General Ban Ki Moon, talking to senior Bahia, Buddhists, Christians, Daoists, Hindus, Muslims, Jews, Shinto and Sikhs in Windsor Castle in November 2009, noted that:

Religions have established or helped to run half the schools in the world; they are among the world's biggest investors; the global output of religious journalism is comparable at least to Europe's secular press.

This may be interpreted as an official acknowledgement that clerics generally are not without overt political influence.

Covert influence and subversion

By definition, we know very little of most covert clerical influence or subversive activities. The notes below are intended merely to show that it goes on, and that pious clerics are no strangers to conspiracy, manipulation and sedition.

In the USA in 1975, the Association of Catholic Bishops issued a 'Pastoral Plan for Pro-Life Activities', which was:

> *... a blueprint for infiltrating and manipulating the democratic process at local, state and federal levels ... controlled by the Vatican ... directed toward creating a highly sophisticated, meticulously organised and well financed ... political machine ... [to] elect officials ... who will adhere to Vatican-ordained positions.*
>
> Stephen Mumford, *The Vatican's Role in the World's Population Crisis,* Center for Research on Population and Security, 1997

According to the *Puritan News Weekly,* the Plan called for the Vatican's role to be hidden behind a Protestant front, and for the enterprise to be promoted as a spontaneous grassroots movement. Four years later, Moral Majority was launched. Maxine Negri (in 'A Well Planned Conspiracy', *The Humanist,* May/June 1982) confirmed the involvement of the Catholic hierarchy in the Moral Majority which, when it was seen to be neither moral nor a majority, was replaced in 1989 by the Christian Coalition. This was devoted to 'stealth' lobbying, training of activists, media watches, planting influential believers into positions of authority, increasing religious influence in schools and, of course, outlawing artificial birth control by whatever means (according to Stephen Mumford in 'Why the Church Can't Change' in *The Catholic Doctrine and Reproductive Health,* published by the Council for Secular Humanism). Lawrence Lader (in *Politics, Power and the Church*) also described the Catholic–fundamentalist alliance, and their bid to kill the First Amendment, which guarantees separation of Church and State.

In 1982, Ronald Reagan told the National Catholic Association: 'I am grateful for your help in shaping American policy to reflect God's will ... and I look forward to further guidance from His Holiness Pope John Paul ...' This guidance led to the withdrawal of US funding for family planning at the 1984 World Conference on Population in Mexico City. In 1986, President Reagan again favoured the pope by electing Catholic activist Antonin Scalia to the Supreme Court – he who in 2000 persuaded the Court to award the presidency of the USA to George W Bush after Bush had lost the election. For the first two years of Bush's second term, the Christian Coalition actually controlled both the Senate and the House of Representatives, effectively holding the power of veto over the government of the most powerful country in the world. This prompted theology professor David Ray Griffin to remark:

> *There are a lot of people worried that America is moving towards a full-scale fascist regime; we are living in a new reality; where a group of people have gotten control of every branch of government – Justice, the FBI, CIA, the White House and increasingly the Supreme Court.*

The Vatican has met tougher opposition in the European Union, prompting Cardinal Ratzinger (now Pope Benedict) to complain, 'it seems to be almost indecent to speak about God, almost as if it were an attack on the freedom of someone who doesn't believe'. Exactly so. The problem with being infallible is that you can't always see your own failings. Nevertheless, Christian

Churches have won special privileges in the EC, such as pre-legislative consultation and regular dialogues with the Office of the Commission President, with working sessions 'on more specific issues whenever the churches ... have a particular concern'.

Flying beneath everyone's radar is the secretive, ultra-rightist cult Opus Dei, whose members do nothing to distinguish themselves from the non- and passively-religious masses, enabling them to infiltrate and operate unnoticed in areas potentially hostile to Catholic activism. Although the cult has only 80,000 members, it has its own 'personal prelature', authorising it to operate worldwide above the authority of local bishops. Being answerable only in secret to the pope himself, it is the most influential secret force within the Vatican, operating in key positions in governments, the civil services, the judiciary, third-level education and the media all over the world. (Notes from *Opus Dei* by John L Allen, Penguin Books, London, 2005)

Part IV has exposed the obsessive interest of many clerics with money and political power, and we are now in a position to draw some conclusions. After considering the history of Christianity, its day-to-day operation, its shaky foundations, its hypocrisy and lack of validity, and the direction of the main Christian leaders away from Jesus' reputed teaching, it seems that Christianity exists primarily for the benefit of a handful of senior clerics. These men stand condemned by the appalling track record of their predecessors, and deserve not reverence, but repudiation. For fifteen centuries, politically powerful Christian clerics consistently showed themselves to be intolerant sadists, as evidenced by their promotion of the Crusades, the Inquisition, witch-burning and the Conquistadors of old, right through to their not-altogether-passive support for the Nazi extermination camps and the murderous antics of the bombers in the skies above Dresden, Hiroshima and Cambodia. These acts of savagery are of ultimate concern, and each of them provides a valid reason for fearing a resurgence of totalitarian theocracy. Yet this could well be what is happening.

Religion is the vehicle these men travel in. It is what provides their self-proclaimed legitimacy as agents of a Supreme Supernatural Being that is so much bigger and more important than mere mortals. Whether or not the Being really exists is seen to be incidental to our investigation, as some religions (e.g. Buddhism) have no need of gods.

What we have discovered is that many religions came into existence, and continue to exist, primarily for the benefit of the men who run them. Many of these men have been corrupt opportunists, a curse and a threat to the wellbeing and happiness of mankind.

PART V

WHAT'S TO BE DONE?

I have identified a scandalous situation, in which society is subsidising one of its own worst enemies, so I will close by listing a few urgently needed changes in our attitudes to God-based religions. But first, I'd like to make a case for Humanism. This is not a religion, but a life stance that simply rejects supernaturalism and promotes secular morality. That's all. Accordingly, it accommodates a wide range of lifestyles, cultures and beliefs. It is available to all people everywhere as a realistic alternative to theologies of helplessness, such as Christianity, and ideologies of superiority, such as fascism. It is aimed at trying to make life good for everyone, everywhere in the world, for all time.

Generally speaking, Humanists reject 'revealed' morality, preferring ethical values that are based on human needs and wishes. To this end, they promote equal rights for everyone. They also reject supernatural explanations of natural phenomena, claiming that the best way of bettering human life is through factual knowledge based on observation and reasoned analysis, combined with sensitivity and compassion, and not by appeals to some imagined supernatural power. Most Humanists aspire to a socially responsible, secular society, isolated from interference by religious interests and free from divisive loyalties or privileges. They support freedom of speech and the right to criticise religious teaching, and they oppose notions of blasphemy and heresy. The Humanist life stance is available to all people everywhere.

Chapter 14

The Lessons

There are a few observations that jump out of the previous pages and demand attention, if our overcrowded world is to become anything but an enormous madhouse. We particularly need to change our tolerant, deferential attitudes to those who would impose what they tell us is God's Will. We now know that 'God's will' is either the product of dangerous psychoses and delusions, or else part of some devious attempt to gain and retain power or wealth for an elite minority, since we also know that God, if It exists at all, either cannot or chooses not to communicate with humankind. Nor does It answer prayers, and nor is It interested in morality or sexuality. We need to recognise clerics as social troublemakers, and start practicing some militant agnosticism. Here are a few of the more urgent topics:

Apocalyptists

We must confront and vilify all those who are eagerly awaiting the end of the world and preparing for the Battle of Armageddon. Jesus was an apocalyptist, but he was generally a nice guy. Modern apocalyptists are promoting nuclear stockpiles, military build-up, pollution and uncontrolled exploitation of our remaining oil and mineral resources, all in the hope of speeding Jesus' return to earth. They may be misled but they are not harmless, particularly in the USA where they have considerable right-wing political and military muscle, and there are fifty million of them! We must challenge their blind support for Zionism and war with Islam 'in order to fulfil ancient prophesies'.

Canon Law and Sharia Law

Clerics claim that their (ScapeGod's) laws, which are often immoral and irrational, should trump the laws of the land as laid down by democratically elected legislators in parliament. They claim that Statute Law is invalid in those areas where it contradicts Canon or Sharia law. So, for example, whereas Sharia deems that apostasy is an offence punishable by death, the Law of the Land sees it as a basic Human Right (Art 18 UDHR). Sharia condemns women wearing bikinis on the beach, but the Law of the Land sees no harm in it. Catholic Canon Law regards the rape of children to be a minor transgression to be confessed away, whereas the Law of the Land regards it as a heinous crime. Canon Law regards abortion as a heinous crime, while the Law of the Land considers it acceptable when properly regulated.

It is clearly impractical to have two conflicting sets of laws operating simultaneously in the same place. The Law of the Land must be upheld at the expense of ScapeGod's laws every time, no matter how historic or traditional they are.

Celibacy

Obligatory celibacy is blamed for many of the sexual perversions of priests, nuns and clerics. Although what they get up to in private may be hypocritical, as long as no one is hurt, then a secularist would see it as no business of his or hers. But when they exploit their positions of trust as self-proclaimed upholders of God's moral law in order to harm others, and especially children, then the matter becomes serious. Obligatory celibacy is unnatural, and whether or not it is the cause of the widespread paedophilia found among celibates (there is evidence both ways), it is quite apparent that celibacy makes people cold and unfeeling. In some cases it promotes sadistic emotions, and it impedes normal adult maturity, which is to say that it is harmful.

It has been suggested that every new priest's ordination ceremony should include not just vows of celibacy but also obligatory castration to help him keep those vows! Conversely, for the sake of society in general, but especially for the sake of the clergy themselves, obligatory celibacy should be dropped.

Census

Clerics are often at pains to emphasise that only those who accept the *whole* of their Church's dogma, including the unpalatable bits, may profess their faith. In other words, if you describe yourself as an '*à la carte* Catholic', or a 'semi-Catholic', then you're not a Catholic at all, you're a Protestant. You must further accept that if you no longer believe everything you profess when you recite the Apostle's Creed, then you're not a Christian, you're an agnostic. If you are one of the 93% of so-called Christians in the UK who no longer practices your religion and who is ambivalent about your religious beliefs, then it is misleading and even dishonest to describe yourself as a Christian. Consider that by continuing to refer to yourself as a Muslim or a Christian, you are giving weight and credibility to clerics who claim to represent you, but don't.

Those of whatever faith who no longer believe in the supernatural should proudly show that they can think for themselves by professing 'no religion' whenever they are asked. This especially applies on national census forms, which are used to guide government policy and spending.

Charitable status

In 1999 in the UK, Scientology was denied charitable status on the grounds that it 'conferred no public benefit'. This should surely have prompted the question: 'What public benefits do any of the other religious organisations provide?' They should provide some very beneficial services to the State to justify the extremely generous treatment that the taxpayers give them, but the reverse is the case. Clerics generally oppose democracy, medical research, population control and basic human rights. They promote sexism, homophobia and racism, and cause division and trouble within whatever societies they operate. How can 'promoting religion' possibly justify tax relief and subsidies?

Charitable status should only apply to specific charitable services actually provided and accounted for. But clerics mostly keep their financial records tightly closed, though we know that most are extremely wealthy (in the United States alone, church properties are valued at $500 billion), and we must wonder if they really need their subsidies in the first place. As churches and meeting halls and schools are typically large buildings, in good urban and suburban locations, which are closed for most of the week, they are wasted resources. The fact that they are untaxed gives churches an unfair advantage over tax-paying commercial businesses in the competition for prime urban locations.

Religious organisations are not charities. Nor are foreign missions 'charities', since they exist primarily to win souls. They may have helped thousands of needy people in many material ways, but this has been incidental to their primary evangelical objective of winning souls by any means. In the immediate aftermath of the tsunami that killed over a hundred thousand Muslims in Banda Aceh in 2005, the *Observer* reported under the headline 'Religious Aid Groups Try to Convert Victims' that US Christians were aggressively proselytising amongst vulnerable and traumatised Muslim survivors. Evangelist Mark Kosinski was reported as saying, 'These people need food. But they also need Jesus,' as he handed out Bibles. This caused much chagrin amongst Muslim clerics, who had meanwhile been telling the Aceh survivors that the tsunami was God's punishment for seeking political independence from Indonesia. This is cruel opportunism, not charity, and taxpayers should not be expected to subsidise it.

Clerics enjoy not only tax exemptions, but many governments also donate buildings, land, subsidies, grants of money and other material assistance without reference to the taxpayers who are paying for them. Surely the recipients should have to explain why they need financial help in the first place, and they should keep audited books showing how they used the financial help, together with details of their annual income and expenditure and their current assets. No genuine charity should have any problem with this.

Children

> *The objective of education is to enable us to make noble use of our leisure.*
>
> Aristotle

> *The aim of education should be to teach the child to think, not what to think.*
>
> Dewey

> *What are schools for if not indoctrination against communism?*
> Richard Nixon

> *Give me a child until he is seven, and I have him for life.*
> attributed to the Jesuits

Article 14 of the UN Convention on the Rights of the Child specifies the right of children to freedom of thought, conscience and religion. Unfortunately, this contradicts Article 26/3 of the Universal Declaration, which gives parents the right to choose the kind of education that shall be given to their children, because some parents will choose a religious education for their children. Teaching religion exploits children's gullibility. It indoctrinates them into belief of the supernatural, thus denying them the right to freedom of belief both now and later in life. It also divides and alienates them from children being taught different faiths.

Religious conditioning is a form of mental and emotional abuse of children, and we should not tolerate it. The State tries to protect young people from addictive drugs, alcohol and tobacco, and it should equally protect them from a toxic addiction to religion. Children are people with rights, not the private possessions of their parents or fodder to swell Church membership. As Stephen Law postulated (in 'Spotting Bullshit', *Free Inquiry*, February/March 2011):

> *Imagine that political schools started opening, a communist school in one town, a neocon school in another, and so on. Suppose these schools start each day with the collective singing of political anthems. Suppose portraits of political leaders beam down from classroom walls. Suppose pupils are selected on the basis of their parents' political beliefs. Suppose they expect children to uncritically accept the political tenets of their ideological leaders, Marx, Irving Kristol etc. What would be the public's reaction?*

Such schools – and there *are* such schools in totalitarian regimes – would be a clear threat to democracy and a healthy society.

In Vatican II, Pope Paul VI's *Declaration on Religious Freedom* (7 December 1965) argues that a person should only adopt religious belief as a result of free and informed choice. In one section he admonishes:

> *... in spreading religious faith and introducing religious practices, everyone ought at all time to refrain from any manner of action which might seem to carry a hint of coercion or of a kind of persuasion that would be dishonourable or unworthy, especially when dealing with poor and uneducated people. Such a manner of action would have to be considered an abuse of one's own right and a violation of the rights of others.*
>
> 'Declaration on Christian Education', Standard translation by Walter M Abbot (ed.), *The Documents of Vatican II*, New York, 1966, p.682

However, this applies only to adults: 'As for Catholic parents, the Council calls to mind their *duty* to entrust their children to Catholic schools ...' (*ibid.* p.637) where they will be indoctrinated into Catholicism. In other words, it is dishonourable to take advantage of an adult's ignorance, but it's a *duty* to exploit a child's innocence.

The Convention on the Human Rights of the Child (CRC) adopted by UN in 1989, Article 29, 1d, states:

> ... *the education of the child shall be directed to ... the preparation of the child for responsible life in a free society, in the spirit of understanding, peace, tolerance, equality of the sexes, and friendship among all peoples, ethnic, national and religious groups ...*

But faith-based schools have a record of social divisiveness and discrimination. In today's culturally diverse society, we especially need a system that will encourage understanding, inclusiveness and social harmony, where children can freely 'seek, receive and impart information and ideas of all kinds'.

Of course, it is really all about aggressive demographics. In order that their respective religions will eventually dominate the world, Catholic and Muslim clerics are adamant that there is an obligation on parents to have their children indoctrinated into Catholicism or Islam respectively. Thus indoctrinated by their schools, homes and peers, these children never get a chance to experience their rights 'to freedom of thought, conscience and religion' as specified in the UN Convention. Religious 'education' should be banned from anywhere that children under eighteen are to be found.

One final point: in claiming the 'human right' to raise their children according to their own faiths, parents demand that education authorities provide faith schools of every denomination in every locality. This is clearly impractical. The only way to avoid ghettoisation and ensure equal treatment to all is to take religion out of education altogether. All schools should be made secular, and those parents with strong religious feelings can arrange for their kids to be religiously indoctrinated elsewhere, at their own or their church's expense.

Church and State

Erecting the 'wall of separation between church and state' is absolutely essential in a free society.
                    Thomas Jefferson, third US president

States used to be sympathetic to organised religion because they recognised clerics as helpful in controlling the masses, keeping them servile, quiet and obedient, unlikely to rise up. Religion is a drug that keeps the masses subdued and keen to maintain the status quo, but a drugged and superstitious nation is hardly what a government should be striving for. State affairs are about managing this life in this world, here and now, assessing priorities and allocating resources according to the needs of living people. Religion, on the other hand, is concerned with some imagined life in a completely different world after we are dead. Unelected clerics therefore have nothing to contribute to secular government. The State should be governed by reason and evidence, not by tradition or by Episcopal whim. Even Vatican II declared that 'the political community and the Church are mutually independent and self-governing'.

Church and State should be formally and constitutionally separated, in order:
a) To protect the State and society from religion. Power corrupts, and if the clerics of one religion gain political power within a state, they will inevitably be intolerant of the clerics of other religions as well as of free speech, democracy, progress and human rights, etc.
b) To protect religion from the State. Knowing nothing of religion, states should be constitutionally forbidden from interfering in religious doctrines or practices that are not illegal. States should refrain from adjudicating in religious disputes.

c) To protect religion from itself. A religion involved in politics is not a religion, but a political organisation. Its religious and moral principles are highly likely to be compromised for the sake of political expediency and realpolitik.

States and religions are similar in that each provides social membership, moral legitimacy and a source of authority. But their interests are mutually exclusive, and there is no reason why they should involve themselves in each other's business. There must be a constitutional separation between the Church and the State, with neither interfering nor claiming expertise in the affairs of the other. The US Constitution provides a simple model, with Article VI stating: 'No religious test shall ever be required as a qualification to any office or public trust under the United States.' The First Amendment (1791) adds: 'Congress may not interfere with freedom of religion, speech, meeting or petition. Congress shall make no law respecting an establishment of religion or prohibiting the free exercise thereof.' Anybody caught breaking these statute laws for whatever reason will be treated the same as any other lawbreaker.

Once separated, it should be constitutionally impossible for any religious interest to exploit the democratic process to gain political power. There should be no question of an 'established' church or, worse, a theocracy.

Civilians

We have been conditioned to acknowledge that some 'co-lateral damage' is inevitable in an all-out war, but since the 1936 Spanish Civil War, we have seen the deliberate targeting of undefended civilians as a tactic of warfare, to 'break the enemy's spirit'. The intentional killing of civilians in order to bring about political change is one definition of terrorism – the firebombing of civilian targets in Germany and the dropping of two nuclear bombs on Japanese cities during WWII, for example, are no more defensible than the atrocities that WWII was fought to prevent.

Killing in war is morally no different from any other killing – self-defence of an individual is a justification, but not self-defence of a political entity. If soldiers want to fight, it is clearly immoral to choose to target unarmed and undefended women, children and old people who pose no threat to anyone. The silence of clerics on these matters, and the notion of 'My Country, Right or Wrong' sometimes blind us to such truths.

Disarmament

Although our religious leaders have little to say about it, being much more concerned with the evils of women clerics, abortion and uncovered female heads, we would all benefit in a world where less effort was devoted to preparing for war. We could eradicate malaria and third-world poverty and find a cure for cancer for a fraction of the money devoted every year to filling our world with means for killing and maiming each other under the euphemism 'defence'. Defence spending is rarely an issue when politicians are elected – it should be.

Disestablishment

In the UK, the established Anglican Church depends on political patronage, and its twenty-six bishops who serve in the House of Lords are clearly compromised whenever the government follows policies that the church abhors. A disestablished church, freed from political control over appointments and doctrine, might be more outspoken in its defence of Jesus' supposed teachings. The monarchy would be free to follow whatever religion (or none) it might wish, and those subjects of other faiths and no faith would no longer feel like second-class citizens. There would also no longer be a requirement to swear religious oaths before giving evidence in Court. As Tony Benn argued,

> *Britain needs a liberation theology which has the courage to preach against the corruption of power by speaking for those*

who are its victims ... The Church needs freedom to challenge the decisions of government, of Parliament and the whole Establishment, and the monetarist values which have elevated the worship of money above all else.

Rt. Hon. Tony Benn MP, 'A case for the Disestablishment of the Church of England', an essay in *The Church and the State*, edited by Donald Reeves, Hodder and Stoughton, London, 1984

Faith Schools

If Northern Ireland has taught us nothing of the divisive effects of State-sponsored faith-based education, the Wahhabist Muslim madrassahs soon will. Since all faiths effectively blaspheme each other by definition, the consequences of such education can only be social tension, hatred and division, and worse. Citizens who bitterly oppose faith-based education reluctantly find themselves subsidising the indoctrination of intellectually defenceless primary schoolchildren through their taxes, which is surely unjust. Religious belief is a private matter, and those who wish to indoctrinate innocent children into becoming pawns of clerics should at least bear the full cost.

The only practical way to ensure that all children get equal treatment is to provide obligatory secular education, in which the children of all faiths and none mix, learn and play together, and grow up together. Supernaturalism is anomalous in a place of learning.

Freedom of Speech

Clerics tend to overreact to any criticism, however reasoned or innocent. They present it as a deliberate expression of hatred, a taunting provocation, or an incitement to violence. In the UK it is against the law to point out that the doctrines of the Established Church are ridiculous, or even to refer to religion in an impious way. The Law Commission has twice recommended the eradication of all blasphemy laws, while Muslim, Catholic and other religious leaders have naturally urged that blasphemy law be extended to cover their respective religions.

One religion's dogma is another religion's blasphemy, and clerics are very easily offended. They claim that 'error has no rights', 'error' here meaning 'any opinion at variance with mine'. So we need to abolish the offences of blasphemy, sacrilege and heresy, and forbid the banning of books on moral, religious or political grounds. We must legislate in favour of freedom of speech, including freedom to criticise, mock and argue. We should be free to ridicule anything that is ridiculous, including religion. One stumbling block here is that the UN Human Rights Council is a highly political body that has little or nothing to do with human rights.

Human Rights

The 1948 UN Declaration of Human Rights (together with the International Covenant on Civil and Political Rights, and the International Covenant on Economic, Social and Cultural Rights of 1966) gained legal force in most countries in 1976 in the form of the International Bill of Rights. Article 18 of the Declaration says:

> *Everyone has a right to freedom of thought, conscience and religion; this right includes the right to change his religion or belief, and freedom either alone or in community with others in public or privately, to manifest his religion or belief in teaching, practice, worship and observance.*

Article 19 says:

> *Everyone has a right to freedom of opinion and expression; this right includes the freedom to hold opinions without interference and to seek, receive and impart information and ideas through any media regardless of frontiers.*

The Declaration was a fundamental step forward for all of humankind.

Of course, Pope Pius IX's *Syllabus of Errors* of 1864 denies that any such human rights exist. Catholic clerics to the present day are uneasy with them, especially rights for women, but from the very beginning it was the Muslim countries that had particular problems with the International Bill of Rights. For Muslims, God-given Sharia Law must take precedence over mere manmade laws, and Sharia Law is seriously contravened by anything that requires equality between men and women, or between Muslims and non-Muslims. Also by anything that permits free movement, apostasy, blasphemy and marriage of choice; and anything that refutes such cruel, degrading or inhuman treatment as amputation, stoning, beheading and female genital mutilation.

And so in 1990, the Organisation of the Islamic Conference (OIC), representing 57 Islamic states, adopted the Cairo Declaration of Human Rights in Islam (CDHRI), which restricts human rights just to those acceptable to Sharia Law. In 1997, the OIC began a campaign of opposition to Article 19, the right to free expression. In March 2008, sixty years after it was first published, they managed to destroy the UDHR with a resolution requiring that henceforth, anyone who criticises any aspect of Sharia Law must be reported to the Human Rights Council for 'abuse' of Article 19. This turned the whole concept of Human Rights on its head, as henceforth the media were to be forbidden from exposing incompetence, corruption, injustice, oppression or denial of rights in Muslim affairs. Fortunately the non-Islamic states rallied, and by 2011 the threat was withdrawn and replaced by a lesser, more acceptable constraint. In this case, we are fortunate that the UN is *de facto* a toothless and irrelevant waste of money, with no intention of enforcing its ban on such 'abuse', but we must nevertheless resist all attempts to allow religious courts to adjudicate in matters of family law.

Intolerance of Intolerance

The majority of monotheist lay believers are considerate and passively tolerant of others, and by their kindness and good works they provide a benign public image for their respective faiths. Unfortunately, some religions include sub-groups of intolerant militant extremists, and such groups capitalise on the goodwill and benign image of the peace-loving moderates. But the moderates' tolerance of the rabble-rousers within their ranks is misplaced, because they alone are in a position to confront their militant co-religionists and defuse their fanaticism. Just as a Muslim would be unable to persuade a band of militant Christofascists of the error of their ways, and an atheist would only upset a Wahhabist sect if he tried to explain where they were going wrong, so it is that only co-religionists stand any chance of being listened to. The moderates' incentive to act is to avoid being tarred with the same brush as the militants, as is happening to some extent with Muslims in the West. Governments only know how to use repression and force, and government intervention in such a situation inevitably exacerbates the problem, so we have the paradoxical situation whereby the tolerant masses urgently need to become intolerant of the intolerant few in their midst.

Morality

Religious morality is largely immoral, as seen in the example set by clerics, e.g. in covering up priestly child abuse, in barefacedly lying with 'mental reservations' about serious temporal matters. We should pay no attention to clerics of whatever stripe who pontificate about God's supposed will. We should openly deride their repeated warnings that without God, there can be no morality, and that law and order will break down if religion (i.e. they) should ever lose its (i.e. their) influence. They are merely sowing their seeds of fear, the great motivator. We saw in Chapter 3 that religious notions of morality are, in many cases, immoral and hypocritical.

Instead we must actively promote secular morality, human rights and mutual cooperation, and we must refuse to allow clerics to judge us. By their obsession especially with sex, they actively distract attention from, and thus render themselves complicit in, the real moral outrages around us: trillion-dollar military budgets; the grossly unequal distribution of wealth; and the absence of human rights for hundreds of millions of humans.

Multi-culturalism

Most religions are mutually divisive and intolerant of each other. For example, Christians believe that Jesus was God – a blasphemous belief that carries the death sentence for Muslims. No wonder that clerics discourage their flocks from mingling with those of different beliefs. They typically urge them to cluster together in ghettoes, where the local schools and church/temple/mosque suits their faith, and they all speak the same language. This could be mistaken for multi-culturalism, but in fact it is a collection of mutually exclusive mono-cultural societies, each alienated by its religion from the others. Secular multi-culturalism is seen to work well, but religiously based 'multi-culturalism' just doesn't happen – look at Northern Ireland or Holland.

Britain provides an example of a multi-cultural society where the non-religious have integrated with ease, but its State-subsidised attempts to provide for religious multi-culturalism have merely ghettoised its Jewish and, especially, its Muslim communities. These have so isolated themselves from outside influence that they even operate Sharia Law in family matters.

The simple solution is to mix all children of whatever faith in secular schools, where they can be taught about the variety of different religious beliefs, but where no particular religion is taught as truer than any other. We must not tolerate State-subsidised faith-based schools, where children are conditioned to believe that one particular religion is true and all others are false. This merely alienates people from each other.

Overpopulation

Overpopulation is perhaps the biggest threat facing humankind. It is responsible for global warming, extinction of species, pollution and the depletion of resources, including water, arable land, oil and raw materials. It leads to starvation, disease, international friction and resource wars. We must, as a matter of urgency, promote population control by educating women, providing them with employment and security, and making available information and means for family planning. The pope and the evangelist and Muslim preachers who promote their brand of 'family values', encouraging their flocks to 'go forth and multiply and conquer the world' can apparently see no limit to the global population which already (2012) stands at over 7,000 million. As a matter of great urgency, we must confront and vilify these agents of God's supposed will. They are demographic aggressors, who would turn the world to ashes in the quest to maximise their own power and influence.

Public Health

We must confront attempts by clerics to interfere with public health measures, such as water fluoridation, essential vaccination programmes, provision of condoms to prevent the spread of AIDS and to reduce unwanted pregnancies, provision of comprehensive medical facilities for pregnant women, and provision of emergency medical and food aid (including GM food) to those who urgently need it. People who would thwart attempts to defeat disease and suffering must bear responsibility for the consequences, and we should no longer show any respect for such unfeeling authoritarianism. Nor should publicly funded hospitals be permitted to refuse certain medical treatments on religious grounds.

Respect

We must define the word 'respect' whenever it is used in the context of religion. I respect your right to worship gods, or even crocodiles, if you want to, but that doesn't mean that I esteem or admire it. I merely tolerate it. Those clerics and others who demand respect for their superstitions should have this explained to them. The respect they want has to be earned, whereas what most of them have earned is contempt.

Toleration

Relativism, whereby we all 'tolerate' each other, giving equal weight to all beliefs, is not acceptable to the proselytising religions, and so it is not an option for the non-religious. Objections to the ringing of church bells and the 'defiance' of civil wedding and funeral ceremonies are petty tokens, which merely give offence. We must confront the clerics head-on, promoting reason over so-called revelation. Our politicians must be persuaded that most of these ultra-rightist clerics are opportunists, exploiting the infantile notion of a vengeful, all-powerful God for their own ends. Appeasement failed the last time the world was forced to face up to fascism, when Hitler took advantage of Western nice-guys' anxiety to live and let live. We must all understand that democracy is threatened more than ever by the Islamofascists, the Christofascists and the Judeofascists, and that appeasement doesn't work.

United Nations Organisation

The glory of individual men may consist in victory over their fellow men, but the glory of man consists in intelligent collective purpose and mastery over the environment as well as what is archaic in his own nature. I believe that in the not very distant future the adversity caused by the pursuit of merely national aims on the part of separate national groups will lead mankind to a more vivid realisation than exists at present of their collective purposes which justify mankind's existence in the universe.

Bertrand Russell, 'Taking Long Views', 30 March 1932

The widespread and unpredictable effects of unregulated globalisation and the consequent decreasing relevance of national governments have driven many fearful people into the arms of religious organisations, which promise to maintain traditional values and to provide safety in numbers. People are frightened by uncontrolled US aggression; by the unregulated power of mega-corporations to do what they damn-well like wherever they damn-well like; by the free movement of goods and untold billions of dollars daily across national borders; and by arbitrary national government regulation of personal freedoms. The world urgently needs a mutually respected global legislature, with a global court of justice, to uphold the original Universal Declaration of Human Rights. This must have the power to investigate, interrogate and enforce its impartial decisions on multinational corporations, nation states, religious organisations and anyone else who scorns those rights. Alas! What we've got is the United Nations.

The UN has produced many valuable documents, specifying everything from the rights of individuals to the actions to be taken in the event of genocide. National governments have piously signed them with great outward solemnity, but with never the slightest intention of honouring them. The UN is worse than useless, it is a powerless talking shop where, years after the event, mediators butter-over their countries' atrocities. It is a forum where diplomats practise hypocrisy and double-talk. It is a deliberate distraction from the fact that there is no proper global legislature. By its very existence, it defuses attempts that would otherwise be made to cooperate meaningfully and to enforce agreements. In this nuclear age, war is no longer an option for solving international disputes. The US superpower that calls itself the world's policeman has shown itself to be no less criminal than those it attacks, and the

UN has shown itself to be more of a hindrance than a help. It is postulated that if the UN had been around in 1945, the Second World War would be raging still.

It is time now to replace the laws of ScapeGod and the worship of money with the Universal Declaration of Human Rights, fairly, properly and universally enforced. The UNHRC should be re-formed and empowered to *enforce* the Universal Declaration in every country in the world, giving rights only to individual humans. There should be no rights or privileges for belief systems, nor for Canon or Sharia law, nor for religious or other organisations, because they are not human individuals. There should be no special rights of veto in the UN Security Council. It should make decisions based on simple majority votes, and if intervention is called for, it should happen the next day, and not five years later, as in Darfur.

Vatican Statehood

That unholy trinity – the Catholic Church, the Holy See and the Vatican City State – should have its claim to international statehood rejected. It shuffles these titles manipulatively to maximise its power and to minimise its responsibilities, but it should have no place in the United Nations, neither as a state nor as a religion.

The Lateran Pact of 1929 which created the Vatican 'State' was a seedy deal between two power-hungry Italians: Benito Mussolini, the fascist atheist who needed the Pope's electoral support, and Achille Ratti who, as Pope Pius XI, needed credibility and political influence. In exchange for the Pope's blessing (and an undertaking that all bishops would be Italian subjects), the dictator Mussolini gave the Pope money to compensate for the loss of the Papal States in 1870. He also agreed to impose obligatory Catholic instruction in all Italian State schools; and he agreed to recognise papal sovereignty over the 108.7 acres of land that constitutes Vatican City. It was a domestic, all-Italian arrangement. It was not a treaty or even a concordat, and the Mussolini--Ratti pact could have placed no obligation on anyone outside Italy to 'recognise' the Pope as a sovereign head of a state. As Geoffrey Robertson QC asks in *The Case of the Pope* (Penguin 2010) 'Would we be happy to welcome the holy city of Qom into the councils of the UN if President Ahmadinejad were to negotiate a Lateran –style treaty with its senior Ayatollah?' I doubt it, yet this is the strength of the pope's worldwide pretension to be a sovereign head of state, immune from prosecution.

In any case, the Holy See fails to meet even the basic requirements for a State as laid down in Article 1 of the 193 Montevideo Convention, which specifies that a State must have at least a permanent population, a defined territory and a government. But Vatican City has no permanent population – nobody was ever born or raised there and the 700-odd priests and nuns who work there are members of the Catholic bureaucracy whose 'citizenship' lasts only so long as they remain in office. Nor has the Pope much in the way of a defined territory: less than half a square kilometre (0.17 of a square mile), with no immigration controls or basic services (they leave such trivia as policing, hospitals, electricity and water supplies, sewerage and access roads to be provided by the City of Rome). As for possessing a government, the Holy See and its bureaucrats are there to administer the worldwide Catholic religion, not the day-to-day affairs of Vatican City which, in the absence of any population or defined territory or service provision, requires no government, in the normal sense of the word.

Further, the 1961 Vienna Convention requires that States have a duty not to interfere in the internal affairs of other States. Yet by citing the Lateran 'Treaty' when hiding its child abusers from prosecution by the police; when demanding that Catholic politicians must follow decrees of Canon Law over their nation's laws on pain of excommunication; or when protecting mafia-friendly Archbishop Marcinkus from arrest after the collapse of the Bank of Ambrosiano, for example, the Holy See, whilst claiming to be a sovereign state, was clearly ignoring its obligations under the Vienna Convention.

Vatican City has achieved its present credibility as a nation state thanks largely to its arrogant brass neck in the presence of diplomatic inertia in the UN. The Holy See gradually insinuated itself into various UN committees and its presence was gradually accepted until, in July 2004, it won the right formally to participate in the debates of the General Assembly. Yet its track record in the UN is disastrous: its diplomats have consistently blocked even the most basic humanitarian measures. In 1995, for example, they wrecked the Cairo conference on global over-population and development aid, and they went on to Beijing where they opposed women's rights and gender equality. They have blocked measures to prevent the spread of AIDS using condoms and needle exchange programmes; they have opposed the provision of 'morning after' pills to the victims of gang rape by enemy soldiers; they have opposed the notion of human rights of any sort for homosexuals; and they have frustrated the workings of the International Criminal Court, as well as attempts by various national authorities to uncover the activities of its paedophile priests.

Every shred of credibility should be taken away from this negative, backward, destructive force in world diplomacy. . The 178 states with which it has diplomatic relations should close their embassies and save their money. The Catholic Church is no more than a special-interest non-governmental organisation, albeit a big one, and it should be treated as no more special than any other NGO, such as Oxfam or *Medecins Sans Frontieres* (MSF).

Despite their loss of visibility and credibility in Western Europe, religious interests haven't gone away. They are busily expanding their influence elsewhere in the world – there are already over 300 million born-again Pentecostals, who pack a powerful political and economic punch; the Vatican is busily exploiting the weight of its claimed 1.1 billion adherents and its extensive diplomatic relations (secure with its multi-trillion dollar stockpile of land and other assets); and the OIC, which represents 57 Islamic nations, is now making big waves in the United Nations. There is no room for complacency, for as Mill pointed out: 'One person with belief is equal to a force of 99 who have only interests.' Though there are only a handful of clerics, they have the dedication, the organisation, the money, the power structure, the contacts and even the tax breaks, while the apathetic masses have none of these things.

We must overcome the inertia, lack of interest and fear that constrain us all at present from standing up and being counted. Clerics must be prevented from ever again having control of the levers of political power, for, as John Gummer noted (*The Times*, 1984): 'Church leaders can no more pontificate on economics than the pope could correct Galileo.' Those who know absolutely nothing about a topic, such as God or Ethics, should say nothing, and stop arrogantly pontificating about it from the pulpit or lectern.

Bob Rees
Dublin 2012

INDEX